What are others saying about Jeffrey Dobkin's information-rich style of writing and his small business marketing and direct marketing advice? <u>Unsolicited</u> comments—

"Your book, How To Market a Product for Under $500, *is one of the best books I've ever read on how to market a product."*
> E. Joseph Cossman

"We doubled the weight of your book: We underlined the important parts!"

"We recommended your book to some friends, and decided to put yellow sticky notes in the pages we especially wanted them to read. Several hundred sticky notes later we abandoned the idea, and finally just bought them their own copy, and told them to read the whole thing."

"I can't give you enough gratitude for writing this book. I've learned more about real-life business in three days than I did in 4 1/2 years of college."

"A much-needed book, very well done."
> Dan Poynter, author of The Self-Publishing Manual

"Your book presents a unique blend of traditional and guerilla marketing techniques in an unpretentious, user-friendly format. What a refreshing change of pace from the stacks of trade mags, newsletters and "how-to" books that clutter my office. I found dozens of pragmatic and affordable suggestions to share with my clients!"
> Henry Berkowitz, President, HB Publishing and Marketing

"I've read just about every book ever written on copy; you definitely belong in the copywriter's hall of fame. Your book is must *reading for any serious seller of goods or services."*

"If an inventor is not sure whether licensing or distributing is the way to go, this book could be his bible. Dobkin cuts through months or years of doing it by trial and error."
> Don Costar, Nevada Inventor's Association Newsletter

"Definitely the best book on marketing I have ever read! I only wish I had read it years ago. It would have saved me many years and thousands of dollars. It is must reading..."

"I ordered your amazing book..."

"Just wanted to tell you again that your book is the best marketing book for small business that I know, and I've read a bunch of them. Terrific, terrific book."

"I've read most of the articles, and even though I am the Director of Marketing for a national association, I must say, I learned something from every one."

"I find your writing to be clear, free of jargon, and full of useful information. You're my kind of writer. Of course, as an old hand with more than 40 years in advertising, I feel like I can be a good judge of the content of your work. Thank you for letting me publish your writing."
    Don R. Blum, Publisher, Savannah Business Journal

"Useful for the author with a book to promote, as well as for the writer who prepares marketing materials for clients." Freelance Writer's Report

"I got your book at the library—they wanted it back. Enclosed is my check..."

"I kept your book out [of the library] so long it would have been cheaper to buy it right from the start."

"I must again compliment you on the detailed thoroughness of your book. There are other books on the subject matter, but they lack the step-by-step panache of yours. Your coverage of the press release was excellent...and I had every confidence in talking to the writer. Thanks to you I must have sounded like I knew what I was talking about. I asked all the right questions."

"When I first read one of your articles, I was impressed by your expertise and your thoroughness. Your telephone consultation and book, How To Market a Product for Under $500!, *were invaluable to me in the process of developing our direct mail program."*

"Your book is wonderful...full of insightful and practical information...has already more than paid for itself...look forward to using your book as reference for years to come."

"This is by far the best book I have ever read on the topics of direct marketing and mail order sales. Well-researched and organized...the book's coverage is exhaustive."

"Again, your section on press releases is great. Have it almost memorized."

"I've been enthusiastically recommending it to anyone who'll listen."

"I was amazed that I could actually start marketing my ideas with a low budget. Your book is beyond excellent. I have read many other marketing books, such as the series by so-called guru Jay Conrad Levinson (Guerrilla Marketing). Your book makes Levinson look like he needs to get a copy, and start studying....Your book has taught me more than I could have ever imagined (and even more than my friends that graduated with business degrees)."

"An excellent resource for ideas on how to sell your products and services inexpensively is How To Market a Product for Under $500 *by Jeffrey Dobkin."*
    Courtney Price, President, Entrepreneurial Education Foundation, featuring the Premier Fast Trac Program

~ UNCOMMON MARKETING TECHNIQUES ~

~ ALSO BY JEFFREY DOBKIN ~

HOW TO MARKET A PRODUCT FOR UNDER $500

ALSO AVAILABLE ON AUDIO CASSETTE & ON VIDEO

UNcommon Marketing Techniques
Reference: Marketing, Direct Marketing, New Product Marketing, Sales,
Small Business, Product Development, Inventing, Brand Marketing,
Multiple Exposure Marketing

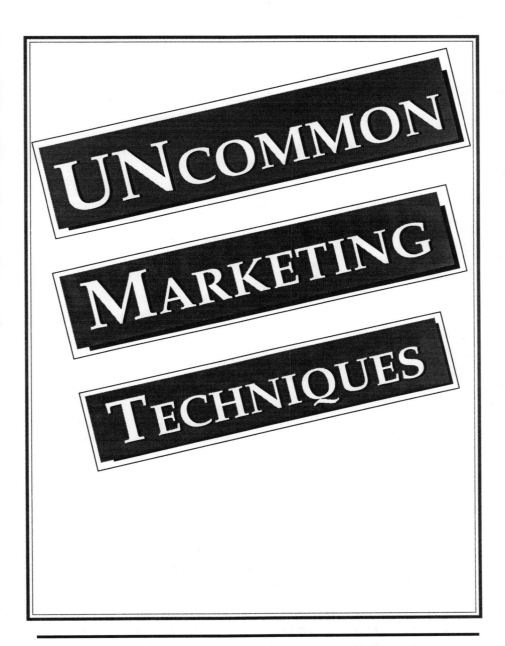

UNCOMMON MARKETING TECHNIQUES

The Most Requested Articles on Small Business Marketing by
America's Small Business Master Marketer

~ Jeffrey Dobkin ~

Edited by Michelle Axelrod

Uncommon Marketing Techniques
by Jeffrey Dobkin

Published by
— The Danielle Adams Publishing Company —
Box 100
Merion Station, PA 19066
Telephone 610/642-1000
Fax 610/642-6832

Library of Congress Catalog Card Number: 97-71742
Printed and Bound in the United States of America
— Printed on Acid-Free Paper —

Publisher's Cataloging-In-Publication

Dobkin, Jeffrey.
Uncommon marketing techniques : practical real-life lessons
in marketing and direct marketing / by Jeffrey Dobkin;
edited by Michelle Axelrod. — 1st ed.
p. cm.
ISBN: 0-9642879-3-5

1. Marketing. 2. Direct marketing. I. Title.

HF5415.D63 1998   380.1
                    QBI97-40498

To My Friend, My Mentor, My Hero, and also My Brother

~ **Robert Dobkin** ~

I must be the luckiest person alive to have a brother like Bob.

Through all my life there has always been a reliable source of experience and wisdom. Now, an elegant and soft-spoken self-made man who would never mention his great wealth or power, Bob has been more influential in my success than anyone.

Robert would never speak of money, yet never let me pay for dinner—or vacations. His multitude of successes has still left him levelheaded and a joy to be with. We've had some fun times over the years, and I cherish the time I have spent in his company. I know that men of this quality are rare, and to be in their presence, a privilege—even as a relative.

Robert has helped me with every business I have ever been in, and has guided and encouraged my entrepreneurial spirit. He's saved me from certain disaster and helped me recover from my mistakes. Thanks, Bob, for all you've done for me. I appreciate it. This book is dedicated to you in my deep appreciation. Thank you so much. I must be the luckiest man alive to have a brother like Bob.

~ Author's Note ~

WITH THIS BOOK AND SUPPLEMENT I HAVE TRIED TO MAKE IT POSSIBLE FOR PEOPLE WITH NO EXPERIENCE TO UNDERSTAND WHAT MARKETING IS AND DOES, THEN BE ABLE TO ACCOMPLISH THIS MARKETING FUNCTION WITHOUT ADDITIONAL HELP.

FURTHER, I HAVE TRIED TO ENCOURAGE SMALL BUSINESS OWNERS TO FIND THEIR MARKETS EFFICIENTLY AND WITH SPEED, THEN REACH THEM AT THE LOWEST COST.

IT IS A PRIVILEGE TO BE ABLE TO SHARE MY MARKETING KNOWLEDGE AND EXPERTISE WITH MY FELLOW ENTREPRENEURS AND FRIENDS. THANK YOU FOR THIS OPPORTUNITY.

UNCOMMON MARKETING TECHNIQUES

~ Foreword ~

How refreshing it is to see such expert attention given to cost-effective and innovative marketing techniques for today's entrepreneurs and small business practitioners! With the increasing clutter in our mailboxes, in our magazines, and even on the Web, it is difficult for our potential customers to separate the wheat from the chaff of advertising.

Throwing money at advertising and marketing efforts is beyond the budget capabilities of most of us who own our own businesses. We must become experts at using the techniques and methods which give us the greatest bang for the buck. This book has provided me with marketing approaches I haven't tried before. I have to wonder why I have missed these gems, and how much more successful I could have been had I known about these earlier.

You have only a few seconds between the time your potential customer opens the day's mail and the time most of it hits the wastebasket. You can learn from this book of gems how to be the marketer who avoids the wastebasket by capturing the imagination of that potential customer in those precious few seconds.

Edward M. Moldt
Entrepreneur in Residence
The Wharton School

~ Preface ~

My book, "HOW I MADE A MILLION DOLLARS IN MAIL ORDER" has sold over two million copies in hard cover. In addition, I initiated:

1) Entrepreneurship courses at Pepperdine University, U.C. Berkeley, San Jose University, University of Albuquerque, and California State University, Los Angeles.

2) American marketing methods to business men and women throughout the major cities in Europe, Canada and Mexico.

3) Created, developed and produced a complete Home Study Program on entrepreneurship.

Why am I telling you this? Because I want to give you a testimony on Jeffrey Dobkin's book, and wanted you to be sure that I have the qualifications to do just that.

When I first read his book, I couldn't believe the incredible wealth of little known secrets on marketing he exposed - secrets it took me a lifetime to learn, and I'm three times his age!

Today I have over one-thousand business books in my library and if I had to get rid of every one, the only one I would save would be Jeffrey's book, "UNcommon Marketing Techniques."

E. Joseph Cossman

THE BIGGEST MISTAKE EVERY FIRM MAKES IN MARKETING, AND WHAT YOU CAN DO TO CORRECT IT IN YOUR FIRM FOR $1.92

H ERE'S THE MISTAKE. One of your 500 absolute best and most qualified prospects calls or writes for information. Maybe the BRC came back from your mailing. Or perhaps his name comes in as a lead from an ad you've placed in a magazine. What do you do?

You send him a brochure and a letter, you wait a week, and you call. When there is no immediate sale, you place his name in a file—to be contacted again somewhere between later and never, and the lead eventually winds up getting lost or thrown out. Some people call this marketing. It's wasting money.

For most industrial sales, it's necessary to have several personal sales calls before a client makes a purchase. Why the heck do you suppose anyone would think this will happen any sooner through a mail campaign? Do mailings defy the law of industrial marketing that states that one contact is not enough for a sale? I don't think so.

A campaign is not a single ad or a single mailing. A campaign is not a single effort of anything—why do you think they call it a campaign?

Enter the phrase **Multiple Exposure Marketing**. It's the philosophy of marketing I teach. Simply stated, you need to contact your prospects more than once to make a sale. Whether it's by ads, phone, or direct mail. Yes, it's true for direct mail, too.

THE MOST EFFECTIVE MARKETING CAMPAIGN YOU CAN CREATE

The MOST effective sales campaign you can use costs under $2. It's a series of letters. In direct mail, a letter is a portrait of the sender. You can send some mighty pretty pictures of your company for just 32¢ apiece. Besides constituting the most effective campaign, letters are the most underused marketing tool of the decade.

To separate your firm from the pack, send qualified prospects a few more letters. It's cheap insurance to get them to notice you and respond. The letters are now a real campaign.

For a short campaign, write five additional letters. These letters are all written up front, then placed in a file—waiting for people to not-respond to your initial contact. I can't think of anyone better to write a tight sales campaign to than your best prospects. Can you?

As campaigns go, let's see how a letter campaign stacks up:

Personal Sales Calls: $175. Nope. Too expensive.

Telephone Contact: $24.50. Not that, either. And ouch, sales rejection; and ugh, call reluctance. Plus, what a waste of time when they're not in.

Letter: 32¢. Hmmm.

A letter is an incredibly powerful marketing tool. With a single page you can get the attention of the world's busiest magazine editor. You can capture the eye of the president of American

Airlines. And you can instill a confidence in hundreds of thousands of consumers that will make them order your products. Hmmm. All this for just 32¢? Yes.

A letter is the most effective component of a direct mail package. If you mail potential customers just a brochure and no letter, you're missing most of your sales, as well as all of the goodwill you can generate with a letter. In fact, a well-written direct mail letter can be so effective, it can be mailed by itself and still draw a terrific response. Ask any fundraiser.

Have you noticed almost every piece of direct mail you receive from any major mailer contains a letter? Actually, there is something in it that *looks* like a letter. A letter is a personal correspondence you write to one or two people. When you send it to 10, 10,000, or 10 million people, it isn't a letter. It's a highly stylized ad designed to look like a letter. In your direct mail campaign, your letters are really highly stylized ads. Yep. People <u>read them</u> (as opposed to <u>just looking</u> at your brochure) and—if they are done well—take them personally.

For a letter campaign to be easy to implement, it all has to happen fairly automatically. When the letters are already in the computer, they're easy to personalize and drop in the mail in a programmed sequence. Send them at regular intervals—mail your first letter, then wait two weeks and mail the second, then send subsequent letters every three weeks after that. Sooner, if you're in a hurry. You will prove your diligence and give up-front proof of excellent customer service. You and your company will look like a million dollars; and I don't mean green and wrinkled.

In the first letter, say it was a pleasure speaking with them, even if it wasn't. Certainly thank them for their inquiry. Mention several of the benefits of your products or services. Don't forget, no one knows you are going to send them five more letters. The second letter explains, *"The brevity of the first letter didn't allow me to tell you of this benefit...."* Now feel free to address additional benefits. Each letter contains benefit-oriented copy and gives additional reasons to do business with your firm.

Letter two always says the exact same thing to each person. Letter three the same. Benefit-rich copy. Courier or typewriter-style type. Make sure they look like letters. Flush left, rag right.

No paragraph over seven lines. Underline occasionally. Bold sparingly. Sign legibly. Show lots of white space around the type to make it look easy to read. And have a PS that repeats the offer in a nutshell and asks directly for the action you'd like your prospect to take. Don't forget a BRC. But mostly orient your copy to generate a phone call; that is the objective of the letter.

The letters get progressively harder-selling. You should make the sales call (if you don't mind making sales calls) after your fourth or fifth letter. Think how much more effective this is than making it earlier. By then all your prospects know you: they know your name, your company, your product. The letters presell your call. And since your letters are benefit-heavy, prospects know the benefits of using your products. They also know you'll be a good person to work with. Everyone likes a responsive firm to work with.

Multiple exposure marketing. A letter is the most effective you can be in marketing for 32¢. Six letters really are six times as effective. A letter series like this is much more effective than a fancy four-color brochure mailed once, don't you think?

Outside of your mailing list and your current leads, those old leads in your files are the most valuable pieces of paper in your entire office. Don't you think it's time you mailed to them again? And again?

QUESTIONS
PEOPLE ASK ME
THE MOST ABOUT
DIRECT MARKETING

WITH 25 YEARS' EXPERIENCE creating marketing action plans, writing ads, direct selling ads and direct mail packages, and assisting small and medium size firms with their marketing and direct marketing, certain questions have come up repeatedly throughout my career. The questions follow.

WHAT THE HECK IS MARKETING, ANYHOW?

So many people are involved in marketing, but most people don't know the definition. Even when you ask marketing people the definition, they hem and haw. Perhaps it's because marketing is such a broad-based term, it's like asking for the definition of "Business." My definition runs seven words, if you count the "a."

"Marketing is selling to a defined audience."

When you offer your products to anyone, that's selling. When you place your customers in groups you can define, and separate them from everyone else in the world, and target your sales efforts specifically to them, that's marketing.

WHAT IS DIRECT MARKETING?

A manufacturer takes out an ad in a consumer or trade magazine. Someone sees the ad and calls and orders the product—or, more likely, sends an inquiry. The firm sends literature, then the customer places an order. Simple. Lots of business sales are direct.

Direct marketing means you have no sales force to move your products into the marketplace, and you solicit buyers by selling directly to them. No representatives to get your products onto retailers' or consumers' shelves. And no retailer or wholesaler link in the distribution chain. You do it all yourself. To me, direct marketing is selling to a consumer or business directly from a magazine or newspaper ad, a telephone campaign, direct response TV ad, or from a direct mail package. I'm not really concerned with whose shelves our goods wind up on, just that they move off our own shelves and we get paid in a timely fashion.

WHAT IS A GOOD RESPONSE TO A MAILING?

Probably *the* most-asked direct marketing question, *ever*. And people are usually looking for a number like 2%, 10%, or 25%.

A successful single mailing (for orders) is any mailing that breaks even or better the first time out. Because you learn from this mailing, the chances of tuning it up for the second time to increase the response even further are very good.

Percentages are no indication of success. If you are offering a free watch, you may get a 90% response for the watch, but no sales on the back end. If you are offering a free brochure about your $2 million printing press, response can be .002%—but if one press is sold, the mailing is a success. Without knowing the mailing objectives, profit per order, the offer, the list, and the audience, any percentages have little meaning.

The simplest formula for success in a direct offer is the cost of the mailing, plus the cost of fulfillment, subtracted from the amount of money you received. Even when you plug in this formula, the additional credibility you get for your next mailing is not taken into account.

Questions...

To take a guess at percentages—which is probably why you're reading this—1% to 2% for an offer is usually considered good to excellent. When planning for success, figure out if you will break even at 1%. If not, better rethink your package, offer, product, or price. As important: Is your offer hard or soft (do you ask for money with the order, or bill later?), and are you asking for an order (direct sale) or for an inquiry (lead generation with a two-step selling process) so you can send a harder-hitting, longer package? Then, what is the lifetime value of the customer (will he order again and how often)? Will all this additional hoopla convert your mailing to being profitable? Most magazine publishers would be happy at .5% conversion to subscription rate; some of our own free-gift-with-inquiry offers have drawn 20% to 25%.

WHICH WORKS BETTER, LONG OR SHORT COPY?

Copy is king, but it can be a real killer. Professionally drafted, well-written long copy works best. But...

BUT—and like my Aunt Mildred, this is a big butt—if the structure is incorrect, if it is anything but the most intriguing, spellbinding, interesting writing, if the benefits are brought in too late, if the offer is too late or misplaced in all the clutter, or if any of a million different bad things that can happen with long copy happens, there is a much greater possibility you will lose your reader, and as he drifts away, your whole package will be trashed rather than read.

If it is poorly structured or uninteresting, most people will place your expensive marketing material in the pile to read sometime between later and never, and it'll wind up just getting thrown out. Unless it's forceful, motivating, and drives readers to read the entire length and act now, they will just file it in the round file without ever a second thought.

Sending a direct mail package is like owning a retail store: the longer you keep your potential customer in your store, the more likely he is to make a purchase. The longer the reader stays in your package, the more likely he is to send for your product. For example: Publisher's Clearing House's big magazine-stamp mailings. They hide the free prize stamps deep in the package— the longer you look for them, the more likely you are to find something you like and place an order.

For the majority of offers and packages, I recommend short copy. And I say that short copy is best because it works best in most packages. However, for the ingenious, and for selling higher-priced products: If you can keep your customer tightly focused, your chance of sales is greater with long copy.

SHOULD I USE ENVELOPE TEASER COPY?

The first word on teaser copy is YES. If your mailing is commercial, sent bulk, and has the look of anything that is not a personal letter, use teaser copy. Yes, yes, yes.

But there is also a grave danger in using envelope teaser copy.

The big danger inherent in teaser copy: being too specific. If your envelope copy is too specific and your teaser is not of interest to the largest segment of your audience, your offer on the last page to give away that new lawnmower to the first 10,000 respondents won't even be seen. The whole envelope, unopened, will be tossed out. It's the biggest danger in all of direct mail.

Teaser copy can make your package really work hard for you, but it can really work hard against you if it isn't appealing to your entire audience. When in doubt, don't. Stick to tried-and-true openers: Free Offer Inside...New Pricing Enclosed...See What's New...Limited Time Offer - Please Open Immediately. They're boring, but still effective.

If your mailing piece is sent first class, chances are it will be opened even without teaser copy, especially if it has just your own name and address in the corner card (no company name). The only copy to enhance this (if you want to) is to say "FIRST CLASS MAIL" under the stamp area.

WHAT IS THE BIGGEST MISTAKE MADE IN MARKETING?

This mistake is made by 99% of the companies marketing products or services. It's a mistake made by almost every firm I have worked with in the past 25 years. The biggest mistake in marketing—and not just direct marketing, but any marketing—is made by people who spend a lot of time, energy, and money on an ad or an inquiry-generation program. When they receive the highly qualified lead it brings in, they send a brochure and a letter. At best, they call about a week later. When a sale is not immediate, they hang up, and they never call back or send another letter. Then they say their campaign failed. What a mistake.

A single letter and brochure is not a campaign. A campaign is not a single effort of anything—why do you think they call it a campaign? A campaign is a sustained effort over time.

I recall some books quoting that a face-to-face sales call costs $172, and that most larger sales are closed on the fifth contact. It always amazes me that otherwise intelligent people send a letter and brochure to their best prospects and call it quits when those prospects don't respond with an immediate purchase.

Why would anyone think it's faster or easier to sell a product off a page or two than sell something in person? Why should it take five in-person meetings to make a sale and only one contact in print? The biggest mistake made in marketing is not contacting a well-qualified buyer, who has expressed an interest in your product or service after the first mailing, a second time with harder-hitting additional marketing material or letters.

What is the biggest mistake you can make in a mailing?

Without a doubt, mailing to the wrong list will ensure your mailing fails. The mistake is not doing enough research into which lists to test and mail to. In direct marketing, the list IS your market. Do your homework by finding the absolute best possible list, then test it. Additional time and thought here won't be wasted. No glitzy brochure, exceptional offer, and great free gift will make a tuna canning factory purchase bottle caps. If you use a list broker, make him do his homework and EARN his commission by digging deep and buying the best.

What is the most important, most effective element in a direct mail package?

The letter is unquestionably the most effective part of your direct mailing package. Some mailers, myself included, have been successful using just a letter with no brochure. People receiving your package look at the brochure, but they read the letter. It is, after all, a personal communication from you, just to them.

Everyone knows that when brochures are printed, they are printed *en masse*. But even when you print a million letters, if you do it correctly you can make the recipient think he is one of a few, or even the only one, receiving it. Interesting: a personal communication from yourself to just a million or so people. Frankly, in my view, a direct marketing letter is really a highly stylized ad designed to look like a letter. Do I refine every sentence, pour over the copy ad nauseam, and call every line break just as I would for an ad? You better believe I do.

WHAT ARE THE BEST MONTHS TO ADVERTISE IN A MAGAZINE?

If your products make great gifts, October, November, and December are good months—if you don't get lost in the advertising clutter of all the Christmas products marketed at this time.

The magazine publishers don't tell you this part. If your products are not gift oriented, special issues and trade or seasonal specialties notwithstanding, the good months are January, February, and March, when most of the country is cold and people tend to stay in and read more. Magazine readership goes up, and so does your response. In June, July, and August, would you rather be inside reading a magazine, or out on the beach sipping a mint julep? And if by some wild chance you did bring your magazine to the beach, would you also bring a pen and your checkbook to respond to an ad? Nah. Response goes down in these months.

Some publishers may give you "pass along" counts of their readers, saying that every month, readers give their magazines to a friend who shares it with other friends, who all then pour over the magazines looking for things to buy. Don't pay much mind to the pass along readership figure. No doubt this was dreamed up by an overzealous advertising man who needed bigger circulation figures in a hurry.

Circulation audit studies aren't much help, either. They stay flat all year—not an indication of readership, just circulation. Also keep in mind that audit figures count how many magazines publishers mail, not how many people actually open a particular issue and read it.

WHAT IS THE BIGGEST MISTAKE IN CREATING AN AD?

Nothing kills off response like not drafting the copy of an ad to a specific, written objective. You start writing all ads the same way: state the objective, then draft the copy to the objective. The objective is generally not to sell a product, the ad objective is to generate a response such as a phone call or, if you are a retailer, a store visit.

All my ads have one or more of the same three objectives: call, write, or come in. If a customer doesn't do any of these, we don't get his business, and the ad fails. All marketing communications should be written to an objective, and somewhere in your ad you should specifically ask your readers to respond to your objective.

WHAT IS THE MOST COMMON ERROR IN PRICING PRODUCTS IN MAILINGS?

The most common error is assuming you know the best sales price for selling your product. Sure, you've seen your product leap off the consumer shelf at $19.95. And you've seen catalogs reorder when they are selling them at a $29.95 list. But if you don't test the price in your direct mail packages, you're making a terrible mistake. A terrible, costly mistake.

The price of your product is determined not only by your product, but by your mailing, the copy, your reader's perception of the product's value, the construction of your offer, your free gift, and any of a multitude of things you've never thought of— including the wealth of your audience and their willingness to send money through the mail. The response can be as variable as what day of the week they get your piece, and it can depend on the individual need of each prospect and the product's perceived value in relation to satisfying this need.

While you may think you know the best price, you will never know or be sure until you test this variable. By testing, you will find not only at what price your product will sell the most, but at what price you make the maximum profit—which may be different. Let the marketplace set the price. Test.

HOW MUCH AD MONEY DO I NEED, AND DO I NEED TO SET A BUDGET FOR ADVERTISING?

The biggest fallacy is to say you are just going to add money to an advertising campaign and expect that the additional funding will ensure its success. In reality, hard work, diligence, dedication, creativity, and devising an action plan, working backward from a set of objectives each step of the way, will increase your chances of success.

Money is not the determinate in marketing a product successfully. If it was, New Coke would have been a tremendous success, as would EuroDisney, the Edsel, and just about every product IBM and Green Giant launched.

There is no correct formula for setting an ad budget for a small firm, I don't care how many books you read, or who tells you there is. Proof of this: there are hundreds of formulas out there, and they are all different.

WHAT IS THE MOST EFFECTIVE TOOL IN DIRECT MARKETING?

Without a doubt, the most effective tool you can use in direct marketing is a letter. For 32¢, you can catch and retain a busy executive's eye, hold the attention of a preoccupied editor, and make a sales pitch that anyone you write to will read.

With a letter, you can slip by a secretary easily, attract favorable attention, create a good impression of your firm or product, and pre-sell or sell your product. It is the most effective you can be in marketing at any price. What a great value—at 32¢! Sending a second letter is also the easiest way to double your marketing effort. Or triple your effort for an additional 32¢. In 25 years of advertising and marketing service, the most effective campaign I have ever written was a series of letters.

"THIS LAWNMOWER MAKES CUTTING THE GRASS SO FAST AND EASY, I BOUGHT IT FOR MY WIFE!"

MAKE SURE YOUR DIRECT MAIL PACKAGES and direct selling ads are the strongest they can be. Make that one extra reader in 1,000 stop, read your ad or package, and send in that additional order. Here's the short course in increasing response.

Every ad or mailing package I write says the same thing: call, come in, or write. These are the objectives. If a person hasn't done any of these, the package failed—we didn't get his business.

Step 1: Start every ad or mailing package the same way: Write the objective in the upper right-hand corner of a blank sheet of paper. Refer to it often. Don't forget, the reason you are writing every word is to fulfill the objective.

Step 2: Draw a line down the middle of your paper. On the left, write down the features of your product. Features are physical characteristics or properties. A feature of a knife, for example, would be a carbon steel blade that holds a keen edge longer.

On the right side of the page, write the benefit that the feature brings to the reader. <u>Benefits are what happen to the reader</u> when the features perform well. The benefits of a carbon blade are easier, smoother, and faster cutting—without any bother of frequent sharpenings.

A lawnmower may have a big engine and a wider cutting blade. These are product features. The benefits are that you can cut your lawn faster and with less effort.

Step 3: Rank the benefits in their order of value.

Step 4: Pick out your biggest and best two or three benefits. Write 20 or so brief, interest-arousing, action-packed headlines highlighting each one. If your headlines are all good, keep writing. You don't need good, you need spectacular. The single greatest one will be the headline of your ad. Or the teaser copy of your mailpiece.

In an ad, you have about two seconds to attract attention and force the reader to continue reading. In a direct mail package, maybe five. These few words had better be irresistible.

These are the most important lines you will write. The wrong headline can decrease ad response by 90%. 90%! You will only get one-tenth of the orders you could receive with a great headline! One-tenth. Instead of 100 orders, you get 10.

In your direct mail package, flaunt your biggest benefits first. Why wait till you lose your readers to pull out your best stuff? Capture attention immediately. Fire all your guns at once, and explode off page one! You'll have plenty of time to lose your readers later.

Step 5: Write a benefit-rich letter. The most effective tool you can use in marketing still costs just 32¢. It's a letter. Or at least it's a piece of paper that looks like a letter.

A letter is a personal communication you send to one or two people. When you send it to 10, 100, or 1 million people, it's a highly stylized ad designed to look like a letter. It's the hardest-working part of your direct mail package. People look at your brochure, but they read your letter. Every piece of direct mail you send should have something in it that looks like a letter.

In your letter, write captivating copy to support your main benefit. Start with a few lines flush right, above the letter salutation, to highlight a sensational benefit, emphasize a terrific offer, or accent your incredible guarantee. Put stars (Shift-8) or dashes around it. This is called a Johnson Box, after its creator.

After your salutation, keep your first paragraph short. Only one line. Two at most.

Explain your teaser copy early on, in an electrifying letter opening. You can repeat the teaser to maintain continuity.

"THIS LAWNMOWER MAKES CUTTING THE GRASS SO FAST AND EASY, I BOUGHT IT FOR MY WIFE!

AS A PROFESSIONAL GARDENER, SHE'LL SAVE TIME AND ENERGY BY CUTTING LAWNS IN HALF THE TIME."

"Now for the FIRST TIME EVER this professional lawncutting system is available to nonprofessionals. For just slightly more than the price of a regular lawnmower, you can **cut your own lawn in half the time** it usually takes you—we guarantee it."

In the body of your letter, keep sentences short. Indent the first line of each paragraph five spaces to start eyeflow. Use a typewriter-style font. Short words. Set margins flush left, rag right. No paragraph over seven lines. Use lots of white space to make the copy look easy to read, even if it isn't.

Use CAPITAL LETTERS once on each page. Use bold twice. Underline a bit more. Use a short-margin paragraph in the center of the page to keep it visually interesting.

Every letter should have a strong PS. Restate your best benefit, what the reader is going to get, your guarantee, and your call to action: ask for the order.

Step 6: Remember AIDA. Attract the attention of the reader. Arouse Interest. Stimulate the Desire. Ask for Action.

Ask for a response two times in your letter and again in the PS. If your reader doesn't act right now, he may put your letter down in that big pile of things to do somewhere between later and never, and eventually it will wind up getting thrown out. Sell the call and the response hard.

Use action words, and stress immediacy: "<u>Send</u> in the card for our free brochure." "<u>Call right now</u> for your free book: 25 tips to cut your lawn faster!" "<u>Call</u> us toll free: Get instant help with your toughest lawncutting questions." "<u>Call now</u> for a free trial offer." "<u>Call now</u> to charge your order...." Sell the call hard.

Step 7. Offer a free gift or incentive for ordering now. This can be as simple as a piece of paper with useful information.

Step 8. In your ad, offer a free brochure, data sheet, or specification sheet. Give the reader an easy, stress-free reason to call. Send a harder-hitting, more benefit-rich, longer mailing package. Can you think of some useful information you can use as a call generator?

Step 9. Provide an easy way to respond. Toll-free phone. Pre-addressed reply envelope. Approved credit, send no money now. Charge orders welcome.

In direct mail, your success may be just 32¢ away. A successful DM package or ad can run for years. The market is out there, and ready when you are.

"INCREASE
YOUR ADVERTISING
RESPONSE BY
10 TIMES!"

A LL MY ADS SAY THE SAME THING: *call, write,* or *come in.* If a customer hasn't done any of these, we didn't get his business. At one point the advertisement has to stimulate this response, or the ad fails.

The process of writing every ad starts exactly the same way: Write your objective in the upper right-hand corner of a blank sheet of paper. Nothing kills an ad faster than having no objective. It should say one or more of the above: call, write, come in. This is a reminder that the response you are seeking is the reason for your ad. Draft your entire ad with your objective in mind. Every line, every word, every graphic—does it increase your response?

The importance of writing the objective of the ad can be demonstrated best by example. I was once called in for a consultation by a large real estate company whose sales were slipping. After an hour's discussion with the owner, who had over 50 years of experience in selling real estate, I outlined the consulting agreement: We'd meet for 10 hours or so, and I'd outline a plan to increase his sales. Disbelievingly, he flatly stated, "I have over 50 years of experience selling real estate—do you mean to tell me in 10 hours of meetings you're going to show me how to sell more houses?"

"Yes," I replied.

"Sir," he said, in continued disbelief, "I have forgotten more about selling houses than you will ever learn in your life." He was right; it was true.

Too bad the reply, "Sir, I have forgotten more about advertising than you have learned in 50 years of selling houses," didn't come to me till months later. Isn't hindsight wonderful? It always lets you know you could have said something more clever, now that it's too late.

We spent a good deal of time reviewing the listings for houses in the real estate sections of the local newspapers. When I asked him the objective of the very expensive one-third-page ads he ran day after day, month after month, he told me quite sincerely, "To sell houses." When I asked him the purpose of the individual listings within these ads, again he replied, "To sell a house."

He was partly right: he had forgotten even more about selling houses than he thought. The objective of the ad was not to sell a house. No one sees a four-line listing and buys a house. The objective of each listing was to generate a phone call. The objective of the entire ad was to generate phone calls. I've never known anyone to see a listing for a house in a newspaper and send a down payment. They see the ad and—if it works—they pick up the phone. Rule number one: The objective of an ad is generally not to sell the product. The objective is to generate phone calls.

TRIPLE YOUR RESPONSE

So I proposed a format change in each listing. *Call now,* the new ads said. *Call for an immediate appointment. For information call!* And we gave the phone number in a multitude of places. After customers read our ads, with all the boxes saying *CALL NOW!* and the phone number showing repeatedly, my client's phone calls tripled in the very first week. That's the value of first writing the objective of the ad, then writing the ad to fulfill the objective. (This lesson was much more expensive for him than for you.)

An axiom in writing direct mail copy also holds true for advertisements, and even more so: AIDA. Attract attention, generate Interest, stimulate the Desire, and ask for Action.

You have about two or three seconds to entice the reader to stop, look at your ad, and read your headline. Which brings us to the second rule of making an effective ad: The headline is by far the most important line in the ad.

GET TEN TIMES YOUR RESPONSE!

Use a headline that will stop the reader dead on the page, capture his attention, and force him to read the rest of the ad. The headline is the ad for your ad.

If you work on writing your ad for 25 hours, make sure to spend 10 of them on the headline. Ten hours on one line? You bet; it can be worth it. The difference between the effectiveness of an ad with a poor headline and one with a great headline can be 10 times. Ten times! Imagine that you take out an ad and get 100 responses. Then, keeping all the other elements of the ad the same, you just change the headline, and now you get 1,000 responses. That's the difference.

Don't write just one or two headlines and pick one. Don't write a dozen. Write 80 or 100. Yes, that's what I do. Write even more if none looks good.

Ask friends to write snappy headlines. Better yet, tell them they'll have the pleasure of seeing their words in print in a magazine if you select their headline to use. If that doesn't work, offer to pay them if their headline is used.

TYPES OF HEADLINES

The most powerful headline you can write contains your biggest reader benefit. One of the best ways to write a benefit-oriented headline for your direct marketing ad is to ask: "What is the biggest benefit of using this product?" In the answer lies the headline of your ad.

For example, if you are selling lawnmowers and yours is the fastest-cutting, cuts the widest path, or has the most horsepower (these are features), you might write in the headline: *Mow your lawn in half the time!*

What is it that makes your product unique and different? This is called your Unique Selling Proposition or USP, and it can be an effective headline if you can show it as a reader benefit. Benefits are an effective way to merchandise your product or service in an ad. A headline that shows the biggest benefit is my _first choice_, and the _safest_ way to write a headline.

"How To"

Another safe—yet effective—headline style is the "How To" format. _How to prepare over 80 meals in under 20 minutes! How to buy any airline ticket at a 50% discount. How to make terrific dinners using only one pot._ If your product lends itself to the how-to-do-it market, even people with mild curiosity will read the ad if the headline shouts "How To!" _How to specify printing to get the lowest price. How to set type without a computer._ (Whoa! Remember those days?) Effective? You bet.

ATTENTION ARRESTER

An attention-arresting headline makes an incredible statement. This is called "teaser copy" when it's placed on the outside of an envelope. Use copy that stirs the reader's interest to such a degree that it forces him or her to read the rest of the ad. Make your headline soooo irresistible people have to read the body copy to see how you support it.

A perfect example is our lawnmower ad with the headline, _This Lawnmower Makes Cutting the Grass So Fast and Easy, I Bought It for My Wife!_ The copy that follows says that she is a professional landscaper, and I bought her this mower to make her job easier. Since it's an unusual occurrence for a man to buy a lawnmower for his wife, it will attract attention and "dare" people to read (or not read) the rest of the ad.

NEW!

Another great formula for success in an ad headline is New! New is always exciting. Is there a new idea, part, feature, or benefit you can show as new? "New" and "Now" are two favorite words of every copywriter, and with great reason: they work. Just check out the shelves of laundry detergent in any supermarket. How many detergents say new? How many really are? Everyone likes a new model, or a newly improved old model.

FREE!

Some words really are magic in advertising. The word "free" in the headline (or in the subhead) beats anything else in attracting attention and getting people interested. For additional value, also include it in the first line of the copy, and again in closing. This is probably _the best_ single word you can use in a headline.

A free offer increases response. Although overplayed and overused, this remains one of the most effective ways to generate a response to an ad. Just be careful to make sure you get qualified responses when offering something for free. Don't wind up sending out mountains of free merchandise or literature and getting back no sales. Ugh. When making free offers, make sure you are advertising to the correct market and that your audience has the money and the authority to purchase your product.

Think of the brilliance of this: A moving company offers in its headline, _Free booklet shows you how to pack your house and valuables for moving._ It offers (1) a free book that (2) directly benefits its ideal audience: people who are moving. I'm sure it produces a ton of the highest-quality and most well-qualified leads.

The formula for the safest, most successful ad headline is simple: Free booklet offers benefit, benefit, benefit. This is my personal recommendation when you are writing any ad. It's particularly helpful when you are having trouble writing a great headline.

Stated another way: _**New Feature makes benefit, benefit, benefit.**_ This formula is an effective and safe way to write any headline, and I don't care what you are selling. Additional variations are: _Free booklet tells you how to get benefit, benefit, benefit_; or _Free item shows you benefit, benefit, benefit._ When you are having trouble, this formula is the answer.

Another example: Suppose you're a printer. Attractive headlines may be: _Free booklet shows you how to specify printing to get lower costs; Free brochure shows you how to select paper; Free brochure shows you how to specify correct colors; Free booklet shows low-cost folding options._ These headlines sound so good, I'd like to get these guides myself. If you already have a promotional mailer printed, *Free booklet shows you how to buy printing at a 10% discount* would be a perfect headline for your ad—just include a 10% off coupon with the piece.

Low-cost free gifts make for great response, too. If you sell typography, the free offer of a type chart on acetate or a film showing character height and leading is always an excellent choice. Or a photo percentage calculating wheel. These low-cost free offers fulfill the requirements of a call generator and a great gift: they (1) are only needed by your perfect audience, those who specify and buy type; (2) are low in cost and ship inexpensively; (3) have a high perceived value; (4) have a useful and long life; and (5) stay in your prospect's view all the time. Nice.

One of the lowest-cost ways to raise your response rate is to create a valuable and useful free gift. Probably the most inexpensive way to do this is to create free literature. Paper is cheap. Create a data sheet that is informative, contains "how to" information, or explains something practical about your industry, product, or service. A safe variation on our free offer can be to give away an educational booklet on the subject. Can you find some "how to" or useful information related to your service or product that potential customers will want?

Make your material as useful as you can, so your free gift has a high value to your audience. In your ad, make your offer sound so great that customers will feel they are missing something if they don't call right away to get it. Use <u>Free!</u> liberally throughout your ad. If you create a useful gift of lasting value, customers will call you for years to use your services. As a lead-generation device, an informational product is an excellent marketing tool. Probably the best.

When drafting your ad, kindly remember you aren't in a contest to see who can be the most unusual or win an award for being the most different. You just want to make money; so create a good, solid ad, built on a traditional format that has proven time and time again it will pay for itself by generating maximum response (your objective). Ads that draw the greatest number of qualified responses have the best chance of success. This is your objective, and the basis for a short ad campaign on a limited budget. If you have a long-running campaign, you can be more flexible in your style and content. If you have an unlimited budget, let's talk.

Get that one extra reader in 100 who was going to whiz right by your ad to stop and read your headline, read the ad, pick up a pencil or the phone, or come in. The headline is the most important line in your ad—don't be satisfied with a good one. Make sure it's a smashing great one. Make a free offer specific to your audience, and make it sound sensational. Don't forget to track the results of each ad to its source. But that's another article.

A Simple Method to Track Ad Response

BY NOW I'VE HEARD EVERY SINGLE EXCUSE EVER IMAGINED about why my clients aren't tracking exactly where each customer heard of us, saw us, or learned about us. The excuses range from the uncreative (I didn't have a pencil) to the absurd (so when I thought it was an earthquake...). While some get credit for imagination, none get credit for effective tracking—which is a most necessary part of every campaign.

Without tracking where each response came from, how are you to know which ad or press release worked? Or which magazine produced better results for each dollar invested? And most of all, how are you going to save money next year by knowing which is the least effective medium—so you can stop running ads and wasting your money in it?

The simplest tracking system is a few pads of paper placed by the phones. These can be 3" x 5" cards, 51/2" x 81/2" sheets, or anything in between. If you feel rich, you can run them through your laser printer or have the top of each sheet printed with the words, "AND HOW DID YOU HEAR OF OUR COMPANY?"

Instruct each employee who answers the phone to ask—at the very beginning of the conversation—how the caller heard of your company. If in a magazine, which issue? If the phone book, what listing? If through a friend, can you get the name and address of the friend for a follow-up "thank you" letter? Assign a centralized drawer for the tracking function, and after every phone call, put each slip in the drawer. In a month, total all the sources and you'll know where your advertising works—and even more importantly, where it doesn't. At the end of 6 months, you'll know darn well where each of your advertising dollars is working the hardest.

If you're a retailer, my favorite tracking method is to question each purchaser when they bring their merchandise up to the cash register. If possible, have them fill out a "Please put me on your mailing list" form at this time also. Feel free to ask tracking questions on this form. My next favorite method is to use a coupon, or a coupon disguised as a gift certificate, in an ad or direct mail piece. When the coupon is presented, you'll know exactly where the customer saw it.

THE ONE
EVENING
MARKETING PLAN
AND THE EXECUTION
OF THE ENTIRE PR
PLAN THE NEXT DAY

A DVERTISING IS KNOWING WHAT TO SAY. Marketing is knowing where to say it. Do all your marketing in one evening? Follow up by completing your entire PR campaign the next day? Impossible?

Marketing. Direct Marketing. Great buzzwords, but what the heck is marketing, anyhow? My definition is seven words, if you count the "a": "Marketing is selling to a defined audience." When you sell to anyone, that's sales. When you narrow your list of prospects, that's marketing.

Most products are marketed nationally through magazines. The best marketing tools are directories of magazines. And a few of the best are the *SRDS* (formerly Standard Rate and Data Services) *Business Publication Advertising Source*™, *Bacon's Newspaper/Magazine Directory*, the *Oxbridge Communications National*

Directory of Magazines, and *Burrelle's Media Directory/Magazines and Newsletters.* All are softcover books weighing well over two pounds each.

In 10 minutes and 1,000 words, you're going to have a great action marketing attack plan and a great PR plan. You'll need a press release and a photo of your product, if you have one. And enough envelopes to send all your releases.

PLAN A.

Go to the main library in your area—they should have a copy of Bacon's. Hopefully a new one, but an old one works OK, too. Good thing you didn't have to buy it—it costs about $280. Worth the money if you use it a lot, but for a single campaign you may not need it.

In the beginning of the directory of magazines you'll find a two-page industry directory broken into 90 market classifications. They're shown alphabetically and numbered from 1 to 90 in their order of alphabetical appearance. Classifications start with 1-Advertising, 2-Amusements, 3-Architecture and so on, ending with classifications 89-Women's and 90-Woodworking. Each market is also shown with the number of trade or consumer magazines sent to that industry.

Larger market classifications are broken into several subgroups. So class 18-Computers is broken into 18A-Computer Technology/Data Management magazines, 18B-General Interest, 18C-Software/Operating Systems, 18D-Marketing/Retailing magazines, and so forth. 450 magazines serve the computer field. Whew.

Each subgroup also shows the number of magazines serving it. Group 89-Women's is broken into the following subgroups: 89A-General Interest (68 magazines), 89B-Parenting (81 magazines), 89C-Beauty and Fashion (7), 89D-Brides (18), 89E-Homemaking (76), and 89F-Romance (6). The layout Bacon's uses is:

Group (Count) Market Classification	Page
88 - (57) Wearing Apparel	**648**
88A - (26) General Wearing Apparel............	648
88B - (4) Men's and Boys' Wearing Apparel.	650

88C -(14) Women's and Children's	650	
88D - (13) Shoes and Leather Goods	653	
89 - (256) Women's.................................	**653**	
89A - (68) Women's General Interest............	653	
89B - (81) Parenting	664	
89C - (7) Beauty and Fashion......................	665	etc.,

Hmmm. I wonder if this means in marketing, as in life, women have taken up homemaking and parenting at the cost of beauty and fashion?

So now we have 90 major markets and their subordinate markets, with the number of magazines serving each field, laid out on two pages. Lotta marketing information on those pages.

But if you're having trouble finding your precise prospects, the next section, the <u>Alphabetical Cross Index of Market Classifications</u>, will help. Outside of its confusing name, this section is simple. It's five pages of products, services, and industries listed alphabetically. The corresponding major market where each is found is shown next to it.

For example, under H you can find "Hairstyling," with references to major classifications: 8-Beauty, Barber and Cosmetics Trade, and 89-Women's (with further reference to the subgroup 89C-Beauty and Fashion). Infants' Wear can be found with references to class 88-Wearing Apparel (the subgroup 88C-Women's and Children's Wearing Apparel) and class 89-Women's (the subgroup 89B-Parenting).

The layout is:

— H —

Hairstyling 8A, 89C
Handicapped 79H
Hardware...............................37A
Hardware, Computer 18A, 18C

After these seven pages, there are almost 700 pages of magazine data. This is the <u>Magazine Listings by Market Classifications</u> section. So if you are marketing to banks, they are all found (regardless of the publication's name) in the same section: 7-Banking and Finance. If you are selling a leather case that would make a nice camera bag, the 39 publications in classification 65-Photography would define your market pretty well. Although if you wanted to sell your leather case to a broader range of markets, you may want to try classifications 86-Travel, 80-Sporting Goods, and 38-Gifts, not to mention 23-Department, Chain, and Specialty Stores, and 27-Export.

Magazine listings in this 673-page section show each magazine's address, editors, phone numbers, ad rates, circulation statistics, and other boring stuff. Data also shows you an editorial profile of the magazine: a one-paragraph synopsis from the publisher of what the magazine is about. This paragraph will give you an idea of whether they take press releases or not.

Before we get to plan B, let's look at the 700-page Magazine Listing Section in brief. This data-intense section is where you do your fine-tuning and figure out if each individual magazine is an exact fit for your press release or ad. In the beginning of each classification here—before all of the data is shown for the 265 banking and finance magazines, for example—there is a short "related market classifications" list of markets you may wish to consider for cross-selling. This makes your marketing even easier and more in-depth. For example, in the beginning of section 29-Fitness and Health, Bacon's suggests that if you are marketing a product to this class, you might also check out classifications 31-Food, 49-Men's, 50-Medical, 80-Sports and Sporting Goods, and 89-Women's.

Each magazine's statistical data is then shown, about 20 write-ups to a page. This is where you do your own analysis in depth. Read each write-up and figure out from this data if the particular magazine is the perfect match for you and your product. This is how it's supposed to be done.

PLAN B. THE ONE-DAY PLAN.

Call Bacon's (800/621-0561) and ask for their order form. It looks exactly like the Major Market Classifications section in their book: two pages of 90 markets, listed alphabetically, showing the number of magazines that goes to each. Note the number of magazines sent to each market you are serving. You'll immediately get an idea of how large your markets are.

Select all the industries where you'd like to sell your product. Each market listed has an open box in front of it so that, with a single check mark, you can order mailing labels for all the magazines in that market. Order them if you have time, and do your own press release mailing.

BUT THAT'S NOT THE ONE-DAY PLAN.

THE ONE-DAY PLAN IS...

...continued next article—see the next article for the conclusion of this terrific plan and, and...just kidding. OK, OK, here's the one-day plan. Check off all the markets where you'd like your releases to be sent. Then send one copy of your release, along with your black-and-white photo, to Bacon's (Mailing Services Dept., 332 S. Michigan Ave., Room 1020 Dept-JD, Chicago, IL 60604), telephone 800/753-6675. Include envelopes they can use (large enough for the photo without bending). They will duplicate the release and your photo and send them to all the magazines in all the markets you select.

Their prices are reasonable. A one-page release costs $75/hundred, $115 for 200 releases, $225 for 500, and $440 for 1,000. A one-page photo release with a 5" x 7" photo costs $138/hundred, $250 for 200 photo releases, $525 for 500, and $1,000 for 1,000. Add postage to these costs; it's not included. You're finished. Depending on the quality of your release and photo, in about three months you'll begin to see leads generated in the write-ups you've received. Instant marketing for the '90s. OK, this article ran over: 1,233 words. It's still a pretty neat plan, though.

MAGAZINES

_____ Mail to the category numbers checked below (quantity for each category is indicated in parentheses).
_____ Omit Canadian magazines (Canadian publications will be included in your mailing unless you specify otherwise).

Group Count Market Classification

___01 (151) Advertising, Marketing & Public Relations
___01A(48) Advertising
___01B(19) Public Relations
___01C(67) Marketing
___01D(17) Selling & Sales Management
___02 (159) Amusements & Motion Pictures
___02A(35) Motion Pictures Trade
___02B(22) Movie & TV Fan
___02C(21) Performing Arts
___02D(49) Local Entertainment Guides
___02E (32) Amusements, Casinos & Gaming
___03 (40) Architecture
___03A(23) Architecture
___03B(17) Interior Design
___04 (404) Automotive
___04A(64) Automotive Trade & Service Stations
___04B (17) Buses, Taxicabs & Public Transportation
___04C(51) Motor Trucks
___04D(23) State & Regional Trucking
___04E (15) Trailers, Motor Homes & Recreational Vehicles
___04F (39) Auto Sports & Racing
___04G (8) General Interest Auto: Consumer
___04H(69) Special Interest Auto: Consumer
___04I (65) Aftermarket, Parts & Repair
___04J (4) Tires & Rubber
___04K (49) Motorcycles
___05 (109) Aviation & Aerospace
___05A(81) Aviation Trade & Aerospace
___05B(28) Sport & Hobby Aviation
___06 (7) Baking
___07 (289) Banking & Finance
___07A(58) Banking
___07B(173) Finance
___07C(28) State & Regional Banking & Finance
___07D(30) Personal Finance
___08 (24) Beauty, Barber & Cosmetics Trade
___09 (73) Beverages
___09A(28) Beverages & Bottling
___09B(35) State & Regional Beverage
___09C(10) Wine Trade
___10 (142) Book Trade, Journalism & Publishing
___10A(41) Book Trade & Libraries
___10B(32) Journalism & Writing
___10C(42) Publishing
___10D(27) Book & Literary Review
___11 (180) Building
___11A(55) Building & Construction
___11B(78) State & Regional Building

Group Count Market Classification

___11C(27) Allied Building Trades
___11D(20) Home Centers & Hardware
___12 (718) Business & Commercial
___12A(105) General Business
___12B(351) City, State & Regional Bus.
___12C(110) Management Methods & Personnel Operations
___12D(39) Accounting
___12E (13) International Business: Foreign Based
___12F (39) International Business: U.S. Based
___12G(37) Meetings & Conventions
___12H(24) Careers & Employment
___13 (17) Ceramics & Glassware
___13A (4) Ceramics
___13B (13) Glass & Glassware
___15 (53) Chemical
___16 (354) Churches & Religion
___16A(12) Religious Administration
___16B(342) Religion
___17 (13) Cleaning/Dyeing/Laundry
___18 (530) Computers & Data Processing
___18A(67) Computer Technology/ Data Management
___18B(94) General Interest Computers
___18C(154) Software/Operating Systems
___18D(33) Internet/Online
___18E (81) Industry Applications
___18F (51) Related Interest
___18G(23) Computer/Video Games
___18H(27) Mktg./Retailing/Reselling
___19 (66) Conservation, Environmental & Nature
___20 (26) Country/Western Living
___21 (22) Dairy Products
___22 (63) Dental
___23 (73) Department, Chain & Specialty Stores
___23A(56) Department, Chain & Specialty Stores
___23B(11) Shopping Center Operations & Design
___23C (6) Vending & Automatic Merch.
___24 (99) Drugs
___25 (152) Electrical & Electronics
___25A(55) Electrical
___25B(86) Electronics
___25C(11) Appliances & Appliance Retailing
___26 (116) Engineering
___26A(45) General Engineering
___26B(62) Civil Engineering & Heavy Construction
___26C (9) Surveying & Mapping
___27 (23) Export/Import & Int'l Trade
___28 (517) Farming
___28A(24) General Farm Journals
___28B(156) Regional Farming

Group Count Market Classification

___28C(13) Farm Chemicals & Fertilizers
___28D(45) Fruit, Nut & Vegetable
___28E (63) Horses & Horse Breeding
___28F(115) Livestock
___28G(14) Poultry
___28H(33) Rural Electric
___28I (8) Specialized Farming
___28J (6) Meat Packing & Merchandising
___28K (6) Farm Equipment
___28M (9) Milling, Feed & Grain
___28N(25) Field Crops
___29 (178) Fitness & Personal Health
___29A(131) Fitness & Personal Health
___29B(16) Nutrition Trade
___29C(10) Health Clubs/Spas
___29D(21) Disabled/Physically Challenged
___30 (115) Florist, Landscaping & Gardening
___30A(74) Florist, Landscape & Nursery Trade
___30B(41) Gardening
___31 (107) Food
___31A(43) Food Industry/Processing
___31B (5) Confectionery
___31C(59) Epicurean
___32 (38) Furniture & Home Furnishings
___33 (37) Fraternal & Club
___34 (514) General Interest Consumer
___34A(65) General Editorial
___34B(323) General Editorial - Metro
___34C(18) News Magazines
___34D(71) Political & Social Opinion
___34E (15) Entertainment
___34F (22) History & Americana
___35 (75) Gifts, Antiques & Collectibles
___36 (82) Grocery/Food Marketing
___36A(42) Grocery & Food Marketing
___36B(40) State & Regional Grocery
___37 (107) Home & Garden
___37A(64) Home
___37B(43) Home Building/Remodeling
___38 (40) Home Electronics, Audio & Video
___38A(20) Consumer Electronics Trade
___38B(20) Consumer Interest Audio & Video
___39 (202) Hospitals & Healthcare
___39A(41) Hospital & Healthcare Administration
___39B(107) Healthcare Trade
___39C(42) Medical & Diagnostic Equipment
___39D(12) Emergency Medical Services
___40 (25) Hotels, Motels & Resorts
___41 (203) Industrial
___41A(135) Industrial
___41B (25) Design & Product Engineering
___41C(18) Security

Group Count Market Classification

___41D(25) Occupational Health & Safety
___42 (21) Instrumentation & Control Systems
___43 (73) Insurance
___44 (18) Jewelry
___45 (178) Legal
___45A(69) Legal
___45B(109) City, State & Regional Legal
___46 (45) Lumber & Forestry
___46A(26) Lumber
___46B(19) Forestry
___48 (106) Marine
___48A(27) Marine & Boat Trade
___48B(65) Pleasure Craft
___48C(14) Commercial Fishing
___49 (36) Men's
___49A(20) Men's General Interest
___49B(16) Adult Publications
___50 (814) Medical
___50A(114) General Medical
___50B(193) Specialized Medicine
___50C(13) Chiropractic
___50D(23) Obstetrics/Gynecology
___50E(33) Veterinary
___50F(75) City, State & Regional
___50G(58) Surgery
___50H(44) Medical Laboratory/Research
___50I (30) Cardiology
___50J (37) Orthopedics/Sports Medicine/Physical Therapy/Rehabilitation
___50K(26) Psychiatric/Psychology
___50L (28) Pediatrics
___50M(22) Radiology
___50N(98) Nursing
___50P(20) Oncology/Cancer
___51 (64) Metalworking & Machinery
___51A(59) Metalworking & Machinery
___51B (5) Welding
___52 (63) Military
___54 (26) Mining & Coal
___55 (18) Mortuary & Cemetery
___55A(12) Mortuary
___55B (6) Cemetery
___56 (149) Municipal, County & National Government
___56A(104) Municipal, County & National Government
___56B(26) Police & Law Enforcement
___56C(19) Fire Protection
___57 (147) Music & Music Trade
___57A(19) Music Trade
___57B(61) Music
___57C(67) Music Fan
___58 (19) Office Equipment & Stationery

Group Count Market Classification

___59 (52) Optical
___60 (18) Packaging
___61 (142) Parenting & Family
___61A(53) National Parenting & Family
___61B(89) Regional Parenting & Family
___62 (24) Paper & Paper Products
___63 (80) Petroleum & Gas
___63A(64) Petroleum
___63B(16) Gas
___64 (37) Pets & Pet Supplies
___65 (39) Photography & Microfilm
___65A(23) Professional Photography
___65B(16) Consumer Interest Photography
___66 (33) Plastics & Rubber
___67 (55) Plumbing, Heating & Air Conditioning
___67A(49) Plumbing, Heating & Air Conditioning
___67B (6) Refrigeration
___68 (50) Power & Energy
___68A(17) Power
___68B(33) Energy
___69 (71) Printing, Graphics & Commercial Arts
___71 (11) Purchasing
___72 (147) Radio, TV, Cable & Recording
___72A(96) Radio, TV, Cable & Recording
___72B (9) Audio/Video Trade
___72C (7) Amateur Radio
___72D(35) TV Listing Guides
___73 (18) Railroad
___74 (132) Real Estate & Building Maintenance
___74A(96) Real Estate
___74B (36) Building Management & Maintenance
___75 (71) Restaurants & Clubs
___75A(42) Restaurants
___75B (6) Clubs
___75C(23) Catering & Food Service
___76 (27) Rock & Cement/Masonry
___77 (208) Schools & Education
___77A(155) Education
___77B(53) City/State/Regional Education
___78 (112) Science
___79 (367) Special Interest & Lifestyle
___79A(34) Children's
___79B(64) Youth
___79C(122) Mature Lifestyle
___79D(71) Gay
___79E (33) Ethnic Lifestyle
___79H(22) Young Adult/Generation X
___79I (21) Student Publications
___80 (574) Sports & Sporting Goods

Group Count Market Classification

___80A(64) Sports Industry & Trade
___80B (77) Sports
___80C(128) Hunting & Fishing
___80D(74) General Outdoor Recreation
___80E (50) Golf
___80F (16) Running
___80G(38) Skiing & Winter Sports
___80H(10) Tennis
___80I (23) Guns & Shooting
___80J (20) Bicycling
___80K(27) Water Sports
___80L (34) Field Sports
___80M(13) Contact Sports
___81 (17) Textile
___82 (124) Telecommunications
___82A(78) Telecommunications
___82B(23) Networking
___82C(23) Mobile/Cellular Communications
___83 (12) Tobacco
___84 (227) Toys, Crafts, Arts & Hobbies
___84A(17) Toys, Crafts, Arts & Hobbies Trade
___84B(140) Crafts, Games & Hobbies
___84C(53) Art
___84D(17) Sports Cards & Memorabilia
___85 (58) Traffic, Shipping & Warehousing
___86 (295) Travel & Tourism
___86A(51) Travel Trade
___86B (41) A A A Motor Club Publications
___86C(31) Airline Inflight
___86D(89) Regional Visitor's Guides
___86E (78) General Interest Travel
___86F (5) Business & Corporate Travel
___87 (132) Waste Management/ Pollution Control
___87A(56) Environmental/Pollution Control/Recycling
___87B (43) Hazardous Materials/ Waste Management
___87C(33) Water & Sanitation
___88 (52) Wearing Apparel
___88A(40) Wearing Apparel
___88B (12) Shoes & Leather Goods
___89 (146) Women's
___89A(85) Women's General Interest
___89B(25) Brides
___89C(28) Beauty & Fashion
___89D (8) Romance
___90 (23) Woodworking

TOTAL LISTINGS - 11,274

OPTIONAL: When selecting by category, you have the option of mailing only to those magazines that accept releases concerning (check only one):

_____ New Products
_____ Personnel News

OR: _____ Omit magazines that do not use photos

The Two-Paragraph Rule of Readership Survival

If you owned a restaurant, you'd only be as good as your last meal. If it wasn't any good, your customer won't be back.

If you owned a print shop, you'd only be as good as your last job. Deliver poor printing, or deliver late—you're outta there.

In direct mail, you're only as good as your last two paragraphs.

You see, in direct mail, you get less of a shot. You can entice your potential customer to open your package with great teaser copy; you can write the most brilliant opening line, then have a compelling set of benefits to keep your reader reading. But as soon as your copy becomes dull, boring, stiff—or worse, less interesting—your mail piece will hit the round file faster than you can get gas eating at Denny's.

And therein lies the danger of long-copy packages in direct mail. Any time you put together two paragraphs that aren't crisp, fluid, and fun reading, your readership drops off dramatically—and fast. So does your response, and your income.

In today's busy environment, readers simply no longer have time for long passages. Just give me the essence; the Cliffs Notes. Don't bother me with the long, lurid details, just give me straight-up information in a fast and easy-to-digest form. Information is presented in catch phrases and synopses. News—and information—is delivered today in bits and bytes. TV news, the ultimate presenter of hyped stories and trivial information, is delivered in soundbites, in three-second bursts, just like videos on MTV.

In direct mail, if you can hold a reader's attention for a couple of minutes, you're doing much better than average. Five minutes in your package is excellent. And if they look for it, can they find the order form in all the clutter? If they do and they can, you're probably about 85% of the way home.

Just keep in mind, the longer your package, the more chances you give your reader to find those two not-quite-up-to-snuff paragraphs, and the faster your mail piece goes from the black "we made money" to the red "we lost money" side of your profit and loss statement.

The biggest danger of long copy: readership fall-off. When in doubt about any copy you write, strike it out, keep it short.

THE 15 PAGE
DIRECT MARKETING
ACTION PLAN

I F THE THOUGHT OF WRITING 15 PAGES of material doesn't scare you, pick up your pen and complete a tremendous segment of your marketing.

Here are the pieces. The material you'll write is a press release, a cover letter, and a short series (two or three) of sales letters to people who respond to your magazine write-ups. In addition, you'll need an introductory letter to better accounts, plus a slightly longer series of letters to send to them over time. This is how all the pieces fit together:

The worst mistake you can make with a high-quality lead is to send a letter and a brochure, call a week later, and when there is no immediate sale, file the lead—never to see it again until you go through the drawer years later to clean it out. Ugh. If your marketing programs sound like this, you're missing some of the easy sales you can get from minimal, inexpensive (32¢) second and third efforts.

While I don't encourage clients to beat a dead horse further, usually more than one piece of communication or advertising is necessary to convert a suspect into a prospect, into a sale that involves any substantial amount of money. The basis for this principle is what I call **Multiple Exposure Marketing**. Everyone has their own favorite number of exposures for this: five sales calls, seven ad strikes, three phone calls—I don't care which number you choose as long as it's more than one. It simply takes more than one contact to make a sizable sale. The larger sales really do go to the people making these additional efforts.

To separate real potential buyers from the universe of everyone who may have any possible interest in your product, including your competitors, you need to get a list of qualified names. In the direct marketing arena, this is accomplished most commonly in two ways: First, by buying a list of all possible suspects, narrowed down as far as possible to actual prospects by creative list procurement, and whittled down further by database enhancements to the list. So call your list broker, and make him work for his money. Keep digging until you find the best list possible; a little extra work here will be well worth it in terms of increased response percentages.

The second way to get suspects is to subscribe to the trade journals sent to the industries where you are marketing. Then take out an ad in each of them, and place those people who express an interest in your products or services on your house mailing list. With this method, you'll find that you'll need to invest about ten grand for what you hope will be a great bunch of leads. Right. OR—for most of my clients, it's go to Plan B. The $25 plan.

Luckily, I happen to have a copy of Plan B in my file. Here's Plan B. (For the money-conscious, and the rest of us mortals who drive old cars.) Go to the library and find the magazines that serve the industries you are marketing to in the *SRDS Business Publication Advertising Source*™, the nicely put-together *Burrelle's Media Directory/Magazines and Newsletters*, or the *Oxbridge Communications National Directory of Magazines*. With any of these tools, you can find your markets—and the magazines that serve them—in less than an evening. These directories make finding the trade journals and consumer interest–specific magazines easier than ever.

Get the magazines (for free) by calling their advertising departments and requesting a media kit. The magazine people know that when media kits go out, the money comes in...and they send them promptly. While you're on the phone with the magazine folks, ask if they print a directory or annual reference issue and request that, too. Usually the publishers sell their annual directory, but if you ask for it at this time under the umbrella of "We may buy advertising space in this," it's always sent for free. It's a powerful industry resource to find the major players.

As they arrive, read through the magazines looking for competitors' ads. If you see a competitor's ad, call the magazine and find out how often your competitor runs it. This will tell you how well it's working for them.

Next, assess the market fit of each magazine. Assign each magazine a letter grade between *A* and *F* according to the likelihood of having an ad ·for your product work profitably in that publication. Write this letter grade on the cover, along with the cost of a full-page ad and a one-quarter-page ad. Finally, note if there is a column or department devoted to new products or product briefs. This will appear as a spread of small product photos, each followed by a one- or two-paragraph write-up. This is the way press releases appear in print. Write the name of this column on the cover, too.

Now throw out the plethora of ads, rate cards, and other extraneous material the magazine folks sent you. Boy, they sure like to write, don't they? Save the magazines in which you are considering placing an ad, and also the ones that may accept your press release. Just save the covers of the other magazines—so in six months, when you can't remember which magazines you reviewed and what they looked like, you'll have a record of it. A thin record.

Read through the remaining magazines that are applicable to your markets. Write a one-page press release and send it to the ones that accept releases, along with a cover letter that mentions how you enjoy their magazine. Say that you have included a release for their column entitled "xxxx," and specifically name the column. This alerts the editor that you are serious about being in their industry, you read their magazine, and you did your homework by becoming familiar with their new product column. This increases your chances for a free press write-up by about 25%.

If you really want to increase the chance of having your release printed—by about 80%—call the editor and ask, "Are you the correct person I should send this release to?" Make sure you have a quality one-minute spiel about your product ready. When you send your press release, be sure to include a cover letter that lets them know it was nice speaking with them, even if it wasn't. This reminds them that you are the one who called and spoke with them personally. This reminder is invaluable in ensuring that your release will be published.

Send all your releases with personalized letters, and include clear, crisp black-and-white product photos (5" x 7"). It will take about three months before the releases get printed and start to generate leads for you. You don't get this time off. While you're waiting for the magazines to publish your release, get busy with the next part.

Part Deux. Create a sales letter campaign which you'll send to people who respond to your magazine press release. Make sure you write about the BENEFITS of your product and what's in it for them. Include reasons to buy now. Offer something special to close the sale immediately. If possible, include a business reply envelope in which they can enclose money when they send an order. And an order form to increase the likelihood they understand they are to order now! Create a second sales letter and data sheet and mail it two to three weeks later. If it's a hot list or the initial response is very good, mail a third letter. As with all approaches, test this two- and three-part mailing for profitability.

Scour the magazines and directories for the names and addresses of better prospects. Make calls to large firms in your markets to find out the names of big purchasers at each firm. No need to talk to them just yet; this is merely an information-gathering call and pretty easy to do.

The rest of the writing is to seduce your very best magazine prospects and your hand-picked prospect list of about 100 people. Write a series of sales letters—maybe six or seven—and send them to these "best of the best" prospects every three to four weeks. This is a short campaign to win the hearts and minds of your newly-acquired prospective customer base.

Create a winning direct mail campaign—with a hard-hitting, benefit-rich letter, data sheet (or brochure if you have one), BRE, and order form. The letter is the key to selling through the mail—make sure yours is benefit-heavy and asks for the order (the objective of the piece) several times and again in the PS.

Start out the series like every other sales letter, with an interest-arousing short opening, then dive right into benefits, benefits, benefits. No need to be pushy here; you still have five or six more letters to go. Second letter: Still casual and friendly, "In my last letter to you on May 9th, I mentioned several benefits we offer over our competitors' models. There are many additional benefits I'd like to highlight that will save you quite a bit of time and work." Now feel free to mention additional benefits.

Over the next five letters, create a friendly dialogue and rapport with your prospect. All letters are personalized, and no prospects know that anyone else is receiving them but themselves. Each letter gets progressively harder-selling. Ask for the order. Cajole. Plead. Be frank. Be sincere. But be friendly (and persistent), and the sales will come.

A letter is a powerful sales vehicle and the most effective marketing tool you can buy for under a dollar. If you decide to call these people after this multiple exposure letter campaign, I guarantee all recipients will know who you are at the first mention of your name. If the letters are constructed to be friendly and persuasive, all of your customers will feel good about purchasing from your firm. Yes, from just a few letters. From just a few 32¢ letters.

A New Angle to Getting Media Coverage

JUST BECAUSE SOME MEDIA DIRECTORIES don't have the distribution the larger magazine directories have, it doesn't mean they aren't as good—or better. Take the *National PR Pitch Books*, for example. Published by the Infocom Group in California (800/959-1059, fax 510/879-4331), the *Business & Consumer Edition* has the weight (over 4 lbs.) and feel (over 700 pages) of any of the other major directories. But there's a big difference, and a new angle.

The editors of this series of PR pitch books have interviewed the nation's top editors, writers, publishers, producers, syndicated columnists, reporters, and journalists on what stories they are looking for, and how they like to be pitched. The responses they received—in many cases the direct quotes from the journalists themselves—are reprinted in each book.

Imagine knowing the inside track on how, when, and what to pitch; editorial hot buttons, quirks and peeves, deadlines, and best times to call. Imagine having the insight to correctly pitch your story or product for the best possible chance of media placement. If you'd like to use the press in your favor consistently, this is valuable information. What a great tool to let you know exactly what to send, what not to send, how and when to follow up, and the editorial mission of each journalist.

The *Business & Consumer Edition* contains over 170 newspapers with circulation of over 100,000, over 460 top business and consumer magazines, over 350 talk radio stations in the largest radio markets, over 100 nationally syndicated radio shows, almost two dozen wire services, over 200 of the top nationally syndicated TV news and consumer shows, and over 450 syndicated newspaper columnists. Granted, it doesn't have 10,000 business magazines or the tremendous depth of some of the other media directories, but it does have all of the top publications, shows, and news bureaus—plus in-depth contact listings that include personal phone lines, fax numbers, and e-mail addresses.

In frank and brutal reality, the *National PR Pitch Books* simply contain *contact dossiers* on the nation's top editors, producers, bookers, and journalists. It's inside information and advice that can get your PR consistently placed in the top markets. This PR reference tool makes an excellent supplement to your PR library. Do we use it in our own office? All the time.

companies." Small companies can hit it big with Collins, but only if they connect with larger market trends. Fax him a short release on your client's product. Avoid the phone.

porter: Claudia Deutsch. Phone: (212) 556-1023. (Pron. "doitch.") Covers manufacturing and industry. Deutsch admits she's willing to listen to -- and sometimes even act on -- tips from the PR world, as long as there is meat to your proposal. "The thing I need more than anything else in the world are story ideas -- but not pitches, not just calls to introduce yourself as representing such-and-such company, who are the leading, the largest or the best something," she explains. "I have no patience with 'the leading,' 'the largest' or 'the best.'" Deutsch is responsible for tracking major manufacturing companies across the nation. She profiles major players, but occasionally pays attention to up-and-comers and sideline players, especially if the company "has a product I'm fascinated by." She prefers to get her pitches over the phone, as long as your call is placed after 10 a.m., is centered on a newsy hook, and is direct and to the point. Cut straight to the chase, and don't include her in any meet-the-CEO lunches. You can phone even after 4 p.m., and even though she might be checking her watch, she says that "it's a myth that we're all on deadline every day. Believe me, if I'm on a deadline, I'll tell you. Just respect that and say that you'll call me back at another time." Avoid sending unsolicited faxes and making follow-up calls. She says to "trust the mail and trust that I'm not shy. I will call if I am interested."

porter: Judith Dobrzynski. Phone: (212) 556-5265. (Pron. "doh brin ski.") Covers management. "I do some management, but I also do a lot of [general] trend stories from a management point of view." "The kinds of stories I do require a lot of access." Be prepared to promise the reporter similar access to your company. Don't pitch follow-ups to stories she has already done. "I prefer a short letter...with enough so I can get a sense of the story." Don't call her; write first.

porter: Geraldine Fabrikant. Phone: (212) 556-1143. Covers the media and entertainment.

porter: Seth Faison. Covers general assignments.

porter: Esther Fein. Phone: (212) 556-7097. Covers publishing. Pens "Book Notes." Also covers gerontology and healthcare.

porter: Doug Frantz. Phone: (212) 556-4076. Covers investigative assignments.

porter: Milton Freudenheim. Phone: (212) 556-4656. (Pron. "FROY den highm") Covers the healthcare industry and writes a monthly column for the business section entitled "Business and Health." His daily reporting tends to focus on pharmaceutical corporations and hospital chains.

porter: Kenneth Gilpin. Phone: (212) 556-3508. Covers general assignments.

porter: Saul Hansell. Phone: (212) 556-5908. Fax: (212) 556-4007. Email: hansell@nytimes.com. Covers banking and Wall Street with a mix of breakers, trends and profiles. Send him real news only -- don't risk it with anything less. He warns sternly, "I ask PR people this: 'would you tell this to

your mother and would she be interested?' And if they say no, then I ask them why they're calling me." This will do more than put you on the spot; you'll lose his ever-important respect. Stress the broad implications of your story. If "big institutions [are] involved and it will affect consumers" he wants to know about it. Mail is best, but if you call, do it in the morning.

Reporter: Diana Henriques. Phone: (212) 556-4397. Covers investigative assignments.

Reporter: John Holusha. Phone: (212) 556-4690. (Pron. "holl oo SHAY.") Covers manufacturing technology and its effect on the environment.

Reporter: Robert Hurtado. Phone: (212) 556-4640. Covers consumer securities and credit markets.

Reporter: (Ms.) Shawn Kennedy. Phone: (212) 556-7344. Writes mainly about public-housing concerns. Kennedy is interested in public-private partnerships formed to develop affordable housing. She likes to talk to sources from banks or corporations involved in economic development or low-income housing. Make sure you're familiar with the newspaper and the reporters' beats before calling her. Contact her by phone, fax or mail. The best times to reach her are very early or very late in the day. She accepts all kinds of materials but usually doesn't need video tapes. Lead time varies.

Reporter: Elizabeth Kolbert. Phone: (212) 556-1658. Covers tv and broadcasting.

Reporter: Steve Lohr. Phone: (212) 556-3814. Lohr doesn't have a product- or company-oriented beat, which makes him a tough pitching target. He is amenable to fielding your press kits and announcements: "It's useful for me to know what's going on." To really get his attention, you'll need a sweeping trend. Lohr writes about the social and business impact of the latest technology innovations -- like Web publishing and the $500 network computer. Prove other people are talking about your company's breakthrough besides the PR person and the CEO: Lohr requires outside analysis. He also prefers to look at "the craftsmen rather than the management" (programmers, e.g.). Mail is the best approach; or phone if you can summarize your news in two sentences. Lohr often files cover letters to keep tabs on future sources. He doesn't like e-mail pitches.

Reporter: Edwin McDowell. Phone: (212) 556-1566. Covers the travel and tourism industry, and pens the "Business Travel" column twice a month, which includes three or four short items of interest to corporate / business travelers, as well as a hard news item. "I cover the business of travel and tourism, not destinations," explains McDowell. He covers both breakers and enterprise stories. Pitch by mail or phone -- if you're leaving voice mail, speak slowly. "I'll tell you when I'm on deadline," McDowell says. Avoid calling to tell him that your CEO will be visiting New York the following week; "There aren't enough hours in the week for me to meet with every president coming into New York...and they probably don't have the time for an interview, either." Lead time varies; he usually writes his column the day before, but will keep ideas on file for future use.

Reporter: Barry Meier. Phone: (212) 556-1917. Covers consumer news.

Reporter: Sylvia Nasar. Phone: (212) 556-1229

Reporter: Iver Peterson. Phone: (212) 556-7231. Covers newspapers, press.

Reporter: Robin Pogrebin. Phone: (212) 556-7789. Fax: (212) 556-4007. Email: pogrebin@nytimes.com. Covers the magazine industry. Send press releases, or pitch via e-mail.

Reporter: Barbara Presley Noble. Phone: (212) 556-1308. Covers workplace issues; writes primarily for the Sun. edition.

Reporter: Anthony Ramirez. Phone: (212) 556-1254. Covers the stock market.

Reporter: (Mr.) Agis Salpukas. Phone: (212) 556-7391. (Pron. "AGE iss sal POO kuss.") Focuses on oil, natural gas, nuclear power and alternative fuels. He's eager to cover energy companies' efforts to expand internationally, particularly into Russia. He welcomes tips. If your company or client has an anecdote to relate, Salpukas wants to hear it. "I'm not just going to do a story about two utility companies competing -- I want to tell a story about corporate strategy." He wants to sit down and talk with industry people on a general basis. He's not adverse to phone pitches, but he doesn't have time to return most calls -- it's better to mail a personal letter. "Tell me why this company is unique."

Reporter: Jennifer Steinhauer. Phone: (212) 556-7453. Covers retail. She covers anything "from Kmart...to supermarket to Bergdorf Goodman." Be direct; "I like people who are straight-shooters and who are really fast." Pitch by fax or mail, but don't phone.

Reporter: Stephanie Strom. Phone: (212) 556-7514. Covers Wall Street.

Reporter: Peter Truell. Phone: (212) 556-1413. Fax: (212) 556-4007. Email: petrue@nytimes.com. Covers Wall Street, financial crime, investment banking and the securities market. Send press releases, backgrounders, graphics, charts and graphs. Pitch by mail, fax, e-mail or phone (especially before noon), but keep it brief.

Reporter: Louis Uchitelle. Phone: (212) 556-1705. (Pron. "YOU cheh tell.")

Reporter: (Ms.) Leslie Wayne. Phone: (212) 556-7192. Covers money management.

Reporter: Laurence Zuckerman. Phone: (212) 556-4212. Covers hardware, IBM, infotechnology and media convergence.

Columnist: Denise Caruso. 1459 18th St., Box 189, San Francisco, CA 94107. Email: dcaruso@aol.com. Pens "Technology."

Columnist: Kurt Eichenwald. Phone: (212) 556-1752. "Street Smarts"

Columnist: Peter Passell. Phone: (212) 556-3833. Pens "Economic Scene."

Contributing Writer: Jane Levere. 515 E. 79th St., Apt. 12B, New York, NY 10021. Phone: (212) 861-4602. (Pron. "le VEER.") Pens the "Business Travel" column once a month on a freelance basis. (See Edwin McDowell's entry for more info on the column.) She looks for trends in products and services of use and interest to the "mobile executive who travels both domestically and overseas for business." Pitch ideas that are truly useful to readers of Business Day. She doesn't mind "unusual, offbeat types of things," but they must have a "consumer angle." Pitch by mail; avoid the phone, fax and e-mail.

Columnist: Felicia Paik. Phone: (212) 416-2348. (Pron. "PAKE.") Writes "A Piece of Paradise," and "Private Properties." "A Piece of Paradise" profiles exceptional residential properties that are up for sale -- the lowest priced homes that are included cost about $1 million. "Private Properties" runs dows the week's biggest buys, sales, trends and growth rates in real estate. She wants to see stories about property owned by CEOs and government officials, rather than celebrities.

INTERNATIONAL TRADE

Reporter: Michael Sesit. Phone: (212) 416-3192. Covers international finance.

Correspondent: Tim Carrington. Phone: (202) 862-6625. Covers international economics and banking.

GENERAL LIFESTYLE / FEATURES

Department Editor: Raymond Sokolov. Phone: (212) 416-2571. Oversees Arts and Leisure coverage.

Deputy Editor: Barbara Phillips. Phone: (212) 416-2579. Edits the "Leisure & Arts" page. Also writes television reviews.

Staff Writer: Amy Gamerman. Phone: (212) 416-2560. Fax: (212) 416-2658. The sole full-time "Leisure and Arts" staff reporter, Gamerman is an important media contact, but don't add her name to regular mailing list. Wait for that gem of a story. "The people who hold back" and don't send stacks of mailings are the ones who will make headway, she says. Her articles most often cover museums, author profiles, oddball characters and cars. Her peeve is stories with a business angle. Send a personal letter by mail, not a press kit. She says, "If it's a nice letter saying in a few paragraphs what this is about, then I can go back to it when I have a slow afternoon."

ARTS / ENTERTAINMENT

Books Editor: Erich Eichman. Phone: (212) 416-2593. One review appears daily. "We try to mix it up quite a bit" in terms of tips. He is open to a variety of authors. Big names definitely get attention, "we've reviewed first-timers, too."

Critic: Dale Harris. Covers dance.
Theater Critic: Donald Lyons
Film Critic: Joe Morgenstern
TV Critic: Robert Goldberg. Phone: (212) 416-2574

HOME / GARDEN

Columnist: John Pierson. RR1, Box 534, River Rd., Woodstock, VT 05091. Phone: (802) 457-4945. Fax: (802) 457-4696. Writes about architecture, appliances and homes.

TRAVEL / HOSPITALITY

Assistant: Debbie Prior. Phone: (212) 416-3284. "The Week Ahead," a short box inside "Takeoffs," offers blurbs about unusual travel offers, money-saving opportunities, events and political news of interest to travelers (she gleans from press releases.) Fax to Prior by Thu. or Fri. the week before.

OTHER TOPICS

Editor: Lisa Vickery. Phone: (212) 416-4217. Is Day Editor. Covers breaking news, domestic news and features. Is interested in fresh business news. Send press releases and product samples. Fax your pitches; if you do call, avoid calling after 4:30.

News Editor: Michael Allen. Allen focuses on South American issues.

Foreign Editor: John Bussey. Phone: (212) 416-2680

Special Projects Editor: Stephen Adler. Phone: (212) 416-3216. Oversees investigative coverage. Adler advises pros to avoid pitching your company as an innovator; tying it to a trend is probably more true and more effective. Avoid personnel announcements and phone calls -- send a short fax instead.

SECTIONS/PROGRAMS

ENTERPRISE:

News Editor: Frederic Wiegold. Phone: (212) 416-3235. (Pron. "WEE gold.")

Department Editor: Roger Ricklefs. Phone: (212) 416-2955. Fax: (212) 416-2653. Supervises "Enterprise." He says column will sometimes address a single company or entrepreneur, if the subject's efforts "illustrate a broader point." Coverage is typically confined to public companies, but will focus on the occasional small, fast-growing firm. Mail brief letters to Ricklefs or the correspondent in your client's region.

Reporter: Rodney Ho. Covers small business.
Reporter: Elizabeth MacDonald. Is Accounting Reporter.
Reporter: Stephanie Mehta. Phone: (212) 416-2502. (Pron. "MET uh.") Covers small business for the "Enterprise & Management" group. She doesn't just showcase up-and-comers -- "I'm interested in stories with an explanatory element that have interest and value to small business owners," she explains. Bigger players sometimes get ink as well, but only when their activities involve or benefit small businesses. Mehta follows national companies with fewer than 500 employees or less than $100 million in revenues (if privately held, up to 1000 employees). She also follows legislation and regulation that affects small business. She prefers trend or explainer pieces to single company profiles, and her favorite topics include female or minority-owned businesses and entrepreneurs. Make sure, however, to offer the deeper issues affecting both these topics and not just the obvious. Always have the pitch in writing, because "even if you call, I'll ask you to send me something," she says.

Reporter: Michael Selz. Phone: (212) 416-4118. Covers small business for the "Enterprise & Management" group.

FLORIDA JOURNAL: A weekly four-page insert that includes economic-indicator graphics, a local version of "Heard on the Street" and regular economic-development pieces. Circulation is 115,000.

Editor: Rob Johnson. Tracks major local industries -- tourism, banking, trade, real estate, healthcare and technology. Company pitches should include its position in the market sector and name the closest rivals and their strengths and / or weaknesses. Prefers faxes over phone calls.

Reporter: (Ms.) Pat Beall. Covers general business issues.

Reporter: Christina Brinkley. Email: brinkley@delphi.com. Covers high technology, real estate.

Reporter: Paul Dillon. Covers banking and finance.

Reporter: Lyda Longa. (Pron. "LEE da.") Covers tourism.

Reporter: Peter Mitchell. Covers public policy and general assignments.

Reporter: Karen Tippett. Covers securities and pens "Heard in Florida."

HEARD ON THE STREET:

Editor: Randall (Randy) Smith. Phone: (212) 416-3151. Responsible for "Heard on the Street," the Wall Street Journal's famed stock-watch column which runs daily in the Money & Investing section. Smith sees the column as a "combination of journalism and prognostication," based as it is on current news events. Smith loves a good scoop: "We recognize it's a scoop that might be favorable to their company, but the definitic of a scoop is a good story." The column can focus on individual stocks or perhaps an industry sector, and writers typically favor stories dealing with larger corporations. Public companies, or those about to go public, are of key interest. It's OK to call Smith directly, but he'll probably just refer you to the writers.

Reporter: Patrick McGeehan. Writes "Abreast of the Market."

Reporter: Bridget O'Brian. Covers municipal bonds. Contributes to the Wed. "Inside Track" feature and tracks brokerage firms.

Reporter: Susan Pulliam. Phone: (212) 416-2137. Reports for "Heard on the Steet."

Reporter: Anita Raghavan. Covers the securitie industry.

Columnist: E.S. ("Jim") Browning. Phone: (212) 416-2221. Is main writer of "Heard on the Street."

MARKETPLACE: Daily Section. Columns: "The Front Lines," "Personal Technology," "Business and Race," "Managing Your Career" and "Health Journal." Daily feature of Marketplace are: "Business Briefs," "Who's News," "Marketing & Media" and "The Mart." Also included on various days in the section are: "Net Interest," "Lawyers and Clients," "The Home Front," "Takeoffs & Landings," "Enterprise & Management," "Advertising," "The Property Report," "Technology & Health," "Industry Focus," "Technology," "Law," "Sports," "Private Properties," "A Piece of Paradise," "Travel, "Food," "Legal Beat," "Enterprise," "Corporate Focus," "Health," "Telecommunications," "Manager's Journal "Autos," "Technology & Telecommunications," "Marketing" and "Online."

News Editor: Kathleen Deveny. Phone: (212) 416-2441. (Pron. "DEV en ee.") Deveny says that she's always looking for a quirky tale to fill the B-front's lower left-hand corner. She sees these "orphan" pieces as providing "comic relief" from the other, more weighty news found in "Marketplace." Deveny welcomes suggestions, but they mu be original. As for the rest of the section, which focuses specifically on marketing, advertising, media and technology, Deveny is looking to make it "newsier." "You have to give [harried executives and inundated readers] a sense of urgency to read the page she says. Some suggestions in your pitches Provide social connections. Suggest hot workplace issues. (Deveny confesses a fondness for labor stories, for instance). Make the story accessible to a wide

How To Find
the Markets for
Your Invention

H AVE A NEW IDEA OR NEW PRODUCT? Here's how to find
the markets for your invention, and what to do when
you find them.

But before I show you how easy it is, and the best tools
available to find your markets, take a piece of paper and write
down all the markets to which you think your product or invention would sell. A market is any group of people you can define
that has the potential to buy your product. Narrow it down as
tightly as you can. This is step one: Figure out exactly what group
or groups are the most likely to need, want, and be able to purchase your product. You've got to define exactly who your market
is before you're able to figure out how to reach it.

The tighter the specifications to find your markets, the lower
your marketing costs will be. If you are selling books to middle
school teachers, most of your money will be wasted if you advertise to all teachers. Your market is teachers, grades 7 through 10.
Any material you send to anyone else just shows up on the red
side of your balance sheet under "expenses."

Let's take a few examples. Your task would be simple if you developed a new camera lens for Canon's line of professional cameras. Find a list of all the owners of Canon professional cameras and you've done all the homework you need to do—you've just found your entire market. Your advertising would have no wasted expense when you mail to them, because every person in that list is a potential buyer for your lens.

If this list isn't available (and a list this tightly qualified usually isn't), your market could be found in the readership of several magazines whose subscribers are a group of people defined as *Professional Photographers*. Although there is some wasted expense in advertising to this group, it is still pretty easy to find this target market.

Suppose you've invented a new tripod to hold any type or brand of camera. Here, your task of finding the specific markets—groups of prospects most likely to purchase your product—is more complex. Surely if your tripod is of good quality, the professional photographers market is a good place to start. But how about the consumer photographic market?

The consumer market is much broader, as well as a little more elusive to reach: consumers don't all read the same dozen or so photography trade magazines the pros read. Since there is a large number of consumers you must reach with the message that your new tripod is available, it's vastly more expensive. Still, sales can be brisk, and you can make big money with a consumer product if you're good and focus tightly on the camera market. Camera? Focus?

Maybe your tripod could also be sold to the video camera market, which is a totally different group of professionals and consumers, who own a different classification of products, who need your tripod. These folks read a totally different group of magazines and shop in vastly different stores and catalogs. But these folks, these video camera owners—they have a lot of money. Now you're going to have to choose which market is better for tripod sales. Who are the more likely users—or better yet, the more likely purchasers?

Hey, how about sales of your tripods to back yard astronomers to mount their telescopes? Or how about selling to the security market, where people need sturdy stands for surveillance cameras? Hey, how about...well, you get the idea. These are all separate and distinctly different markets. All the people in these markets can be reached through the magazines they read, but each group reads a completely different set of magazines. Now you're learning about the finesse of marketing. Think about all the market niches where your products would sell. In a minute you'll see how to reach them.

Take another example. For a while I owned a company that manufactured I.D. tags. It wasn't too exciting, but we did some nice numbers—we placed about 25,000 pounds of mail a year into the mailstream. For a quick study of in-depth marketing, take a one-minute look at where we marketed our I.D. tags.

First, the pet industry was a big market for us—we marketed pet I.D. tags to the owners of 54 million dogs and 57 million cats, give or take a few million. In a completely separate industry, we made emergency medical I.D.—personalized identification bracelets and neck pendants for the medical community, specifically for the subspecialty markets of people with diabetes and people taking heart medication.

To the child care industry, we sold I.D. tags to parents, to lace onto their child's sneaker so young children would have some sort of identification on them. To the running industry, we sold them as runners' sneaker identification tags. We marketed through runners' magazines and through race directors of marathons.

Besides these industries, we marketed our product to laboratories and laboratory equipment manufacturers as permanent, indestructible name plates for equipment.

To the machinery industry, we marketed the same product as valve tags; to the luggage industry, as baggage tags; and to golf bag manufacturers and through golf and pro shops, as golf bag identification. To the woodworking industry, we personalized plaques for woodworkers' custom cabinetry and hobbyists' handmade wood projects. To zoos, we marketed our I.D. tags as name plates for animal cages; to the equestrian industry, as horse halter, tack, and saddle identification tags.

To medical and veterinary doctors, we marketed the same I.D. tags as identification tags for their stethoscopes; to art museums, for photo and picture nameplates; and to the commercial fishing industry, as identification tags for lobster and crab pots—as required by law. So what other markets did you say your product fit into? By the way, we manufactured only five shapes of tags and offered only one style of engraving.

HERE'S THE PLAN

Think of all the markets where your product can be sold, then rank them—starting with your primary market as number one. Exactly what groups of people will be most likely to buy your product? As you can see from the examples, if you came up with only one group, you can probably go back and find several more.

Figure out all your markets, then find all the magazines that go to these markets; then, finally, create and send a press release to all those magazines. A press release is a one-page document you send to magazines describing your product and its benefits. The magazine then publishes it for free. Simple plan, isn't it?

From the response you receive from your press releases, you'll be able to see exactly which markets have the most interest in your product. If you're not familiar with writing press releases and sending them to magazines for free write-ups, see the article in this book on writing press releases. Or buy my first book, *How To Market a Product for Under $500* (ISBN 0-9642879-2-7), and read the first chapter: almost fifty pages on writing press releases and how to submit them with the best possible chance of having them published. OK, so I plugged my book, sue me. It's a great book.

STEP II—FINDING YOUR MARKETS

There are several great reference books found in most libraries that list all markets and the magazines that are sent to each. All the reference tools are easy to use, and you will be able to use them after this five-minute introduction.

The main players are the directories of magazines. Big, thick, 1,000- to 1,500-page books of easy-to-use information. The best ones are *Burrelle's Media Directory/Magazines and Newsletters, Bacon's Newspaper/Magazine Directory,* the *Oxbridge Communications National Directory of Magazines* (also their *National Direc-*

tory of Newsletters and the *Standard Periodical Directory*), and the *SRDS* (formerly Standard Rate and Data Service but now officially called by just their acronym) *Business Publication Advertising Source*™.

Each of these directories has a similar setup, with easy-to-use features. Why do I say they're easy to use? In the front of each book the publishers have a *single page* of instructions. From this you can understand that using these marketing tools is quite easy—quite a contrast to using your VCR, for which you received a 30-page instruction manual! All the directories group the entire universe of people into about 90 to 110 distinct markets or industries, and they're all listed alphabetically by subject in the *market classification section:* two or three pages that are found in the front of each book. How convenient. If you can remember the alphabet, you can perform the marketing function.

Examples of industries you can look up would include everything from accounting, banking, firefighting, or heating, to tourism, veterinary, or woodworking, to name just a few. Any profession or industry you can think of has one or more magazines published for it, and larger industries may be served by hundreds of magazines. All the industries and markets and all their accompanying magazines are listed in these directories.

For example: If you were marketing a product to the motorcycle industry, you'd pick any directory and look up "M" for "Motorcycles" in the *market classification section.* Then you'd turn to the main section of the book—the *magazine data section*—where all the motorcycle magazines are found in a single location under "M" for motorcycles. There you'd see all 38 magazines sent to the motorcycle industry, along with their data: circulation, ad costs, publisher, phone and fax numbers, and other miscellaneous information.

Another way to use these books to find the markets you're researching (and the magazines that serve them) is to know the name of any one magazine sent to that particular industry. Each reference book has an alphabetical title directory; if you know the title of a magazine, look it up there.

While *American Photographer* would be listed under "photography" in the *market classification section*, in the *title index* you'd look under "A" for American, and scan down to *American Photographer*. The directories then show you the page in the *magazine data section* where the magazine is found. Turn to that page and, lo and behold, *American Photographer* is grouped with all the other photographic magazines.

Fast and easy; and you thought marketing was hard. Nope. Just time consuming: some industries have dozens of specialty magazines, and the lucrative markets have even more.

While the lawn and garden supplies industry may have only a dozen magazines, the computer industry has over 450 magazines that go to every niche of the computer market. Man, those computer geeks must like to read. But you don't have to worry about reading all of the magazines now. You only have to read them if you're going to place an ad in one. Right now, you're just going to be exploring the markets with press releases.

Finding a single market would take you about five minutes, if you're a slow reader. Once you've found the markets you're prospecting to, and you see all the magazines sent to those industries, you'll have a pretty good idea of how you can reach your prospective buyers through those magazines, and of how large each market is.

Here's an optional step, but I recommend it. If you think your product will really fit in well in a particular magazine, call the magazine publisher and ask for a media kit. It's free. Ask for a couple of recent samples of their magazine, too. Media kits contain the magazine's ad rates and are always sent free to potential advertisers. If you'd like to get the annual directory the magazine publishes, ask for a sample of that, too.

There's never a charge for any of this material if they think you're serious about advertising. If the directory is normally expensive, here's your chance to get it free, by mentioning how you may take out an ad in it and would appreciate a sample copy for evaluation. This is also a great way to get the directory if it's published at a different time of the year and is no longer attainable through normal channels.

If you don't want to call, you can also write to the publishers and ask for a media kit. Use business stationery so they know you're a serious player and have the money to place an ad. The magazine publishers are pretty good about getting their promotional material right out—it means revenue to them to have an ad come in, so they strike while the lead is hot.

The media kit contains all the hype about the magazine and why you should spend all of your advertising money in that publication. All kinds of information about the industry are also included. While most of this package is usually fiction, there are always some industry insights that will help you with your marketing.

Now that you've found the magazines that serve the industries compatible with your product, create a press release and cover letter and send them to the magazines with a photo of the product. In about three months you'll start to receive inquiries from the readers of the magazines who saw your published press release and are interested. Good luck.

What do you do with these inquiries? Well, that's another chapter: "How To Create a Winning Direct Mail Package."

TABLE OF CONTENTS

Reprinted with permission from Oxbridge Communications

Domestic Classification Groupings

EDITOR'S NOTE: The asterisk (*) denotes a duplicate listing.

0. AFFLUENCE

AUDITED
ABA Journal*
Departures
Economist, The North America Edition
Ivy League Magazine Network, The
Medical Economics*
Men's Health
Mutual Funds
Preservation
Private Clubs
Robb Report, The
Smithsonian*

NON-AUDITED
Art & Auction
Bay Window, The
BMW Magazine USA
Chicago Social
Chronos
City & Country Club Life
Dimensions
Homecoming
Independent, The
Jerusalem Report, The
N. Focus
Palm Beach Society Magazine
Watches 1997
Zarposh International

1. AIRLINE INFLIGHT/TRAIN ENROUTE
(See also: Hotel Inroom.)

AUDITED
Aboard Inflight Magazines
American Way
Delta Air Lines Sky Magazine
Frequent Flyer
Hemispheres
KWHI
Northwest Airlines WorldTraveler
Southwest Airlines Spirit
TWA Ambassador
US Airways Attache Magazine
Washington Flyer Magazine

NON-AUDITED
Air Travel Journal
Air-Currents Magazine
Alaska Airlines Magazine
America West Airlines Magazine
American Eagle Latitudes
Continental
Horizon Air Magazine
Japan Airlines Winds
Midwest Express Magazine
Pacific Connections Magazine
Pan Am Clipper
Publishing Group, Inc. Inflight Division, The
Roaring Fork Valley
SkyMall
Spirit of Aloha
Tower Air Magazine

1A. ALMANACS & DIRECTORIES

AUDITED
Old Farmer's Almanac, The

NON-AUDITED
Almanac for Farmers & City Folk, The
Blum's Farmers & Planters Almanac and Turner's Carolina Almanac
Farmers' Almanac
Grier's Almanac
J. Gruber's Hagers-Town Town and Country Almanack
Ladies Birthday Almanac, The
Trail Blazers' Almanac and Pioneer Guide Book

2. ART & ANTIQUES
(See also: Crafts, Games, Hobbies & Models; Entertainment Guides & Programs; Literary, Book Reviews & Writing Techniques; Music.)

AUDITED
American Artist
Antiques, The Magazine
Art & Antiques
Art in America
Artist's Magazine, The
Artnews
Native Peoples
Southwest Art
Tattoo

NON-AUDITED
American Collector

American Country Collectibles
Antique Trader Weekly
AntiqueWeek
Art Now Gallery Guide
Art Revue
Artforum
Collector Editions
Collector Magazine & Price Guide
Collector's Mart
Collectors News
Collectors' Showcase
Fiberarts
FMR
Sculpture
Shuttle Spindle & Dyepot
Today's Collector
Treasure Chest
Watercolor Magic
Wildlife Art

3. AUTOMOTIVE
(See also: Crafts, Games, Hobbies & Models; Mechanics & Science; Motorcycle; Sports; Travel.)

AUDITED
American Rodder
Automobile Magazine
AutoWeek
Car and Driver
Car and Driver Buyers Guide
Car and Driver Road Test Annual
Car and Driver Truck Buyers Guide
Car Craft
Chevy High Performance
Circle Track
Drag Racing Monthly
du Pont Registry
European Car
4-Wheel & Off-Road
4 Wheel Drive & Sport Utility
Four Wheeler
Hemmings Motor News
Hot Rod
Lowrider Magazine
Motor Trend
Motor Trend's New Car Buyer's Guide
Motor Trend's Performance Cars
Mustang & Fords
NASCAR Winston Cup Illustrated
NASCAR Winston Cup Scene
Off-Road
On Track
Open Wheel
Popular Hot Rodding
Racer
Road & Track
Rod & Custom Magazine
Sport Truck
Stock Car Racing Magazine
Street Rodder
Super Chevy
Truckin'
Vintage Motorsport
VW Trends

NON-AUDITED
Alfa Owner
American Woman Motorscene Magazine
Area Auto Racing News
Auto Racing Digest
Auto Trader
Automobile Magazine's Field Guide
Automobile Magazine's Guide to Buying & Leasing
Automundo Magazine
Big Truck & Equipment Trader
Bracket Racing USA
British Car
California Sports Car
Car Collector & Car Classics
Cars & Parts Magazine
Chevy Truck
Chrysler Power
Classic Trucks
Collector Car & Truck Prices
Corvette and Chevy Trader
Corvette Fever Magazine
Corvette Quarterly
Custom Classic Trucks
Delorean World
Drag Racer Magazine
Driva Magazine
Dune Buggies & Hot VWs
Excellence
5.0 Mustang
Ford & Mustang Trader
Forza
4 X 4 Performance
4x4 Power
Grassroots Motorsports
High Performance Mopar
High Performance Pontiac
High-Tech Performance
Indy Car Racing Magazine

Kit Car
Kit Car Illustrated
Mini Truckin'
Mopar Muscle
Motor Trend's Road Tests
Motor Trend's Sport Utility/Truck & Van Buyer's Guide
MotoRacing
Muscle Mustangs & Fast Fords
Musclecar Review
Mustang Monthly
National Dragster
National Speed Sport News
Official NASCAR Preview and Press Guide, The
Old Car Trader
Old Cars Price Guide
Old Cars Weekly
Open Road
Professional SportsCar Racing Newsmagazine
Professional SportsCar Racing Yearbook
Road & Track Specials
Sand Sports
Special Interest Autos
Speedway Scene
SportsCar
Sports Car International
Super Ford
Super Street
Today's Truck & Sport Utility Vehicle
Truck Trader
Turbo & Hi-Tech Performance Magazine
Vette

4. AVIATION
(See also: Crafts, Games, Hobbies & Models; Travel.)

AUDITED
AOPA Pilot
Flight Training
Flying
Kitplanes
Plane&Pilot
Private Pilot
Sport Aviation

NON-AUDITED
Aero Trader and Chopper Shopper
Air Line Pilot
Air Progress
Flight Journal
General Aviation News & Flyer
Mountain Pilot
Rotorcraft
Soaring
Sport Pilot & Ultralights
Ultralight Flying!
Woman Pilot
World Airshow News

5. BABIES
(See also: Children's; Women's.)

AUDITED
American Baby
Baby Magazine
Baby Magazine's Infantcare Guide
Baby Talk
Child Birth Planner
Child First-Year Planner
Child Pregnancy Planner
Childbirth
Childbirth Instructor
Embarazo
First Year of Life
Guide for Expectant Parents
Lamaze Parents' Magazine
Lamazebaby
Parenting's Healthy Pregnancy
Parents Baby
Parents Expecting
Revista Lamaze para Padres
Twins
Una Nueva Vida

NON-AUDITED
Baby's World
Bay Area Baby
Leaven
New Beginnings
Prenatal Educator
That's My Baby Magazine

5A. BLACK/AFRICAN-AMERICAN

AUDITED
American Legacy
Essence*
La Vida News-The Black Voice
Today's Black Woman

NON-AUDITED
about...time
African Times, The
American Minorities Media
American Visions
Black Diaspora
Black Elegance
Black History Is No Mystery
Black Pages
Career Focus
Central Florida Black Family Today
College Preview
Crisis, The
Directions
First Opportunity
New Orleans Tribune, The
Personalities
Sisters In Style
SuccessGuide Vol. VI

Upscale

6. BOATING & YACHTING
(See also: Fishing & Hunting; Sports.)

AUDITED
Boat/U.S. Magazine
Boating
Boating World
Chesapeake Bay Magazine
Cruising World
Ensign, The
Florida Sportsman*
Lakeland Boating
Motor Boating & Sailing
Power & Motoryacht
PWC Magazine
Sail
Sailing World
Salt Water Sportsman
Sea Magazine
Showboats International
Splash
Trailer Boats
WoodenBoat
Yachting
Yachtsman's Guide to the Virgin Islands

NON-AUDITED
Bass & Walleye Boats
Boat Trader
Boating For Women
Boating Life
Embassy's Complete Boating Guide & Chartbook
48 Degrees North
Go Boating
Great Lakes Boating
Heartland Boating
Hot Boat
Jet Sports
Log, The
M.P.C.—Marine Publications Company
Marlin
Norwesting
Northern Breezes Sailing Magazine
Ocean Navigator
Offshore
Ohio Fishwrapper
Pacific Boating Almanac
Personal Watercraft Illustrated
Powerboat
Sailboat Buyers Guide
Sailing
Santana
Soundings
Southern Boating
Watercraft World
Waterlines
Waterway Guide
Yacht Trader
Yachtsman's Guide To The Bahamas

7. BRIDAL
(See also: Fashion, Beauty & Grooming; Home Service & Home; Women's.)

AUDITED
Bridal Guide
Bride's Magazine
Elegant Bride
For the Bride by Demetrios
Modern Bride

NON-AUDITED
Bridal Crafts
Bridal Fair
Bride & Groom
Celebrate
Chicago Bride
Marblehead Publications, Inc.
Minnesota Bride
Modern Bride Connection, The
New England Bride
New Jersey Bride
La Novia Linda
Signature Bride
South Florida Bride
Wedding Day Magazine
Wedding Pages, The
Weddings West

8. BUSINESS & FINANCE
(See also: Fraternal, Professional Groups, Service Clubs, Veteran's Organizations & Associations.)

AUDITED
Better Investing
Black Enterprise
Business Start-Ups
Business Week*
Costco Connection, The
Economist, The North America Edition
Entrepreneur
Financial World
Forbes
Foreign Affairs
Fortune
Harvard Business Review*
Hispanic Business
Inc.
Independent Business*
Individual Investor
Institutional Investor
Journal of Accountancy
Kiplinger's Personal Finance Magazine
Media Networks Business Network
Money
Mutual Funds Magazine
Nation's Business
Scientific American*

INDEX OF SUBJECT CLASSIFICATIONS
MAGAZINES AND NEWSLETTERS

Magazines and newsletters published in the United States, Canada and Mexico are separated into 388 subject classifications which f
Each classification contains alphabetically arranged listings for the magazine and newsletters dealing with that subject. Many classifica
also contain cross-reference listings for publications, referring the reader to a different classification for full listing information on that public
The reader is encouraged to refer to the Index of Subject Classification Cross References, beginning on page 1609, for further assistar
locating a particular topic.

MARKETING REFERENCE TOOLS

DVERTISING IS KNOWING WHAT TO SAY; marketing is knowing where to say it. Here's where to learn where to say it. A brief look at three directories—and how to find and reach your markets in each.

BURRELLE'S MEDIA DIRECTORY/MAGAZINES AND NEWSLETTERS

Burrelle's Media Directory/Magazines and Newsletters is an excellent reference tool for researching markets—and figuring out where to place your hard-earned advertising and PR dollars. It's designed to be an easy-to-use reference tool from the get-go, with information presented clearly, concisely, and in a logical format. It's in-depth coverage at its best.

Even though the book is big, over 1,400 8 1/2" x 11" pages containing over 12,000 magazines and newsletters, you can find a particular market you are searching for in about a minute, faster if you have a little experience. Subjects or markets are arranged alphabetically. Looking for 'B'ankers? Well...that was easy. All the magazines going to the banking industry are found in the market index under B.

The listing for each magazine contains the following data: publisher, address, phone, fax, e-mail, editors' names, circulation, cost of ads, frequency of publication, and my personal favorite—whether or not they accept publicity material. Burrelle's also gives a short description of the market the magazine serves and its editorial slant. This tells you if you're barking up the right tree when searching through the ground pulpwood for the correct magazine.

In addition to the subject index—where markets appear alphabetically by market name—there is an index of magazines listed alphabetically by magazine name. In this index, you would find a magazine under its proper name. *American Banker*—check under A. Hey, that was easy, too. All in all, if you can remember the alphabet, you can find your markets pretty darn fast in *Burrelle's Media Directory/Magazines and Newsletters*.

Burrelle's actually publishes a five-book set of in-depth media directories: Magazines and Newsletters, Newspapers and Related Media (2 volumes), and Broadcast and Related Media (2 volumes). Once you spend ten minutes or so figuring out how to use each, an incredible amount of information is at your fingertips and accessible in seconds.

The staff at Burrelle's is approachable for questions (yes, even tough marketing questions) and is exceptionally friendly and helpful—a big, big plus that sets the value of the product (and the firm) at the very peak of the information industry. Five stars for directories and customer service. Magazine and newsletter directory, $225 and worth it. *Burrelle's Media Directory/Magazines and Newsletters*, telephone 800/USMEDIA for a free descriptive brochure. We use this directory in our own office.

THE ALL-IN-ONE DIRECTORY

Gebbie Press publishes the *All-In-One Directory*, which includes sections on magazines, newspapers, and electronic media, all in one book.

Magazines and journals are shown in a tight 25-to-a-page format. But the folks at Gebbie Press cram enough information into their list of 3,000 business, consumer, and farm publications for you to be able to send a press release campaign to the proper magazines.

Each listing contains the publisher, the main editor, address, phone and fax numbers, circulation, and a short description of the magazine's audience. This is bare-bones information, but enough to find the correct market, locate the magazines that serve it, and direct a press release to the editor by name. It is also enough information to call the editor and inquire if your product will fit well in their particular market.

The newspaper section is contained in the center third of the 6" x 9" spiral-bound directory and includes over 7,500 entries of news syndicates and daily and weekly newspapers. Newspapers are arranged by state, and listings show name, address, and phone and fax numbers, along with circulation figures.

The final third of the 500-page *All-In-One Directory* is all electronic media and includes listings of TV network headquarters, news services, and over 1,200 television stations. The bulk of this section follows with the data for over 7,000 radio stations. As you would suspect, all the necessary data is shown so you are able to find a station, then send them a press release or inquire about placing an ad. A good value at $85. Gebbie Press, 914/255-7560.

BRADLEY'S GUIDE TO THE TOP NATIONAL TV TALK SHOWS

What if you're not looking for depth, but just need the names of, say, the top 100 national TV news, talk, and magazine shows? Well, for $75 and a charge card you can get just that from Bradley Communications in Lansdowne, PA.

No fancy anything—just a spiral binding and a nicely laid-out book. If you are looking for just the top 100 shows, why buy anything else? The talk show market is hard to break into, but with enough phone calls, an incredible amount of persistence, and a good hook, perhaps someone, somewhere, will bite. You never know what's going to turn on a producer. *Bradley's Guide to the Top National TV Talk Shows* offers listings of show name, address, phone and fax, contact person for pitch, hosts, times the show runs, and subject interests. Also included: pitch angles that the show's producers like. It shows some suggestions on how to get in, and where and how to send your story.

While *Bradley's Guide to the Top National TV Talk Shows* does not contain the deepest of listings, and limits its listings to the top shows in the country, if you think you've got the right stuff, here's how to get to the country's hottest top show producers. For $75, can you afford not to try? Bradley Communications, telephone 610/259-1070, orders 800/989-1400. Bradley also publishes a wealth of reference publications on public relations, publishing, and selling books. Call for a free catalog.

Staff:

Editor	Kirk Bell
Publisher	Gary Schmidt 414-783-7740
Advertising Manager	Katie Mennenoh
Subscription Manager	Emmy Kincaid

Classic Toy Trains   414-796-8776
21027 Crossroads Circle   Fax 414-796-1383
Waukesha, WI 53186-4055   800-558-1544
Data:
Circ: 70,000 (PS); *Freq:* 8x/yr; Paid; *Language:* English
Category: Consumer; Magazine; *Sub. Cost:* $26.50
Coverage: United States & Internationally
Ownership: Kalmbach Publishing Company
News Release: 3 mos prior pub
Uses: Book, Calendar, Letters, Movie, New Product, B/W & Color Photos
Content: Regular issue features include Feedback, Q's & A's, Product News, and Product Reviews.
Staff:

Editor .... Roger Carp	Publisher .... Russell G. Larsonau
Art Director .... Lawrence Luser	Advertising Manager ..... Fred Hamilton
Circulation Director .... Marc Liu	Associate Editor .... Martin McGuirk
Associate Editor .... Marshall Poindexter	

Fine Scale Modeler   414-796-8776
P.O. Box 1612   Fax 414-796-1383
Waukesha, WI 53187-1612   800-446-5489
Data:
E-mail: rhayden@finescale.com
Web Site: http://www.kalmbach.com/fsm/finescale.html
Circ: 80,000 (PO); *Freq:* 10x/yr; Paid
Category: Consumer; Magazine; *Est:* 1982; *Sub. Cost:* $32.95
Coverage: United States & internationally; *Ad Rate:* $2,215.00
Ownership: Kalmbach Publishing Company
News Release: 10 wks prior pub; *Ads:* 2 mos prior pub
Uses: Book, Calendar, Industry, Letters, New Product, B/W & Color Photos; Accepts publicity material
Content: Publication contains technical how-to information for scale modelers.
Staff:

Editor .... Bob Hayden	Publisher .... Walter J. Mundschau
Senior Editor .... Paul Boyer	Managing Editor .... Richard McNally
Art Director .... Lawrence O. Luser	Book Review Editor ...... Mark Hembree
Advertising Manager ... H. Michael Yuhas	Advertising Director ...... Fred Hamilton
Circulation Director ... Diane Margenthaler	

Flying Models   201-383-3355
Phil Hardin Road   Fax 201-383-4064
Newton, NJ 07860
Data:
Circ: 26,000 (ABC); *Freq:* 1x/mo; Paid; *Language:* English
Category: Consumer; Magazine
Coverage: United States & Internationally; *Ad Rate:* $653.00
Ownership: Carstens Publications, Inc.
Accepts publicity material
Content: Publication covers the model airplane industry, including static display, remote control planes, and boats.
Staff:

Publisher .... Harold H. Carstens	Editor-in-Chief .... Frank Fanelli
Art Director .... Larry Deitch	Advertising Manager ..... John A. Earley
Circulation Director .... Henry R. Carstens	

Garden Railways   303-733-4779
1040 South Gaylord, Suite 203
Denver, CO 80209-4652
Data:
Circ: 17,000 (PS); *Freq:* 6x/yr; Paid
Category: Consumer; Magazine
Coverage: United States & Internationally; *Ad Rate:* $554.00
Ownership: Sidestreet Bannerworks, Inc.
News Release: No press; *Ads:* 1 mo prior pub
Uses: Book, Calendar, Letters, New Product, B/W & Color Photos; Accepts publicity material

Staff:

Publisher .... Marc Horovitz	Managing Editor .... Marc Horovitz
Garden Editor .... Barbara Horovitz	Advertising Manager ...... Irene Shafler
Circulation Director .... Mary VanZet	

Kit Car   213-782-2000
6420 Wilshire Boulevard   Fax 213-782-2704
Los Angeles, CA 90048-5502
Data:
Freq: 6x/yr; *Language:* English
Coverage: United States
Ownership: Petersen Publishing Company
News Release: 2 mos prior pub; *Ads:* 2 mos prior pub
Accepts publicity material
Content: Publication is a magazine for kit car enthusiasts.
Staff:

Editor .... Steve Temple	Publisher .... Skip Johnson
Editorial Director .... Drew Hardin	

Kit Car Illustrated   714-572-2255
744 South Placentia Avenue   Fax 714-572-1864
Placentia, CA 92670-6832
Data:
Circ: 72,700 (PS); *Freq:* 6x/yr; Paid
Category: Consumer; Magazine
Coverage: United States
Ownership: McMullen Argus Publishing Inc.
News Release: 1 mo prior pub; *Ads:* 1 mo prior pub
Accepts publicity material
Content: Publication is geared toward kit car enthusiasts.
Staff:

Editor .... Bill Moore	Publisher .... Tom McMullen

Kitplanes   714-855-8822
P.O. Box 6050   Fax 714-855-3045
Mission Viejo, CA 92690-6050
Data:
Circ: 65,000 (PS); *Freq:* 1x/mo; Paid
Category: Consumer; Magazine
Coverage: United States & internationally; *Ad Rate:* $3,500.00
Ownership: Fancy Publications Inc.
News Release: 1 mo prior pub; *Ads:* 1 mo prior pub
Accepts publicity material
Content: Publication contains design and technical articles and flight and product reports; geared toward the home craftsman.
Staff:

Editor .... Dave Martin	Publisher .... Norman Ridker
Managing Editor .... Keith Beveridge	Art Director .... Paul Zeek
Advertising Director ...... Chuck Preston	Circulation Director .... Harry Saller

Live Steam   616-946-3712
2779 Aero Park Drive   Fax 616-946-3289
Traverse City, MI 49686-9101   800-773-7798
Data:
Circ: 12,000 (PS); *Freq:* 6x/yr; Paid
Category: Consumer; Magazine; *Est:* 1966
Coverage: United States & internationally; *Ad Rate:* $577.00
Ownership: Village Press, Inc.
News Release: 3 mos prior pub; *Ads:* 2 mos prior pub
Content: Publication is a hobby magazine for steam engine enthusiasts (locomotives, boats, traction, automotive, and stationary), particularly those who are interested in building miniature scale models that operate on steam power.
Staff:

Publisher .... Robert L. Goff	Editor-in-Chief .... Joe D. Rice
Art Director .... Luana Dueweke	Book Review Editor ...... Clover McKinley
Advertising Manager ...... Kathy Booth	Circulation Director ..... Debby Neuman
Marketing Director .... Steve Smith	

Mainline Modeler   206-743-2607
13110 Beverly Park Road   Fax 206-787-9269
Mukilteo, WA 98275-3449

     Reprinted with permission from Burrelle's Information Services

Mining--Coal--Ore 43---continued

UNITED MINE WORKERS JRNL. 900 15th St. NW, Washington, DC 20005 Eileen Goldsmith, editor. Monthly tabloid. — **200,000** to members of United Mine Workers of America; labor leaders, legislators; labor relations. Fax 202-842-7227 **202-842-7321**

Mortuary--Cemetery .44

AMERICAN CEMETERY 100 S. Wood Ave., Islin, NJ 08830 Nick Verrastro 6M **908-767-9300**

AMERICAN FUNERAL DIRECTOR 100 S. Wood Ave., Islin, NJ 08830 Nick Verrastro, editor. Kates-Boylston. Mo. mag. — **11,300** to funeral directors, embalmers, casket manufacturers, salespeople, mortuary colleges. Fax 908-767-9741 **908-767-9300**

CEMETERY MANAGEMENT 1895 Preston White Dr., Reston, VA 22091 Mo. 6M **703-391-8400**

DIRECTOR 11121 W. Oklahoma Ave., Milwaukee, WI 53227 Gretchen Schaefer, editor. NFDA Publications, Inc. Monthly magazine. — **15,000** to owners, directors, key personnel of funeral service establishments; equipment mfrs. Fax 414-541-1909 **414-541-2500**

MORTICIANS OF THE SW 2514 National Dr., Garland, TX 75041 Monthly 4M **214-840-1060**

SOUTHERN FUNERAL DIRECTOR PO Box 1147, Beaufort, SC 29901 Mo. 6M **803-521-0239**

STONE IN AMERICA 30 Eden Aly, Columbus, OH 43215 Pennie Sabel Mo. 2M **614-461-5852**

Music--Music Trades .45

ALSO SEE: Amusements-Films .2 and Radio-Television .58

ABSOLUTE SOUND 58 School St., Glen Cove, NY 11542 Harry Pearson, editor. Absolute Sound, Inc. 8-issue magazine. — **27,000** to general public interested in high-end audio reproduction, engineering, technology, equip. Fax 516-676-5469 **516-676-2830**

ACOUSTIC GUITAR PO Box 767, San Anselmo, CA 94979 Jeff Rodgers, editor. String Letter, Inc. Monthly magazine. — **69,000** to players interested in instructional articles, music transcriptions, instrument care. Fax 415-485-0831 **415-485-6946**

AMERICAN MUSIC TEACHER 441 Vine St., Cincinnati, OH 45202 Michael Oxley, editor. Bimonthly magazine. — **24,000** to members of Music Teachers Natl. Assn.; Advisory Council on Materials; students. Fax 513-421-2503 **513-421-1420**

AMERICAN ORGANIST 475 Riverside Dr., New York, NY 10115 Anthony Baglivi, editor. Am. Guild of Organists. Monthly magazine. — **19,500** to members of American Guild of Organists; church musicians, choir directors, composers. Fax 212-870-2163 **212-870-2310**

AUDIO 1633 Broadway, New York, NY 10019 Michael Riggs, editor. Hachette Filipacci Magazines. Monthly magazine. — **125,000** to stereo music listeners; hobbyists, musicians; stereo equipment manufacturers, distributors. Fax 212-767-5633 **212-767-6940**

AUDIO/VIDEO INTERIORS 21700 Oxnard St., Woodland Hills, CA 91367 Maureen Jensen, editor. Avcom, Inc. Monthly magazine. — **63,000** to residential, commercial space owners requiring interior designer assistance. Fax 818-593-2274 **818-593-3900**

BAM 3470 Buskirk Ave., Pleasant Hill, CA 94523 Bill Crandall, editor. Bam Network, Inc. Biweekly magazine. — **115,000** to general public interested in musical personalities in L.A., San Fran., Calif. music scene. Fax 510-934-3958 **510-934-3700**

BASS PLAYER 411 Borel Ave., San Mateo, CA 94402 Jim Roberts, editor. Miller Freeman. Monthly magazine. — **59,000** to serious electric bass, acoustic upright bass interested in how-to techniques, repair. Fax 415-358-8728 **415-358-9500**

BLUEGRASS UNLIMITED 9514 J. Madison Hwy., Warrenton, VA 22186 Mo. 26M **540-349-8181**

CAR AUDIO & ELECTRONICS 21700 Oxnard St., Woodland Hills, CA 91367 Doug Newcomb, editor. Avcom Publishing. Monthly. — **148,000** to general public interested in audio components, cellular phones, security, new products. Fax 818-593-2274 **818-593-3900**

CD REVIEW 86 Elm St., Peterborough, NH 03458 Robert Baird, editor. Connell Communications. Monthly magazine. — **96,000** to owners, buyers of compact discs, CD players, related stereo components; suppliers. Fax 603-924-7013 **603-924-7271**

CIRCUS MAGAZINE 6 W. 18th St., New York, NY 10011 Gerald Rothberg, editor. Circus Enterprises. Monthly magazine. — **100,000** to young people with interests in modern music, audio, instruments, tapes, records. Fax 212-242-5734 **212-242-4902**

Bimonthly: once every two months   **Semimonthly: twice a month**

Bradley's Guide to the Top National TV Talk Shows

Sally Jessy Raphael

Universal Entertainment
515 W. 57th Street
New York, NY 10019-2981
Phone: (212) 582-1722
Fax: (212) 265-1953

Airs: Monday—Friday 4:00 p.m.
Audience: Women

Profile: Syndicated talk show with guests covering all subjects. What sets Sally apart from the other daytime talkers is that she gets emotionally involved with her guests and their problems. Her staff follows up on their stories and they try to help the guests if they can.

How to pitch: They read every pitch. Mail your complete package and make a follow-up call to be sure they received it. They will let you know if they are interested. The producers share information and Amy Rosenblum will pass material along. Pitching individual producers is usually a waste of time unless you know for sure that they produced a similar segment in the past or have a particular area of interest. The producers look for guests who have dramatic stories of overcoming terrible odds and celebrities who will talk about real problems and not just their latest movie. They use many therapists and human behavior experts on the show.

Exectives and Talent:

Co-Executive Producers: Maurice Tunick & Amy Rosenblum
Host: Sally Jessy Raphael

Booking Contacts:

Producer: Christina Pane. She's the best contact for authors and books.
Producer: Jill Pollack
Producer: Holly Jacobs
Producer: Jill Blackstone
Associate Producer: Risa Saslow
Associate Producer: Stacey Credidio
Associate Producer: Taha Howze

THE MOST
IMPORTANT PART
OF AN AD

NOTHING KILLS A GREAT AD like having no purpose. To be considered well drafted, an ad must first have a written, stated and defined objective. To draw up an ad without first writing an objective is self-defeating.

The *objective* is a one- or two-line definition of the function of the ad. Most commonly in traditional advertising, it is "to generate sales leads." Another objective may be "to increase public awareness of our company or our products." In business to business ads, it's usually "to bring in qualified inquiries and leads." In retail advertising, it's usually "to generate maximum store traffic."

It is quite common for an ad to have primary and secondary objectives, such as "to increase our firm's industry visibility and uplift our market position," or "to alert consumers of our safety features and stimulate sales." More often than not, objectives aren't written, or are written poorly and end up being vague and hazy. The advertising follows suit.

In direct marketing, there should be no delusions about the objective. In direct marketing, the ad objective is "to bring in orders!" Further, the function of the ad is to bring in the maximum response by generating phone calls, orders, and write-in inquiries, or if the direct merchant has a store, by stimulating an in-store visit. 95% of the ads I write are to generate calls or orders. Without this response, my value to my client diminishes.

The objective becomes the yardstick to measure the response. The success of the ad is based on how well it fulfilled the objective. Although I have mentioned the most important part of any ad in the preceding paragraph, the objective is the _first_ part of an ad, but not the _most_ important.

The main requirements of an ad are that it be seen, read, and acted upon. The elements of graphics, illustrations, and copy are blended to entice the reader to do all three. If your advertisement isn't designed to attract attention right from the get-go, you won't have to worry about your competitors reading it. No one will read it. The response will show this.

Over the years, rating services for advertisements have consistently named one common point for ads having the greatest readership. It is having a simple illustration or photo two-thirds the size of the ad. When designing your ad, this parameter should be one of your utmost considerations. A large illustration or headline will entice the readers to look deeper into your ad and respond.

While attracting attention is crucial to any advertisement, it isn't the most important element, although I have mentioned the most important part again. Did you pick it up?

OK, so you've designed your ad to be attractive. If your copy isn't compelling, it will be read mainly by people in your firm. Then the only other readers will be your competitors. To be read in its entirety, ad copy must create compelling interest. As soon as you lose a reader's attention, your nicely designed ad loses any chance of success.

It's just too easy to turn the page. You don't get so much as a hesitation—not even for a nanosecond. And you don't get a second chance without paying for a second ad. Heck, anybody can pay for a second chance; the trick is to draw your response the first time. Is copy important? You bet. _Most_ important? No, although the single most important part of your ad has been brought up again.

After arousing interest, a successful ad will direct that interest—to the product, to the firm, to the coupon, to the phone number. To stimulate the response.

Buy. Inquire. Call. Come in. Feel good. Agree. Disagree. Take notice. Get mad. Get even. Do something, anything. But do it. Respond. And that's pretty close to home. Because the most important part of any ad is the response.

If your ad objective (remember the objective?) was to generate inquiries, the inquiries generated are the single most important element of the ad, followed very closely by your follow-up to them.

Do your inquiries die quietly in a drawer? "No," you say, "I sent them a form letter, flyer, and price sheet." Swell. Don't get carried away with yourself. If that's your answer to what's in store for your very best prospects, your competition will love you for it.

Think about it. Your crack (cracked?) ad team designed the perfect lead-generating ad. With loving care—and considerable expense—they placed it in the best magazine for your market. It got great position, as requested. And it worked so well, it brought in tons of mail.

Then what did you do? You say it was too expensive to send everybody your catalog (even to your best prospects?). I'll buy that. I don't like it, but I'll buy it. Too expensive is too expensive.

But a form letter, a flyer, and a price sheet aren't the ultimate answer, either. Although they are a start. You now have a list of prospects. They wrote in. They're interested. Don't lose them now, and don't let them get away.

Qualify the leads tightly or loosely, at your discretion. Include in your mailing piece a catalog request form, or let your leads know a catalog is available upon request. Don't stop there— the people who didn't respond to this mailing are still prospects, they just need a little more convincing. A second mailing will help. Be sure to ask if they want to be placed on your complimentary mailing list. Make it sound attractive.

A third or fourth mailing should be enough to stimulate a response from any genuinely interested party. Remember, a campaign isn't a single mailing, or a single effort of anything—why do you think they call it a campaign? In the final mailing, alert people that it's final by saying so. Ask them again to express interest by filling out your enclosed business reply card, even if it's just to remain on your mailing list. Include a "just curious" box to be checked by those who are. You may elect to mail to them less frequently.

But keep in tune with your ads by keeping in touch with the respondents. And don't be afraid to mail again to those old inquiries sitting in your drawer. They're still more valuable than your old ads.

GETTING YOUR PRESS RELEASE INTO PRINT

THE PRESS RELEASE SELECTION PROCESS is simple, fast, and brutal—and very unforgiving of mistakes or poor work.

I seldom recommend an ad campaign until a press release has tested the media and has proven we can get a qualified response from the target audience. We don't always get in with our press releases, but we always try.

On the flip side: For industrial marketing, an ad is the logical conclusion to a successful press release campaign. A client should be willing to take out an ad schedule after a successful press campaign shows that the media and the market can be profitable.

Press releases can be both simple and complex instruments to write. Simple because they can take almost any form and still be published. Complex because every element adds to or detracts from your chances of being published. Additionally, releases can be so general that they serve very little of the marketing function (i.e., they produce no inquiries, no prospects, and no sales), or they can be written to draw the maximum response from the best-qualified prospects. Which would you like to have published?

This article will spend a paragraph or so on the basics of a press release, then give the formula for making your releases effective. Finally, I'll reveal the secret formula (shhh—make sure no one is reading this article over your shoulder) the magazine editors use to select the press releases they will publish. Engage.

A press release is a one- or two-page write-up of your product or service in a "news" style of writing. It's sent to magazines and newspapers, usually with a black-and-white photo. The magazine sets the type, and when the release appears in print it looks like an article the publication wrote. It's always published for free. Everyone likes new products, even magazine editors, and they know their readers do, too.

The chance of having your release published depends on the quality of your release and the publication. Industrial magazines are easier to get published in because their circulations are smaller, their audience is more focused, and less publicity material is aimed at them. They are also more "market friendly"—what's good for the market they serve is good for their readers.

It's much harder to get your release published in consumer publications. It's like shaking hands with the Pope—you can do it, but usually not without a great deal of trouble and expense. The numbers tell you why. Industrial publication circulation figures are usually 5,000 to 30,000, the latter being a fairly big industrial magazine circulation. They are almost always under 100,000. In consumer publications, circulation of 100,000 is small when you are shooting for the general interest magazines (like Newsweek or House Beautiful). Targeted market publications (like Runners World or Field and Stream) can be lower, but either way, the number of releases they get is quite staggering.

First, let's make sure your release is strongly considered for publishing, then we'll make sure it's written effectively to generate the maximum response. Then we'll look at the (shhh) secret process.

The closer you can come to the accepted standard for writing press releases, the greater your chances of being published. Why? (1) The standard format makes it easier for editors to read, scan, and edit. (2) It lets editors know that you know what you are doing and that your organization will be a responsible firm when dealing with their readers. (3) Well-presented releases add credibility to your offer, and editors will feel that their readers will receive a good product. Any editor in his or her right mind would never accept a release from a firm whose marketing material is poorly formatted or is full of typographical errors—knowing their product is probably like that, too.

Finally, number 4. Most editors get so many releases that they simply can afford to be choosy, and they are. With good reason: it's their neck on the line when the release is published. A poor selection of editorial write-ups can get the editor (or publisher) a lot of calls from disgruntled subscribers.

Parts of the Release

The top of the release is called the header. It is separate from the body copy and contains background information about the release material. Make sure it contains a release date—for example, "For Release May 1998." If your news can run anytime, say "For Immediate Release" in large bold print. Send a release two to four months prior to the publication date of the magazine or one to two weeks prior to the publication date of the newspaper in which you'd like it to appear.

The header also contains a line stating, "For Additional Information Contact:" followed by your name, company, and phone number. After that, give editors a kill date—state "Kill Date" and the date after which you no longer want your release to run. If it's OK anytime, state "No Kill Date." The header presents information about the background of the release to the editor at a glance.

Writing the Perfect Release: The Biggest-Benefit Headline, and the Benefit-First Release

As with all the ads I write, I write the objective of the release first. Since I can't sell the call as hard as in an ad, my marketing objective in a press release is usually to generate the maximum number of inquiries and orders from qualified prospects.

Start with a great headline. Write the headline with as much thought and care as you would write a headline for an ad. Capture the major portion of your market at a glance. An easy way to do this is to start the release with a headline that offers your biggest benefit. The formula for an effective release headline is NEW PRODUCT OFFERS BENEFIT, BENEFIT, BENEFIT.

Just like when you create an ad, the headline of your release will determine how many people will read the rest of the release. So offer benefits, benefits, benefits. And you'll get response, response, response. An example: "New lightweight tennis racket offers easier swing, faster ball speed, and is less tiring." When this is your headline, every tennis player will read it and continue reading the rest of the release.

Editors cut releases from the bottom, so keep all the important stuff at the top. The editor knows anything cut from the bottom of a correctly structured release won't be missed. So continue the benefit of the headline into the first few lines of your body copy. "A new lightweight tennis racket that won't tire you out when you play has just been introduced by the Racketeers. It offers more accurate ball placement, better control, and is easier on the elbow than heavyweight rackets."

See how many benefits are crammed into the first two lines? And chances are 98% they won't be cut because they're the first two sentences. In the Benefit-First type of release, the most important information is found at the top of the story. Benefits presented in the first two sentences won't be cut. Nice formula, eh?

Continue writing the body of your release in an inverted pyramid style, with the most important information at the very top of the story. Whatever style of writing you select for your pitch, make it sound like it's "news." If it sounds too much like an ad, or if the body of the release is written with too much sell, it will take too much time for an editor to rewrite; so it won't get rewritten, it'll get tossed out.

Then double space the body copy of the release. When releases are reviewed, the editor goes over them with a red pen and strikes out anything that does not conform to the style and content of the magazine. He then marks brief copy changes inside the double spacing and writes instructions to the production department in the margins. So leave big margins, too. *Anything you can do to make the editor's job easier and faster gets your release closer to being published.*

At the very end of the body copy of the release, write "For Additional Information Contact:" and then your company name, address, and phone number. After your street address, put the word "Dept. ____" with an underscored line after it. The magazine editors will insert their publication's initials in this block when they publish your release, so when you get inquiries, you'll know from which publication they came.

Try to confine your release to one page, with the body copy double spaced, and ixnay on the very small type to cram more in. If your release runs over one page, don't break a paragraph in the middle—end the first page at the end of the last full paragraph, then type "MORE" at the bottom of the page so editors will know to look for another page. If there isn't one, they'll know it's missing. Start the next page with a fresh paragraph.

Releases end with the number sign typed three times (###) or three asterisks (***); either set of marks signals the end of the release. Busy editors appreciate this.

If you are writing a release to be published in a particular magazine, read some of the other releases in the magazine and copy the magazine's particular style of writing. Write directly to the audience of the magazine. When you send your release, mention the name of the column in which you'd like it to appear. Editors are flattered by people who take the time to know their magazine and direct their energies specifically to it. To increase your chances of being published even further, include a personalized letter to the editor with your release.

If it's a photo release, include a crisp black-and-white 5" x 7" or 8" x 10" glossy finish photo, unfolded, so note: the envelope size you'll need for mailing photo releases is larger than a standard number 10. If there is a crease or fold in the photo, it won't be usable since the crease will show up when printed.

The correct way to identify a photo—and your release photos should always be identified—is to take a shipping label or file folder label, write the product name and your company name and phone number on it, then stick it on the back of the photo.

If you write directly on the back of the photo, chances are the pen or pencil will push into the emulsion side of the photo (front) and scar the photo, making it unusable. Editors know this scar will show up if the photo is printed, so it won't be.

If it's not obvious which end of your product is up, write "TOP" in very small letters in the top white photo margin. If an editor doesn't know which side is up, he won't guess—he'll simply toss it out and use another firm's release.

Send a photo with each release (not separately). Photos are never returned, so don't ask. If you need it, have a duplicate made before sending it.

THE EDITORIAL SELECTION PROCESS—
PART DEUX: YOU ARE THE EDITOR

Let's take a look at a press release from the other side of the desk. You are the editor.

It was unusually cold and damp when you awoke this morning, but the building super doesn't put the heat on till October 1. Too bad you ran out of coffee over the weekend. Through bleary eyes you shower and dress and get into your car still groggy and tired. As you drive to work, it starts raining hard. You can't remember ever seeing such a heavy volume of cars on the expressway, even for a Monday.

Even though you left 15 minutes early, you arrive at 10:15, an hour and fifteen minutes late. There are nine phone messages written in various hieroglyphics on scraps of paper on your desk. You can read only four of them. There are 12 voice mails, including one from the publisher asking you to come into his office when you get in to prepare for a 9:30 meeting with the magazine's largest advertiser.

Sitting at your desk, you look at the imposing volume of press releases. Three days are left till the closing of your gala Back-to-School issue. In a stack to your immediate right are about 80 releases. In a stack to your left, there are four unfinished stories and three uneaten slices of Monday's pizza in a box from Luigi's.

Everything except the pizza is marked for your "Immediate Attention" for the upcoming issue. This backlog of work happens every month around the closing date of the publication.

So how do you, the editor, pick out releases? First, you look through them and throw out all the ones that don't give you double spaces between the lines so you can make your corrections comfortably. This cuts the pile by about a third. It gets rid of the novices. (Now you understand why your releases should be double spaced.)

As the editor, you also trash all the releases that don't look good—smudges, typos, fingerprints, poor photocopies—figuring if the release doesn't look good, or if the photo isn't crisp, the literature your readers will receive—if any—will be of the same quality. This may reflect poorly on your magazine, so you throw them out. These first two steps take about a minute. (This brings us to Lesson 2: Submit neat, clean-appearing releases, double spaced, with good sharp, in-focus photos.)

Now you go back through the pile of about 40 releases, knowing you have room for about eight in this issue. Each month some people write with a ball point pen on the back of their photo exactly what the photo is, the release information, or their own version of *War and Peace*. So you check for writing on the back of the photos—you won't be able to print these without the writing showing through—and you toss them out, too. You see this mistake every month. Some people never learn.

The pictures with no identifying information on them could get imposed incorrectly in the production department, so you throw them out, too! Well, that was easy. If it were earlier in the month, you could now take a break. You'd go for a nice lunch, or for a beer. But since things always back up around the closing dates, you have to keep working. You start eyeing the pizza carefully. Is that a mushroom, or did it just move?

The acceptable product releases are now reviewed for newness, freshness, and newsworthiness and evaluated for proximity to your editorial style. Is there a good industry match? Will it be of interest to your readers? Does it look like a good product to introduce? Is it designed well? Are your readers going to be happy or disappointed if and when they get the literature, or if they order the product? If everything clicks, the release advances to the next level.

With about 20 releases surviving, and no other possible way out, you read them. The ones needing the least amount of rewriting make your job easier—and that slims the pile down to about 15 high-quality releases. But this month you have room for only eight.

SHHH. THE SECRET PROCESS.

So you, the wild-eyed editor now with eight cups of coffee under your belt at just 11:30, go to the top of the stairs and throw all the remaining releases up in the air directly over your head. The eight that land on the top few stairs get in, and the rest that floated downward are trashed or saved for next month's consideration. And that's why they call it editorial, because they don't all get in, and marketers like yourself have to submit to this "part hand-picked" and "part random" selection process that dictates what runs and what doesn't.

What I mean by this is, there is a great element of risk that your release won't run, no matter what you do. At the last moment you can get bumped for any reason, or no reason at all. You have to accept this as part of the mystique of the press release, as opposed to an ad for which you purchase space and which absolutely does run.

What are your chances of being published? For a new consumer product release, 5%. In an industry trade journal, 20%. If you are known to the industry or your product is industry specific, perhaps 40%. If you call the magazine and speak to the editor personally, the chance of your release being published may be as high as 80% or 90%, from just the one phone call. But the release still must be formatted and written correctly.

Keep your releases as close to the standard format as possible; it shows you know what you are doing, the product is probably good, and readers will be happy with you—as well as with the magazine, for giving your product and firm editorial support. Doing this will also get you to the top of the stairs. After that, it's up to gravity and the luck of the float to get your release into print.

THE DANIELLE ADAMS PUBLISHING COMPANY

~ Office of the President ~
Box 100 ✢ Merion Station, PA 19066
Fax 610/642-6832 ✢ Telephone 610/642-1000

Mr. Jeffrey Rogers
Excellence In Business
6782 Sylvia Drive
Huntington Beach, CA   92647

Dear Mr. Rogers:

Reluctant Entrepreneurs.

The Corporate Fallout. Corporate Refugees.

Even the long-employed and trusted upper management isn't safe
from the drastic downsizing of big business.

> *In 1995 even the U.S. government laid off over 800,000 personnel.*
> *If federal jobs aren't safe, how can the baby boomers of mid-*
> *America protect themselves from the ravages of the corporate*
> *layoff, not to mention gaining weight and middle age?*

Where have the corporate jobless gone? Home.

Over 40 million businesses are run from small offices/home offices.
The corporate surplus has turned into an army of entrepreneurial small business
owners. Many downsized victims have shortened their commute to a walk down-
stairs - and a chair by a computer. Millions of Americans have plunged headfirst
into a new life for the opportunity to be master of their own destiny. And the
chance to orchestrate their own success - or failure.

But launching a new product - or a new business - doesn't have to be scary.
Marketing doesn't have to be a big black hole. My new book, *How To Market a
Product for Under $500*, is for home office pioneers and small business owners
who need an *immediate education in real-life marketing*. **It cuts right through
the theoretical crap,** and straightaway gets to the usable, low-cost marketing
techniques that entrepreneurs need to run their businesses day to day.

In under 6 months, with under $500 to invest, anyone can market a product
working from any office - or their home. You can prove it to yourself in just a
few nights of enjoyable reading.

How To Market a Product for Under $500 is almost 400 pages of lean,
practical marketing information. No theory, no history, and no B.S. Just
concise How-To solutions for real-world marketing problems.

If this is the type of information you'd like to provide to your
readers, please **ask for a FREE review copy**. Please call 610/642-1000 for
your complimentary review copy. Your readers will thank you.

Kindest regards,

Jeffrey Dobkin
Publisher/Author

PS. Don't believe it? Please call now - 610/642-1000 - get your own
FREE review copy and see for yourself! It's like no other marketing book
you've ever seen. It's explicit. It's funny. And it works! Call now,
then decide for yourself if it's worth your readers' time. Thanks.

How to Market/Small Business 7/8
More Information - Jeffrey Dobkin (Owner) at
Danielle Adams Publishing: 610/642-1000
No Kill Date!

New Book Helps Small Businesses Market Products Cheaper.

How To Market a Product for Under $500 is a step-by-step action plan for marketing a product nationally, without phone calls. Readers can learn the inside secrets of direct marketing in just a few evenings with this book. Information-rich text and examples are crammed into a 21/2 lb., easy-to-follow marketing reference book.

"Anyone can market a product nationally, working just by themselves, from their home or small office - for under $500," says the author, Jeff Dobkin, who spent over two years researching and writing the reference data. The methods in the book provide in-depth direct marketing techniques to increase the effectiveness - yet lower the cost of any PR, marketing, direct marketing, or advertising campaigns.

"A few evenings with this book will change the way you market products, forever. You'll never, ever even consider going back to your old style of marketing again," says Dobkin. A 100% satisfaction guarantee is offered, and Dobkin states his return rate is under .0003%.

The book is written to make it easy for anyone to bring a product to market: from inventors with little or no experience in marketing, to home-office pioneers, to owners of small businesses with sales up to $20 million annually. The heavily referenced book is also for the professional marketer looking for innovative or new, low-cost marketing techniques. *How To Market a Product for Under $500* provides a firm foundation in marketing and direct marketing, with plenty of examples, then offers advanced techniques in traditional and nontraditional marketing.

Unusual marketing techniques are discussed, including how to do all your marketing in a single evening, and how to complete your entire publicity campaign the following day - even just working by yourself. Also included: how to write publicity releases for maximum response, and how to increase the chances of having your release published from 10% to 85%. No brochure? You don't need one - really - to use Jeff Dobkin's Multiple Exposure Marketing techniques. The last chapter - "The $500 Campaign" - is a unique, easy-to-follow national marketing plan and, as promised, costs less than $500.

Almost 400 pages of information-rich reading in Mr. Dobkin's breezy-to-read conversational style of writing, crammed with inside secrets of direct marketing. "You never learned this stuff in college. It's lean and concise marketing information," says Dobkin. "You know the boring historical part you always skipped over in your college textbooks? I left that part out." *How To Market a Product for Under $500* is $29.95 + $ shipping, available from Danielle Adams Publishing, Box 100-   Merion Station, PA 19066. Visa/MC, AMEX. Phone: 610/642-1000, orders: 800-234-IDEA. Sample excerpts are available. Publisher guarantees satisfaction or money back.

###

How To
Write Direct Mail
Letter Copy

PLUS, THE SINGLE GREATEST COPYWRITING TRICK
I'VE EVER LEARNED.

A LETTER IN DIRECT MAIL ISN'T REALLY A LETTER. A letter is a personal correspondence you send to one or two people. In direct mail, a letter is a highly stylized ad designed to look like a letter. Any arguments?

So now you know: What you are writing is really an ad. Like any ad copy, direct mail letter copy isn't something you can dash off in a few minutes. You wouldn't write an ad in ten minutes, would you? Your letter is going to take longer to write, too.

It takes me 5 to 8 hours to write a crisp, one-page direct mail letter. Sometimes longer. And most of the time I know what I'm doing, and it still takes that long. No, no TV on; not even in the background. If you think you can do it in less time, please send me the secret formula.

If your letter is going to many recipients, it's worth the extra time and effort you're going to spend making it tight. Allow yourself more time and take it. You may spend up to a week on a single one-page letter. That's OK, too. I still have tough assignments that require a week or more to write and design a single page. Some letters are more difficult than others.

Above all, the letter in a direct mail package is a compelling set of benefits that directs the readers to the objective: to call or write or, if you own a retail store, to come in. This can be to place an order or to inquire. In consumer direct marketing, it's usually to place an order, by phone, with a credit card.

Smooth writing transitions, editing, and more editing make the copy tight. Keeping the words fresh, exciting, and stimulating while continually pointing the reader toward the order form or the phone call takes time. Have those credit cards handy? Why don't you call us and order right now, while you're thinking of it. Oy, how many times I've written that line.

Every direct mail piece starts the same way: Write the objective in the upper right-hand corner of a blank sheet of paper. This reminds you that the reason you are writing every word is to fulfill this objective: call, write, come in, send in the card, inquire, place the order.

Next, draw a line down the center of your paper and write the features of your product (or service) on the left, the benefits of those features to your readers on the right. For example, a 400-watt receiver in a stereo system you sell is a feature. The benefit to the purchaser is no matter how loud you turn it up, the music always sounds crystal clear. In my case, an added benefit: I can turn it up so loud I can annoy my neighbor who owns that stupid barking dog. With 400 watts, I can probably blow out his windows if I place my speakers just right. Hmmm. Now that is a compelling set of benefits. I'll take one. Stupid dog. Stupid neighbor. Hrumph.

One of the best ways to write benefit-oriented copy is to ask, "What is the biggest benefit of using this product?" What happens to the reader if everything works perfectly? In the answer lie your ad headline, envelope teaser copy, first sentence, and even the lead paragraph of your letter.

Once you have all the benefits written down, rank them in importance. Which are the biggest benefits to the widest segment of your audience? You'll use these first.

When you begin writing copy, write everything that pops into your head. Write down even the silly stuff. Even the far-out ideas. Don't leave anything out. You never know what's going to look good later, or work well in print, or sound good in context. This isn't the time to edit. When you edit, you stop the flow of words and ideas. Editing comes later—you can't do both at one time. After your writing session, take a break. Let your writing sit. Come back from a fresh angle. After two or three good writing sessions, begin editing. Edit severely to get the writing focused and tight. Maybe three pages down to one.

All copy is drafted to fulfill the central theme of your objective, so look up at the top of the page often so you don't lose sight, and...

OK, pick up your pencil and begin. Start with a rough draft; everyone does. You are going to write several drafts and do several revisions to get the copy crisp and electric. So just start writing anywhere.

Here's the best trick I've ever learned in writing copy. After you have about a page of writing, go back and delete your first sentence. This brings your copy into a fast start, and 99% of the time it works. Simple, isn't it? If you are having trouble starting, just write anything. Start anywhere. Then go back and strike out your first two or three sentences. Another nice trick. If you are really having a bad day, strike out your first paragraph. You're already over the hardest part of copywriting, which, as in all jobs, is to start.

Use every square inch of your paper to fulfill your objective. Start at the top of the page; use a single selling line incorporated into your letterhead to let readers know what you're about, or use your first line to convince them to buy your product or service or to call you. Examples showing quality would be "A Tradition of Excellence," "A Tradition of Quality," "World's Finest...." Examples of selling the call would be "Call Us Toll Free," or "Your Call is Welcome at...."

Use the area directly under the letterhead (but before the salutation and body of the letter) to get in an additional short sales message. Words above the salutation do not appear to the reader as part of the letter. Insert a couple of lines dedicated to the most important selling features, a strong enticement for your best offer, the biggest benefits, or a few lines to arouse additional interest. Some mailers even leave off the letterhead of company logo, name, and address in favor of an early heavier block of selling copy. I recommend this, also. Both ways work well.

Information presented here should be brief and in shortened form. This copy is separated from the body of the letter, and the space may be incredibly effective for arousing interest. A few major benefits set off with bullets can also be effective. No need for full sentences: "Get this benefit"; "This one, too."

The salutation "Dear Reader" can always be used. It's safe, but it's usually my last choice because it's boring and impersonal. This is a personal medium. The closer you can get to the heart, the occupation, or the passion of the person, or the market, the better. If you're writing to physicians, open with "Dear Doctor" or "Dear Physician"; to veterinarians, "Dear Animal Lover." If you're writing to business people, "Dear Colleague" is one of my universal favorites and has a wide application. Common sense prevails.

Other favorites are Dear Neighbor, Dear Friend, Dear Enthusiast, Dear Valued Customer, and Dear Valued Patron. Dear Fellow Shopper—actually, Dear Fellow Anything—is also a friendly greeting. My very favorite idea to enhance all of the general headings is to put "and Friend" after the greeting. An example of this is "Dear Customer and Friend," or "Dear Neighbor and Friend." Don't take a chance with something too cute here—it may turn people off or appear insincere. You'll have plenty of time to do that later. Stay with the basics at the beginning.

Create an interest-arousing opening sentence. Make this line so compelling that people must continue reading or they'll go crazy from the suspense. The purpose of the first line is to get the reader into the letter. If they trash it, make sure they'll drag it out of the trash at midnight to read the rest of it. If you can bring your biggest benefit into this line, great. If not, that's OK, too. Just make sure the first line is of exceptional interest to every reader, to keep them reading.

Like the headline for an ad, the opening line has got to be the biggest, the best, the smashing greatest line in your whole package. If your teaser copy in this line isn't great great—and I mean great great, not just great—don't use it. Keep searching.

With the first line of your letter compelling readers to continue reading, show them early on how they can get your biggest primary or secondary benefits. Why wait till you lose your readers? Benefits are what the reader gets for himself when he buys your products. Benefits are the reason people buy. Benefits are also the reason people continue to read your letter. They want to see what they get. They want to see "what's in it for me." Show this to them early.

If you can't decide if a block of copy should stay or go, strike it out. Your readers won't be so kind: when they get to that wishy-washy block, they'll simply toss everything out. With the objective in the upper right-hand corner of your paper, compare every line you write to it. Does this sentence help fulfill the objective? Does it hold the reader's intense interest?

Lead off the letter body with an opening paragraph that is one, maybe two lines at most. A single line can be most electric. It's oh-so-easy to read a short line, and most people do. Now's your chance to hook them. Catch their attention at their first glance.

Use an exciting and provocative opening sentence. Or simply start with your biggest benefit first, then expand on that benefit. The secret of success in direct mail: Show the features in the brochure, flaunt the benefits in the letter, and sell the response hard. That is the secret of successful direct mail.

The copy should be written so the weakest, most inexperienced portion of your audience can read it easily. Write in a conversational tone—like this article. The text should read as though you're speaking to someone, man to man, woman to woman, one to one, whatever you are.

If your offer is to businesses, or more technical people, you can use longer words. But for the best response, I still recommend your letter be in short words and conversational in tone. In fact, I never recommend big words. Scientists and technical people are just people with different sets of skills who don't know how to dress (plaid shirt, plaid sport coat, plastic pocket pen protectors!). In every English class I've ever taken, the instructor has always told me to increase my vocabulary. It's a good thing I never let my education get in the way of effective writing. Short words work best, so why chance it?

The body of the letter should be a compelling set of benefits leading the reader to the logical conclusion to pick up the phone right now and order, inquire, or send in the reply card. (You do have a reply card, don't you?) Mention every important benefit you can think of. If you have a ton of them, list them in brief bulleted statements of one or two lines apiece. Picture your reader successfully using your product, and paint this picture in his mind, too.

Focus on how easily he can accomplish the tasks at hand. How simple things become after he orders your product. How soon he'll be finished with his unpleasant tasks. How much he'll enjoy using it. And how much better life will be, if he picks up the phone right now and calls to order.

Now hammer that in. Don't be afraid to ask for the response several times in the letter, and again in the PS. If you are seeking a phone call, mention the number several times in the letter after you say, "Call now to place your order: 800-876-5432!" or "Call for additional information: 800-987-6543." This reinforces the number and encourages customers to call. I usually don't repeat myself too many times, but asking for the response is the exception. If you don't get the response, all has failed and your whole piece has no value other than to look pretty. In direct mail, we evaluate our packages by different criteria. They need to bring in money.

The PS is an important part of a direct mail letter, and every letter-like ad should have one. It gets read first, and sometimes again last. This is the best place to restate your most powerful benefit and your offer. Give the phone number again. It's your last chance to get your order; make it sound fantastic.

Keep your letters as short as you can; you risk an early death otherwise. If it looks like it's going to be too much to read, the whole thing gets tossed out. If it's excessively long, the benefits can get lost in the clutter instead of being presented first in the logical sequence pointing to the response, and the whole package winds up as landfill fodder. Long copy only works best if the recipient reads the whole thing and then orders. For long packages your writing must be totally electric, and even then a good portion of your readers will fall off way before the order form. So keep it short. It's safer.

All writing should be based on "you will receive." Avoid starting any paragraph with the first-person singular "I." Write in terms of reader benefits and speak in terms of "you." Use "you" throughout the letter. Instead of writing "I will send you," write "You will receive." Think in terms of what the readers will get, and let them know. Tell them. Then tell them again. Ask for the response three times in the letter.

To rate your letter copy with a numerical grade, give yourself 10 points for every time you use the word "you" or "your," 20 points for each benefit you mention, and 30 points for mentioning the best benefit. Add 5 points for each action word and 10 points for each action or command word directed at your objective (send in the postage-paid card). Add 25 points for each time you use the word "Free." Deduct 25 points each time you use the word "I," and deduct 100 points if you use "I" to start a sentence at the beginning of a paragraph. Wish I had these tips when I started out. Oops. Minus 50.

~ *Features & Benefits* ~

A *Feature* is a property of a product or service.

A *Benefit* is what the consumer receives as a result of the feature.

Features may be shown in long brochures, technical specifications, pseudotechnical sales brochures, and informational data sheets. Benefits are shown in ads, sales letters, and selling brochures. When selling to consumers, always address the satisfaction of their needs by stating the benefits.

Automobile Features and Benefits

Feature	Benefit
ABS Brakes	Stopping on ice won't kill you
Automatic Climate Control	Always be comfortable
50-Watt Stereo	Can't hear kids
Quartz Halogen Lights	Blind oncoming drivers who won't dim their lights
Rear Wheel Drive with Limited Slip Differential	Do doughnuts in snow
Cloth Seats	Never get cold
Childproof Locks	Kids won't fall out
Rear Window Defroster	Wife won't need to stand in cold to scrape window

THE ART
OF A DIRECT MAIL
LETTER

A LETTER IS A SELF-PORTRAIT OF THE SENDER in a direct mail campaign. Here's how to design one that makes you look like Sharon Stone.

A letter is the most effective you can be in marketing for 32¢. A letter is the most effective you can be in marketing at any price. In direct mail, your success may be just 32¢ away.

But is it really a letter? In truth, a letter is really a personal communication you write to one or two people. When you send it to a few hundred, a few thousand, or a few million people, it's an advertisement. Specifically, what you see in most direct mail packages is a one-page, highly stylized ad designed to <u>look</u> like a letter. It's the hardest-working part of the package you mail. People look at the brochure, but they read the letter. The letter is far more important than a brochure, and it can be effective if used just by itself.

Unless you are exceptionally long-winded like me, most commercial direct mail letters should be typed on a single side of a standard 81/2" x 11" sheet of paper, then folded copy-side out so the recipient sees the copy as soon as he opens the envelope. If it requires more than one page, it's least expensive to use the back of the sheet. Although this never looks as good as two pages printed on the face only, its lower cost may justify this format. It should still be folded with the first side facing out.

If you find your letter is slightly too long for one page, let the right and left margins out a total of perhaps 5 to 10 spaces. This will allow your typing to go a little farther out to the side edges of the paper. Additionally, extend your letter almost to the paper's bottom edge. The longer line lengths and more lines per page will allow more copy to fit on a single page. Before printing the final copy, reduce the letter by 5% or 10% on a quality photocopy machine. You can also ask a printer to shoot it down. This reduction will give your letter slightly smaller type, as well as the added bonus of additional white space around the top and sides. I sometimes reduce the size of a letter just to make it appear shorter and easier to read.

If the package requires even longer copy, my first choice is to use an 11" x 17" sheet folded in half for a four-page letter. This is also the most effective format for a three-page letter—leave the back of the second page blank. This allows for plenty of selling copy and plenty of white space around it.

Above all, the letter must look attractive. It should have lots of white space, making it look easy to read, even if it isn't. Frame your copy with a broad white border—this "breathing area" makes it look more inviting. If your letter looks like it's going to take a long time to read, it's just tossed in the pile to be read sometime between later and never, and it eventually winds up getting thrown out. So Rule Number 1: Your letter must look good so people will read it.

Use typewriter-style type to make your letter look like it was just typed on a typewriter. The size of the type in a letter is determined by the amount of copy you have and the amount of space it needs to fit. Courier is my favorite typeface for letters and is used 12/12 (12 point type on 12 point leading) because it looks OK in a slightly larger size. It can be used 11/12, 11/11, and 10/11 if the copy is long, but the believability of "this just came off my typewriter" falls off fast if the type used is too small. American Typewriter typestyle from ITC Corporation works OK for very commercial letters.

Make the first line short and compelling to read. Like this.

Here you can see the value of a line that stands alone. Since it's short and set apart, everyone will read it. The first line of the letter is the single most important line because it must interest the reader enough to convince him to continue reading. Grab the reader and demand he read further. To do this, an opening paragraph should be one line—maybe two lines at most. A single line can be most electric. A single line is too short to pass up. Inspire your reader at his first glance to read the rest.

To start the eyeflow of the reader, indent the first line of all paragraphs five spaces. This also breaks up the copy from the monotony of squared-off visual blocks of text. Set the paragraphs to rag right (ragged edge of type on the right-hand side) to further break up the look of the block of copy. Never justify the body of the letter.

To make the letter look less forbidding and faster and easier to read, make the top line of each paragraph shorter on the right-hand side than the lines in the rest of the paragraph. This makes the paragraphs appear shorter and encourages reading. If it creates a bad break, poor copy flow, or an awkward sentence ending, forget it. Since we are dealing with letters as both copy and art, consider each and every change; notice and make a deliberate call on where each line breaks on the right-hand side of the letter. I do.

Limit paragraph length to seven lines at most. If a paragraph runs longer than seven lines, break it into two paragraphs. Artificially broken paragraphs are OK—this isn't English class, it's real life.

Stagger paragraph lengths so they don't all look the same, keeping the copy looking fresh and visually interesting. One short, two long, two long, one short, etc. Vary the text block design to make it look inviting. No one wants to read a wall of type where each paragraph looks exactly the same.

Next, to keep the letter visually stimulating, and to direct the eye of the reader to the parts you wish him to see, underline one or two words or a short phrase in all but one or two of the paragraphs. Use bold in one or two paragraphs. For words in a list,

Letter Design
— Before —

****
TAKE 10% OFF YOUR
NEXT PRINTING BILL!
****

Dear Colleague:

You're invited to call our TOLL-FREE number and get our remarkable new DISCOUNT ENVELOPE CATALOG. It's FREE.

Look over our incredible LOW PRICES, then call us toll free and find out what exceptional service really is:

TOLL-FREE QUOTE LINES - Call 800-987-6543. Call our toll-free phone lines - they're staffed by friendly, knowledgeable personnel - who know our products and can help you with your selections, questions, or press and delivery schedules. Call EARLY with questions or for quotes. For your convenience, our phone lines open at 7 AM.

Call LATE. We're open LATE, too - until 6 PM. Call with last-minute questions, quotes, or inquiries. FAX orders or quotes: Call 800-987-6543, 24 hours!

Call us and get INSTANT QUOTES on most any envelope printing. Need a price in just a few moments? Just call and we'll be happy to help you immediately! There are NEVER any hidden charges with us - you'll know your total costs up front.

Call to place your order - and receive it FAST. Standard delivery: just 5 days. Rush service, 3 days. Special windows and nonstandard envelope sizes, delivered in 10 days or less. Fastest delivery you can get. Need it faster? Please call and inquire.

Compare our pricing to anyone, anywhere, anytime. We are consistently the lowest-priced envelope manufacturer in the East. Many customers use our catalog as a handy pricing reference. No catalog? Call toll free and get one: 800-987-6543!

Please call now for a fast quote on any style envelope, or get your FREE CATALOG. See how easy it is to get a quote or order envelopes. CALL TOLL FREE: 800-987-6543. Thanks.

Kindest regards,

Jeff Dobkin
President

PS - I've included a 10% GIFT CERTIFICATE - so please call and get our catalog right now. Let us give you an immediate price quote. Then place any order and enjoy additional savings of 10% off our already low prices. Call 800-987-6543. Thank you.

****
TAKE 10% OFF YOUR
NEXT PRINTING BILL!
****

Dear Colleague:

   You're invited to call our TOLL-FREE number and get
our remarkable new *DISCOUNT ENVELOPE CATALOG.*   It's FREE.

   Look over our incredible *LOW PRICES,* then call us
toll free and find out what exceptional service really is:

   [✔] **TOLL-FREE QUOTE LINES - Call 800-987-6543**
           Call our toll-free phone lines - they're staffed
           by friendly, knowledgeable personnel - who know
           our products and can help you with your selections.
   [✔] **Call EARLY** with questions or for quotes.
           For your convenience, our *phone lines open at 7 AM.*
   [✔] **Call LATE.** We're open LATE, too - *until 6 PM.*
           Call with last-minute questions, quotes or inquiries.
   [✔] **FAX** orders or quotes: Call 800-987-6543 *24 hours!*

   Call us and get **INSTANT QUOTES** on most any envelope
printing. Need a price in just a few moments? Just call and
we'll be happy to help you immediately! There are NEVER any
hidden charges with us - you'll know your total costs up front.

   Call to place your order - and receive it FAST. Standard
delivery: *just 5 days.* Rush service, *3 days.* Special windows
and nonstandard envelope sizes, delivered in 10 days or less.
Fastest delivery you can get. Need it faster? Call and inquire.

           Compare our pricing to anyone, anywhere,
           anytime. We are consistently the lowest-priced
           envelope manufacturer in the East. Many customers
           use our catalog as a handy pricing reference. No
           catalog? Call toll free and get one: 800-987-6543!

   Please **call now for a fast quote** on any style envelope,
or get your *FREE CATALOG.* See how easy it is to get a quote
or order envelopes. *CALL TOLL FREE: 800-987-6543.*   Thanks.

                        Kindest regards,

                        Jeff Dobkin
                        For Envelopes & Stuff!

PS - I've included a **10% GIFT CERTIFICATE** - so please call and
get our catalog right now. Let us give you an immediate price
quote. Then place any order and enjoy **additional savings** of 10%
off our already low prices. Call 800-987-6543.   Thank you.

bold can be used more frequently. Use all capital letters only once or twice on a page for a short phrase that describes a really attractive benefit.

Finally, to break up the copy and keep it visually interesting, in the center of the letter you can list bulleted information to catch and hold the reader's attention. Bulleted copy:

- Directs the eyeflow to this area
- Draws attention to the important parts
- Shows the strongest benefits
- Enhances the best offer
- Highlights the guarantee
- Pulls the eye to features you want your readers to see
- Increases the response you want

If your heart is set on showing the features of your product, the way to list them is in this brief, bulleted style.

Another visual trick in commercial direct mail letters is to use a shortened paragraph:

> You may also use a shortened paragraph in the center of the page to direct the reader's eyes to the important points. Indent a paragraph on both sides with wide margins, and justify the type to set it apart from the rest of the letter even further.

This paragraph can be in a smaller or different typeface. A paragraph like this increases visual interest. When used with a smaller typeface, it can also increase the amount of copy you can get on a single page without making it look crammed or forbidding to read.

If it gives a clean impression, you can just use that old Smith-Corona portable typewriter you have in your closet—I used one for years. An IBM Selectric isn't a bad choice, either. Nowadays most folks use a computer, I suspect. Don't get lost in all those fancy typefaces. Just make it look like a letter. Use typewriter-style type. Sorry, no exceptions.

Begin your letter at the very top of the page. Way before the salutation, your letter should start to sell the response. (Remember the objective?) To further the impression that your highly stylized ad is really a letter, use a letterhead with your company logo. But since you can use this area more effectively for selling and the logo is not a reader benefit, make it smaller than usual. Then reduce your letterhead so it doesn't get in the way. Perhaps you can squish it over to the left and drop in some early sale copy on the right.

The copy above the salutation and body of the letter can be set in any style and any size type, since it's not really viewed as part of the body of the letter. It can almost be an ad in itself, but don't use a border—it will take away from the intended image of the page as a letter. Following this area comes the letter itself, in traditional form and format.

Following the letterhead and its accompanying pre-selling copy, it's best to show a date, even if it's just the month and year (September 1998). If you're unsure about your mailing date, leave this out. Once printed, a stale date can sink a mailing like a stone and waste every single sheet of paper it's printed on. So think carefully about putting in a date.

As in any piece of art, each element of the design enhances or detracts from the appearance, and in this case it directly affects the response. The more elements you consciously control, the less you leave to chance, the better the letter will work for you. This will also ensure that your letters will consistently be effective.

When you are finished and happy with your letter's appearance, run your eye down the right-hand side and bring down any words that stick out too far into the margin. If your letter is commercial-looking and not too personal, one or two handwritten marginal words or a short phrase can call attention to a strong benefit. Hand-underlining can also be effective, if used sparingly.

Sign with a legible signature, and don't forget to enhance your letter with a powerful PS. Shorten the right-hand margin of the PS one inch to tuck it in attractively. A handwritten PS can also work if it's short, but if your handwriting is less than perfect, don't chance it.

Always keep in mind that you are not writing a letter, you are writing copy and inserting it into a piece of art. The objective of the art is to create an attractive design that makes the copy appear easy to read. The objective of the copy is to guide the reader through a set of benefits leading to a desire to inquire (pick up the phone) or order the product.

How To Create Your Own Great Ad - Or Get One You Like From An Agency, The First Time

ARMED WITH THE SOLID KNOWLEDGE of who your audience is, grab a pen and come up with a great headline. Not a good headline, a GREAT headline.

This is usually accomplished by showing, offering, providing, or proving the biggest benefit of using your product. An easy way to do this is to think, "What is the best, the ultimate result that can occur when a customer uses my product?" Now cleverly craft that into a headline with impact. You have under three seconds to capture the attention of the page-scanning reader. Man, today's readers are tough.

The headline is the ad for the ad. If you have a mediocre headline, no one will read the brilliant copy that took you three weeks to write. No one will see the great offer you're making. They won't get that far. If your headline isn't the most captivating headline on the page, no one will bother reading the rest of the ad. They'll simply turn the page. You won't even get a second glance.

Your headline must make an immediate impression on the reader about what your product is going to do *for him.* The secret formula I personally recommend is "NEW PRODUCT OFFERS BENEFIT, BENEFIT, BENEFIT." When writing the headline, if it's not great, or it doesn't stress an immediate benefit to the reader, nothing else matters.

When I write an ad, I usually write between 50 and 100 headlines. Then, over a period of a few days, I sift through them and select the one great one. And people wonder why ads from me are expensive—after all, I had to write only one line.

The sole purpose of the headline is to catch and hold the reader's attention and demand that he read the rest of the ad.

Space permitting, I use a subhead next. This appears in slightly smaller type, but it continues to show the compelling reasons why the reader should keep reading the ad. That's the purpose of the subhead. Expound on the main benefit, or if there is a strong secondary benefit, add it here.

When you are developing your copy strategy, consider exactly what you want readers to do. Call? Send money? Inquire? The body copy of the ad depends on this, and on whether you plan a one-step sale—asking the reader to make a purchase directly from the ad—or an inquiry-generating two-step sale, which asks the reader to request more information and gives you the chance to send a longer, harder-hitting direct mail package.

Smaller or classified ads demand a two-step selling posture. Since you have only a few words, there isn't really enough copy to sell a product—so you must go for the inquiry.

Next, decide how tightly you want to qualify your prospects. Throw as loose or as tight of a qualification net as you like. A loose net is asking anyone and everyone to contact you: to check off the reader service card, call you on your own toll-free 800 number, or send back a reply card that is postpaid by you. This increases the response, but it adds plenty of expense from people who have no intention of buying. Your competitors will love you for this! So will the "just curious."

A tight qualification net screens respondents in some way, and the value of each response increases depending on the toughness of your qualifier. A minimal qualification may be to make respondents call on their dime, make them send back a reply card that they have to place their own stamp on, or say that response cards won't be processed without phone numbers. On the high end, a tight qualifier may say a minimum investment amount of "so much" is required, or that your sales rep will personally call on each inquirer in person.

You can also offer an interim package for a nominal amount to prequalify interested parties. I send excerpts from my book, *How To Market a Product for Under $500,* to potential prospects who want to see what it's all about without buying it, but I charge $2 for postage and handling. It's a good deal for them—they get a lot of information from the excerpts for two bucks, and I get only the more serious inquirers. If I just said FREE EXCERPTS—CALL TOLL FREE AND REQUEST THEM, everyone and their mother would call because it's a free offer with a free call. Ugh.

I once ran a campaign to the teaching profession. We received thousands of responses from a reader service bingo number, but further mailings to respondents resulted in a scant few sales. I asked the magazine publisher for some of the response cards and found out why our response was so poor: half the cards had ALL the numbers circled. Some teachers even drew one big circle around all the numbers *en masse.* What did I learn from this? Not who liked my product, but that teachers just like to get mail. I guess if you're a teacher in rural Nebraska, the Saturday mail delivery is a whopping big event.

Write the body copy, enhancing the benefits. Make your offer sound sensational. To increase response, offer a free trial or a money-back guarantee. Hammer home the benefits, and ask several times for the reader to call you and place an order. Give your phone number several times in the ad also.

The Secrets of a Direct Response Ad

Go for the call. For an ad to be successful, it must generate a response. So get the call. This is your number-one priority and the objective of the ad. That's right, the objective of the ad is not usually to sell the product, it is to generate a response, and that's usually a phone call.

Show the benefits to the readers—then sell the call hard. That is the secret of direct response advertising.

"Call now for free information. Call for a free sample. Call now to place your order at this special price. Call toll free and order right now—you'll get...." If a person doesn't call right now, your chance of any response drops off significantly with each passing moment. Request immediate action; offer a great deal or a limited-time special.

Place your phone number again on the bottom of the ad in fairly large type—so that someone who is thinking about calling can find it easily while reaching for the phone.

Read your ad again from the eyes of a prospect. If you haven't persuaded someone to call you by the end of the ad, start over and compose the ad again; no one will know you had to create the ad twice, they'll just see the final product and think it's great. You should see the first efforts in my wastebasket.

Place a small copy of your logo, if you have one, on the bottom of the ad. The value of a logo is that people will recognize it and your firm when they see it *again.* If you are running a solid schedule of ads, your logo should be distinctive enough that people will remember it, but it should not necessarily be large. Large is not usually a memorable trait except in people, buildings, and fish. If you place ads occasionally, the logo is not a benefit to the reader and not that important to you, either—use the space more wisely and show a bigger phone number.

Concentrate on anything that may increase your response. With every element in your ad, with every conscious decision you make, ask, "Does this increase my response?" If yes, leave it in. If no, trash it.

Finish writing your copy by letting it sit for a day or two, then coming back to it for a final editing and polishing. Edit severely. Then edit severely again. Cut out everything that doesn't make someone pick up the phone. If you don't cut your copy by at least one-third, you aren't nearly tough enough on yourself—let someone else do it.

The last step is the design. My first choice is to use a compelling photo or illustration to capture the eye of the page-flipping audience and direct their attention to your space. Too bad I can't draw even a reasonable resemblance of a stick figure without everyone wondering what the heck it is. So I usually rely on tastefully laid-out large type in the headline with copy that is strong enough to make people read it—along with the rest of the ad.

If you use a photo, make sure it has a caption and that the caption is a strong benefit or makes the reader call. A photo caption has exceptionally high readership, but what a great opportunity you waste if you describe the photo—readers can already see what it is. Better you should increase your response with this universally read hot spot.

DESIGNING A GREAT AD

Start out with some thumbnail sketches of how your ad will lay out. Pick up any magazine and find an ad to emulate. Draw some fast, smaller-than-actual-size likenesses of all the elements in your ad. Hand-letter the headline. Does it look better on one line or two? Can you logically break the wording? Instead of hand-lettering the body copy in the layout, just use straight lines to represent it. One column or two? Will all the copy fit? Are you sure? Hint: better edit again.

When you get a thumbnail ad you like, move up in size. Draw a border that is the same size your actual ad will be. It's easiest to trace the border of an ad of the same size in a magazine. Now pencil in your ad copy, following the thumbnail sketch you made as a guide. Don't spend a lot of time on this one, this is just a "rough." Does everything work? Everything fit? Enough room for the photo? You don't have to write the body copy, but rule some lines in its place to get a feel for what it will look like. Sketch in your logo and your company name and address at the bottom. Pencil in your phone number.

Now—do all this again. Yep, it's part of the process, and everyone does it. Tighten up the ad. Make your headline more perfect. Tighten where the copy will print. Exactly where will you place the headline, and where will the line break? Pencil in the subhead to size. Where does the break fall? Define and refine all the elements. Work out all the details.

Sorry: now make a third and final ad, crisp enough to show people. This is called a comprehensive layout or "comp." If there are colors, show them. Show the border style. Everything should be as it will appear in the final ad, except in pencil. Don't hand-write the body copy, but have it represented with straight ruled lines. Hand-letter the head and subhead to approximate size. Shade in where the photo or illustration will be placed. Complete with your logo and name at the bottom, and don't forget the large phone number. It should be nice enough to show around.

Now show it around. Does everyone like it? Get opinions. Do they read it? No, don't just ask if they would read it, hand them the ad and the typed copy on another sheet and SEE if they read it. Hint: If they don't smile the moment you show it to them, you're in trouble. If they don't read it in its entirety, you're in deep trouble.

Everyone like it? Read it? Good. Now you have several choices: (1) set the ad on your computer, (2) set the ad at a type-setting house, (3) set the ad at a copy shop like Kinko's, or (4) take it to an advertising agency and have them set it. If you've selected door number 1, you're almost finished: just do it. If you'd like to choose option 2, yes, everyone at a typesetting house (if you can still find one) will respect you if you come in with a tight, well-thought-out composition. They'll set the type in your ad for you. If you've elected option 3, the people at Kinko's are generally friendly and helpful. Create your ad on their computer. Ask them to help you if you need help. Best of luck. Drop a sample to me for a fast review.

But I recommend option number 4. Since your ad is already written and in final layout form, it shouldn't be too expensive to have an agency look it over and get the type set. Included in the price, you'll get someone qualified looking over your work; they should let you know if you have any gross errors in your ad, or anything wrong at all. They'd be stupid to set a typo or misspell-ing. And they should be happy to give you some feedback on it—like if it has a structural defect and will not be effective—and why.

Having the agency set your type is the final frontier for your ad before you place it—it's nice to have a knowledgeable stranger look over your work. It becomes very expensive to make changes in hindsight, embarrassing to print with an error, and/or very expensive to run twice to get it right. But then, an ad is only expensive if it doesn't work.

12 Do's AND DON'TS FOR SMALL BUSINESS

1 Do: SEND PRESS RELEASES EVERY MONTH. I don't care to whom, or where. Unless, of course, you have all the business you can stand—and I mean you're running three shifts. If you can use more business, press releases are no longer a luxury or sent on a whim. In these days of tight marketing, schedule them as any other marketing function gets scheduled. Put them on the calendar for mailings on a regular basis, like every month.

2. Do: use personal letters as sales tools. Right from your computer, you can wage the cheapest, most effective sales campaign ever. A letter is an incredible sales weapon. More effective than any ad, and lower in cost than any other sales campaign, bar none. A whole campaign can be waged without ever having to pick up the phone. The most effective campaign I have ever written was a series of personal letters.

3. Don't: send one letter and call it a marketing campaign. A campaign is not a single effort of anything. Think of it this way— that long, boring three-page letter you have been sending would make three excellent, vibrant one-page letters in a three-letter sales campaign. Write a short series of letters, and send them to

your best prospects over a selected time frame—in a program that takes your best prospects more seriously than just sending one letter.

4. Don't: mail 25 letters to inquiries from an ad, then when you get only one response say, "I tried direct mail and it didn't work for us." Direct mail is a game of numbers. One response in 25 is 4%—not a bad draw in the direct mail domain. I wish some of my low-percentage clients' mailings did this—we'd all be rich! Well, now mail 100, get four more sales. Now mail 1,000—get 40 sales. By the way, to test a new list, the direct marketing industry standard is to mail 5,000 pieces.

5. Do: have open business discussions with consultants or your peers. As broad as your vision may be, you can only see your business from your own singular perspective. Ask open-ended questions, then listen. For example, "What would you do to advance my business? What do you think I should change? What is our company's greatest opportunity? Our gravest weakness? Where are we missing the boat? How can we be more profitable? How can we move forward? Where can we save money?"

6. Don't: forget to put money in a growth fund. Don't paint yourself into a nonprofit business or a nongrowth corner. How many times have I seen clients who have no potential to grow even though they want to? If you make a comfortable living and that's all you want, then fine. But if you want to grow, you need to know how—and have the money earmarked as a growth fund. Every business peaks out at a certain level—if your level is high enough, you can be pretty comfortable. But if not, you need a plan to break through that level and into the next phase, and chances are you're going to need money to do it. Assign a certain percentage of your income to a growth account.

7. Do: learn to delegate. You can't do everything yourself; this is a given. To grow, you're going to need to assign tasks and functions to others and figure out if they are doing their jobs effectively. Learn benchmarking. Let others know how you are going to judge their success, so they will have overall goals. Be quick with rewards, slow but fair with discipline. Learn early how to lead and inspire—so people will want to do their best for you (and your company). No one likes a dictator for a boss, although

some put up with it. Learn to motivate the people who work with you, and their 110% effort will help ensure your success—and theirs, too. There are plenty of great books on leadership in the library.

8. Do: have clear goals. Know what you want and what you expect from your business. These goals should be set for both immediate rewards and future expectations. So if you say, "I'd like to produce this product for one year, perhaps without making any money," you then need to say, "The next year I'll take out some cash, and in five years I'll grow to a firm this size." This puts things in perspective and lets you know what it will take to get where you'd like to go. Once you know where you're going, the roads to get there become more self-evident.

9. Don't: proceed without a realistic time frame. Know in advance how long each step will take and what time allotment you will allow for it. I know, I know, it's easier said than done. But if you don't start roughing in the time element now, how will you know when things have taken too long, when to celebrate because you finished early, or when your time is up?

10. Don't: forget to go to the library every month or so. More often if you need new information more frequently. Use the library as a reference source for your business. To the dismay of my college professors, I'm pretty much all self-taught. When I couldn't afford books at a bookstore, I read them at the library. I've never been to the library without knowing, when I left, how valuable the time I spent there was, how much information I received, and how much it helped me.

11. Don't: forget to create Plan B. While success is nice, and necessary to stay in business, you should have a contingency plan in case what you are doing isn't working. What happens if... is a scenario you should deal with up front, before it happens. (Even if there is no Plan B, you should know that in the beginning.) I'll give you an example. When I started Merion Station Mail Order, I mortgaged my house to the hilt and jumped into business. My older and wiser brother asked, "What happens if the initial mailings don't work?" "Well," I coughed reluctantly, "I'll refinance what's left on the house and try new offers and new mailing packages." That was Plan B. What happened if that

didn't work? The options at that time all looked worse. "Fail" was one of them. But you know, I'd rather have tried and failed, than never have had the courage to try.

12. Do: have an exit plan. No one likes to call it quits, but you should decide up front how much time you'll devote to a project that isn't living up to your expectations. An exit plan is one of the hardest strategies to write—no one likes to think there is even a chance of failure. To complicate issues, failure may not be so clear-cut. Your successes may be only partial. How long do you settle for second best to your dreams? If you're not at your maximum potential, know when to call it a day, and where to go from there—and how.

5 RULES OF STARTING AND STAYING IN BUSINESS

RULE NUMBER ONE

IT IS A PRIVILEGE TO SERVE YOUR CUSTOMERS. This guiding principle (and some start-up money) helped my old manufacturing firm grow with one of the most loyal followings in the pet industry, where we marketed our products. Be honest and fair in all your dealings.

Along with this in today's marketplace, remember to let people know that you appreciate their business. Thank your customers—it comes back to you in repeat business and referrals. An example: One day I was approached by the owner of one of the larger magazine groups serving the pet industry. He asked me what I thought about his firm, where I placed about $6,000 a year in advertising. I told him they were ugly to do business with, and if my ads ever stopped drawing, I would withdraw them in a second.

Horrified, he asked why. I told him: In seven years of placing ads in his magazines, and seven years of receiving bills every month for those ads, I never, ever received a single thank-you.

As fate would have it, a competitor started running ad space, and instead of working out a new test schedule, I withdrew my ads, never called the magazine owner, and have never run again despite his phone calls and requests.

When I look at our own shipping form, I see that in a 31/2" x 8" form we said "Thank you!" to the customer SEVEN times. (Then, just to be sure we got more business, we gave customers a free gift that they could glue on their front door—so they always had our name and phone number handy for reorders.)

RULE 2

Make money. Remember, your numero uno reason for being in business is to make a profit. This is the reason for business and, in fact, the heart of business. The owner of a pharmacy is not in business to cure you, he is in business to make money. The airlines are not in business to take you from point A to point B, they are in business to make money; the way they do it is incidental. The goal of restaurants is not to feed you, it is to make money. If they do this correctly—with good food served properly—you pay them and come back to further their goal and send them referrals.

If you don't make a profit, you won't be in business long. I've seen way too many inventors—and normal people, too—who start out saying, "I don't need to make any money now, I'll just do this till the product gets off the ground." Nope. The reason to go into business is not to market your product successfully—that goal just strokes your ego. It is to make money on your product, so you can stay in business and grow and expand.

RULE 3

Don't worry about your mistakes—everybody makes them. Everybody. And that crap about learning from them—don't worry, you won't. From most of them, you won't learn a thing except ouch, that hurts. You'll do it again. Maybe not the exact same thing, but it'll be pretty close.

You're in good company. Henry Ford went bankrupt two times before coming out with the Model T. John Wanamaker's just went belly-up. Macy's went bankrupt, and came back. New Coke, wow—what a screwup. EuroDisney—how many re-fi's till they turned the corner? The Edsel—geez, am I that old already? All of these were losing propositions. Well-financed, well-thought-out, big, big errors. Errors in judgments, in predictions, in executions—by people with plenty of research teams and focus groups...and experience.

If these executive giants can screw up, you can, too. Even the pros hit into the sand traps once in a while. Big companies have the money to power through their marketing blunders—and I mean big, expensive marketing blunders; hopefully you can survive, too. If not—well, I'll tell you a little story.

About ten years ago I decided I wasn't happy with what I was doing. Being a one-person advertising and marketing consultant had its limitations—I made good money, but if I didn't work, one day somewhere down the road I missed a payday. I wanted a company that would earn money even if I took a day off.

So I mortgaged my house to the hilt and took a shot. And I felt—and still feel—this way: I could live with failure, and even with a failed business. Yep. Others have failed and regrouped to try again. Sure, it's heavy, but you survive.

But I decided I couldn't live with this: I didn't want to wake up ten years from now and know I had had a chance to start a new company, should have taken the chance, but didn't have the courage. I couldn't live with that. So win or lose, take your best shot, and if you fail, it's not the end of the world.

By the way, when you start up, it's a wild ride, and things go up and down in a radical fashion. I don't know of any business that started off on an even keel, much less stayed there.

Here's something to go with that: If you find yourself short on cash, with excellent long-range probabilities, sacrifice some of your vendors to stay in business. Pay them what you can, when you can. When my company had hard times—and I had plenty of hard times—I sent the people I owed money to whatever I could—every week. I called them to let them know I wasn't running from them, told them times were tough and I was paying them off as fast as I could. Every week. 50 bucks. 100 bucks. $500 or $1,000—whatever I could. It showed them I was trying, making an effort. They respected that. Only two vendors dropped off, and they were paid eventually, too—just like everyone else.

And you know, the ones that stuck it out—they have my undying gratitude and my continued business. I don't even get quotations from other companies on those parts they supply—whatever they charge me is just fine. They saved me when I needed it. Vendor credit is a valuable part of any business, and it is appreciated when needed. Sacrifice a vendor if you have to, but stay in business. Pay them when you get the money in. Declaring bankruptcy is just the beginning of a new headache—a migraine.

My priorities when paying bills: Employees are #1. They earn it every day, just for putting up with me. I have missed many paychecks myself, but I have never missed an employee payday. #2, rent. #3, phone. Even after ten years of prompt payments every month, those bastards will cut you off after a couple of months. You need a phone to be in business, or you could fail the Jeff Dobkin 75¢ credit check: I call Information and ask for your business number.

Rule 4

Read books and magazines. (Especially the other book I wrote on low-cost marketing, *How to Market a Product for Under $500!*) You can get any information you need at the library. Bookstores are a lot of help, too. And magazines present valuable trade information, along with precisely targeted, market-specific educational material. Learn everything about your primary industry, your markets, your competition, and all the secondary and tertiary industries you hope to serve. Gather information.

I receive over 100 magazines a month. More than that number of catalogs. I always have a dozen business books on my coffee table that I am reading or skimming. I am entirely self-taught and learned everything through reading. You can, too.

Rule 5

Just start. Don't know about payroll? When you have a staff, you'll figure out how to pay them. Don't know about taxes? There's no income tax if there's no income. Just start. Jump in. Don't worry—if you're successful and you make a lot of money, all the questions you have now will have been answered. Money solves a lot of problems and answers a lot of questions.

I've seen too many people not start because of one reason or another. You're never going to know everything you need to know, so if you're waiting for that day, hell will freeze over first. Don't wait, just start. There are millions of excuses, but no real reasons not to start right now. Let me know if you come up with a valid excuse—ain't never seen one yet. See you at the library.

How To
Write a Small
Classified Ad

Y EARS AGO, A REAL ESTATE AGENT HIRED ME to increase the
phone calls from his listings. We met for about 10 hours,
reading over the real estate section of the paper and discussing his ads. I then told him I was ready to increase his phone
calls—and although there are no guarantess in advertising, I could
probably double them.

"Sir!" he said in startled disbelief. "Do you mean to tell me we
can meet for 10 hours and you can tell me how to sell more
houses? I've been selling houses for forty years. I've forgotten
more about selling houses than you will ever learn in your life." It
was true.

Too bad the reply, "Sir, I have forgotten more about advertising than you have learned in forty years of selling houses," didn't
occur to me till a few weeks later. Isn't hindsight wonderful—it
always lets you know you could have said something more clever
now that it's too late.

My client was right. He had forgotten more about selling
houses than he thought. The structure of his entire advertising
campaign was incorrect.

What my client was trying to do was sell a house in his ad. You do not sell a house in a four-line listing. No one sees the listing and sends a down payment. The objective of the ad was not to sell a house. The objective of the ad was to generate a phone call. He paid me a lot of money to hear me say that last sentence.

So we changed all the listings. "Call now!" they all said. "Call to see this beautiful four-bedroom..." "For additional information sent to you in the mail, call..." "For a free brochure with pictures of this house, call us at..." "Call and get a free..." and we gave the phone number. If you read all of our listings, you saw our phone number dozens of times. The new ads were structured correctly. The objective of the ad was defined and written: to generate phone calls. The ads were drafted to this new objective. My client's phone calls tripled, starting in week number one. This is where I became worth all the money he paid me to hear that one sentence.

How To Sell Your Car

Take an example: selling your car. When you place an ad in the paper to sell your car, what is the objective? If you answered, "To sell my car!" no, no, no! Read the first part of this article again. The objective is not to sell your car. You do not sell your car in an ad; no one sees your ad and sends you a check. If your ad works, people call. The objective of the ad is to generate a call. Now structure the ad to generate calls. Call 876-5432 for immediate information. Call now for low price. Must sell. Great shape. Call for photos. Low mileage. One owner. Call now. Ready to go, call for immediate delivery.

And do you put a price in? I say only if it's an incredibly amazing low price that will make everyone call. Otherwise, let everyone call to find out the price. This fulfills the primary objective of the ad. People call.

OK, I admit you're going to get a lot of calls from people who only ask the price. These calls will be very quick. I didn't say it wasn't going to be a pain in the neck to sell your car yourself. But then, you're not doing it for fun, you're doing it to get the best possible price you can for your car. If you wanted to get a lousy price, you could sell it to a dealer—it's quick and easy, but ouch, you're going to take a hit on your asking price.

By the way, I hate to sound like a mercenary, but when someone calls, the objective is to have them come out to take a look at the car. They won't buy it if they don't see it. Again, the objective is not to sell the car, it's to get the person out to look at it. While they are on the phone, don't forget to mention how it's your grandmother's car, and she kept it in her heated garage and drove it only on weekends. Don't mention it was only a quarter of a mile at a time, in B modifieds.

THE TWO-STEP SECRET

Here is the two-step secret to creating successful small classified ads. (1) Start by writing the objective of the ad in the upper right-hand corner of a blank sheet of paper. This reminds you that every word should be crafted to fulfill this objective directly.

(2) Unless your product costs under $5, the objective of a small classified ad is not to sell the product. The objective is to generate an inquiry—a response by mail or phone. This is called a two-step marketing approach. Now you can draft your ad.

FREE MONEY!

Now, let's get serious. Here's where we generate the **maximum** response we can possibly get.

How can you best generate the most response? Let's see, would "Buy my product" get readers' attention? No, not really.

Would "Get this benefit!" excite them? Yes, that's a nice start. But surely there must be something better. Much better. What would attract everyone? How about "Get this FREE MONEY!" Yes, that's it. Now you have everyone's attention.

So the best way to generate maximum response is to give something away for free. Any arguments? But we don't want people outside of our market—people who are most likely not going to buy our product—calling or inquiring. No offense, but you can waste a lot of money on literature and postage by mailing to people who have no intention of buying. So while "Free Money" may generate maximum response, let's not use it. Let's intentionally limit the response to people who are more likely to purchase what we are selling. Let's still give something away, but let's make sure it's of value only to the people in our market. How about an informational booklet or brochure?

If you're trying to get people to call, "Call now for a FREE BOOKLET" is my favorite for two reasons. This specific line is so strong because it not only promises prospects something for free, it gives people a REASON TO CALL. The free brochure overcomes reader inertia: A body at rest tends to stay at rest unless the ad offers something really incredible. The purpose of the call—to get something free—overcomes call reluctance: people no longer must figure out what to say when you answer the phone, since they can ask for the brochure. You may not think this is important, but it's a big factor with folks who have problems calling anyone other than friends.

A big bonus for the advertiser: When people ask for something for free, they are generally pleasant and in a giving mood. They're happy to talk to you—after all, they're getting something free! This is the time to poke around for information you need from them in your own marketing. This is the time to qualify the caller as a serious prospect, a literature collector, or someone with a phone and nothing better to do.

When someone calls and asks me to send information, somewhere between rarely and never are my next words, "OK, what's your address?" Instead, I always qualify prospects at this point. "Oh, when were you thinking of buying one of these?" You can describe your product in brief and ask, "Does this sound like what you are looking for?"

Nothing to give away? How about your new brochure, dressed up as a helpful educational and information-rich *resource guide?* Just a few pieces of paper become a powerful sales tool to attract customers and generate response.

QUALIFYING THE RESPONDENTS

Well, now that we know we can get everyone and their mother to call or write to get something free, let's talk about the quality of the leads you're going to get with a free offer. If your offer—free money—is too general, your leads won't be worth anything. You'll only attract people who want free money, and who doesn't? To get true prospects, you need to prequalify inquirers.

The best way to generate a "qualified" response is to give away information or a small free gift that will only benefit people who need your product or service. For example, imagine the moving company that offers a "Guide to Packing." This offer must produce a ton of the highest-quality leads. Now imagine that when a person calls and says he'd like to get the free guide, the moving company responds with, "I'd be happy to send it right out. How soon are you moving?" Instant qualification.

If you're selling material from another source, product information is usually available from the manufacturer—just ask them for their literature. The best literature to give away is educational material, instructional booklets, or how-to literature.

For example, suppose you're a roofer. Offering a book from a shingle manufacturer that shows how to install a new shingle roof will bring in a good number of highly qualified leads from people who need new roofs. Will they read the book and do it themselves? I doubt it. If they were inclined to do it themselves, they'd get a book out of the library and shingle their roof. Their current interest shows only that they are viable prospects for your services.

When fishing for prospects, there are different types of nets you can throw. A loose qualification net generates all the calls it can from just about anyone and everyone, regardless of their intent or ability to buy your product. A tight net further qualifies the respondent in some way.

Free offers can generate a large response up front, but with a very loose qualifying net you may receive no orders on your back end. You wind up getting lots of inquiries to your initial ad, send out lots of literature or brochures, then get no sales. Ugh. Many respondents aren't real prospects.

There are as many different opinions on this aspect of marketing as there are marketers. My feeling is, if your unit of sale is large, it's generally better to get all the calls you can and sort them out yourself later. You never know who in this list will turn up as a viable prospect and purchase your product.

You should limit your response by placing more of a qualifier in your advertisements if your product is inexpensive, or if your literature is expensive. In these examples, it's better to qualify your respondents more tightly up front so you send your direct marketing packages only to the most likely prospects.

Qualifying the respondents is already partly done for you based on where your advertisement appears. To a great extent, the quality of your leads will reflect this. In our automotive example, we defined our market by placing an ad in the cars-for-sale section. Respondents were shoppers looking for cars. In the real estate section, shoppers were looking for houses.

This is the difference between advertising and marketing. Advertising is knowing what to say, marketing is knowing where to say it. Marketing is selling to a defined audience. When you are advertising to everyone, that's selling; when you define your audience and advertise just to them, that's marketing. When you precisely define your exact target market and advertise just to this market, that's intelligence.

To increase the value of each response to your free offer, you may elect to qualify inquirers slightly by asking them to send a self-addressed stamped envelope (SASE for short). This will wash out the least serious, as well as cut down on your postage costs. To separate the literature seekers from the rest of the inquirers, you may further require a dollar or two for postage and handling. This will cut your response way down to the very serious. Voilà: more limited response, and only from better prospects.

It's your choice: more respondents who may be less qualified, or fewer respondents who are more qualified and more likely to purchase your products or service. Do you go with the bigger numbers or the better percentages? That's up to you. This is the point where the science of marketing meets the art of making money.

Either way, take out an ad in the best possible place to generate a response from the folks most likely to buy your products. Write small classified ads using a two-step selling approach. Qualify suspects in a tight or loose qualification net, and when you get an inquiry, send the hardest-hitting direct marketing package you can write. You can be successful in direct marketing.

PLAN B.
BEFORE
BANKRUPTCY...

USINESS IS NOT ONLY LOUSY, IT STINKS. Every one of your accounts—or at least the ones still with you—is slow pay. You owe money to a lot of people, and it's not getting any better. Former business associates and suppliers no longer call to speak with you, they just have their accounting departments call and ask for money. Smaller vendors call, demanding immediate payment. Some call you names. You can hear the disgust in their voices. As an honest person, you cry a little inside at each of these calls. Since your business start-up, these calls are the toughest part of business you have ever had to endure. This, my dear, sucks.

After a couple of months of this, when the phone rings, you cringe. This reaction accompanies any call. Now you dread answering the phone. The ringing pierces your every thought. When the phone rings, it penetrates your stomach with a sharp pain, like a stab with a pencil. Then the feeling comes back up your throat, accompanied by an acid burning. The bad taste remains in the back of your mouth the rest of the day. It's only Monday; you have the rest of the week to look forward to. Is this what business is really about? I don't think so. What a mess. What now, *mes amis*, what now?

Well, I'm not going to tell you not to worry; you're in a hell of a pickle. But you're not alone. Yes, it has happened to others. Many others. Bigger companies than yours, I'll guarantee you that. And lots of companies, too. Way more than you have ever imagined.

Sometimes companies fail. Big companies—with the biggest and best minds—sometimes still crap out. And all through the decision-making process—with the best advisors and the best advice, with research money out the wazoo, with enough focus groups to choke Rhode Island—some companies still go belly-up. Chrysler almost went out. International Harvester, same. Look at EuroDisney—only heavy backing saved them. So if things are going down the tubes, don't feel too bad, because you're not alone. In fact, you're in good company.

More common than failing businesses are product failures. New Coke—remember that? The Edsel, the Ford Falcon, and the Chevy Vega. Remember IBM's OS/2? How about Apple's Newton? Lots of products fail. You don't think Green Giant says, "Oh, let's just stick with frozen peas!" do you? They launch a new product every single month. They get six feet of freezer space from the Acme, so whatever fits, goes in. Whatever sells, they keep marketing. The rest of the products just die. Your products can, too. It's fantastically easy to have a product that doesn't do well—and if you're a one-product company, *c'est la vie.* Or, more appropriately, *c'est la morte.*

The hardest part is, if you're like me, you're as honest as the day is long. You take all the dunning calls and letters personally—just like I did when my company went through hard times. Although you may think you have some new ones, I know every feeling you're going through. Tough, tough times. And hand to mouth is no way to run a company. But it may have to do for now. So until you can get back on your feet, here's what to do.

Numero uno. The first rule of order is to reassess being in business. The further beating of a dead horse to try to bring him to a gallop is neither practical nor feasible. If you really have no possible alternative, and no bright hope on any horizon, let it go. In the final evaluation, is your business worth saving? If not, engage your exit strategy. What! You don't have one? Oh well, I don't have one, either. Most people don't. Just being realistic. So now what? So whatever happens, happens. Just get out, cut your losses. Don't ruin the rest of your life—it's not worth it.

Rule 2. Follow your reassessment plan. If it's to close your doors, then dissolve the business as best you can, and start looking forward to your new life. Hey, no one said that you could only start one business in your lifetime, and that if that one didn't work out, you could never start another. Or that you had to live in grief for the rest of your life, either. Sure, it's heavy. But life is short, and you absolutely have multiple chances.

If your business is big enough, and you do have high hopes of bringing it back to life, filing for bankruptcy is an option. For a small firm, this is always my *last* option—like right before death and taxes. Don't go bankrupt. This is always the worst choice, and it's just the beginning of a headache. It's dragging you through the court system, endlessly. Lawyers, all of whom will insist on payment up front, are expensive. It's a horror, and then you drag the government bureaucracy in. I don't know about you, but I've found that whenever the government gets involved, everything gets worse; it gets more expensive, and your money buys about one-third as much. I don't recommend you even think about declaring bankruptcy until it's forced upon you.

If you've opted for getting out, then get on with your life. Pick up the pieces as best and as fast as you can, find the next road going from where you are now to where you want to be, and get on it. Walk away. You now have experience—which is what you get when you don't get what you want. You'll get another chance—maybe even later this week. Maybe next week. Or in a month. It'll come, don't worry.

If you've opted for staying in business, this is where you tough it out and get to work. It's probably the best option for you, and certainly for your suppliers. As long as you have some cash flow, you may be able to work things out. If you go belly-up, no suppliers get paid at all, and they know that. If your business ends, you won't have anything worthwhile left, and your vendors won't get any money at all. So if it's at all possible, hang in there. I know, no one told you it would be easy, but then no one told you it would be this hard, either. A decision to stay and fight is always hard, and you have a tough new round of parameters to deal with, and new decisions to make. But you also have more options than you may think. Here they are.

Plan B: Call all of your suppliers, and let them know you're having a difficult time. Tell them you are paying them off on a regular basis and that things will be better soon. It's the truth. Always tell the truth. As bad as it ever gets, it's always best to tell the truth. Hey, don't necessarily spill your guts out on their conference room table, but always be truthful.

Rule 1: Stop money from coming out the bottom. Plug unnecessary holes. First, cut staff. Yep, always hard to do, but it's a fact of life. Downsizing is a popular word until it happens to your firm, then it's more like devastating. Letting friends and loyal employees go, I hated that the most. But there was no other way. If you've gotta do it to stay in business, then do it.

Rule 2: Cut your square footage. Renegotiate with your landlord for less space. Or maybe move. Serious problems demand serious solutions, and if you're going to have to cut your expenses to the bone, rent is probably a big chunk of them.

Rule 3: Cut back on everything. Limit calls. Mail less-expensive brochures. Reassess everything to see where you can cut down on expenses and save money.

Rule 4: Negotiate with your suppliers. Show good faith by sending payments. Even if it's just $100 a week, send it every week. I've never seen a merchant who wouldn't take a regular payment, as promised, over starting legal proceedings. Your vendors know that if you declare bankruptcy, they'll likely go unpaid. And if paid, they'll get only 10¢ to 25¢ on the dollar. While you're not bargaining from a position of power, you can still show some strength and resiliency.

Rule 5: Prioritize your income. Write out a list of your most likely sources of cash. See exactly what options are there. Prioritize expenses, then call up the merchants you owe money to and tell them you're going to make payments, and do it. Any amount is OK; sure, they'll want more than any offer you make, but pick a number that's realistic *to you* to send, and make the payments. I don't care if it's $10 a week—make the offer and do it.

Rule 6: Sacrifice some of your suppliers. Face it, you need your suppliers as much as they need you. In my business, our vendors are as valuable (or more so) than some of our customers. But when the chips are really down, stall them. Some will drop you. It's a sad fact of life. Sorry, but it's a necessity to let them go to save yourself. Others will support you—and that's what business is about.

I'll tell you a little story. We sold our products to a catalog house, and they went out in a big way. My company had money on their books when we got the notice, and I knew I wasn't going to get paid. It was a big account for us. So what did I do? I wrote them a nice letter. "Chin up," I said. "Even Henry Ford went bankrupt before coming out with the Model T. We appreciate all the business you have sent us over the last five years. Thank you so much for that. We are happy to do anything we can for you."

You know, I never did get paid in money from that account, but I knew I wouldn't. They continued to use us (with prompt payment on current bills) until they finally went terminally out of business. Imagine, though, all the suppliers who called them up, yelling and screaming at them. Man, it must have been ugly. My letter must have been a breath of fresh air, and a godsend to them in time of need.

What did I get out of it? The director of merchandising, who I wrote the letter to, left and went to Hanover House, one of the largest catalog houses in the U.S. His first call was to my office, requesting that samples of our products be sent to him for photography—to be in their catalog.

Rule 7: Be prepared. You're going to lose not only some of your suppliers, but some friends, too. If you do well and make a comeback, you'll get them back—even though you may be on COD for a while. I've lost suppliers. Keep in mind you still must pay them off, but first pay off those you need to in order to stay in business. As you recover, pay off old debts, including these old vendors. A debt is a debt.

Face reality with the truth and a positive attitude. No one said you had to work at only one business for the rest of your life, and that if that didn't work out, you were doomed! BS. Come on, even the pros hit into the sand traps once in a while. We're all living on borrowed time, so make the best of it.

This burn, this desire they call the entrepreneurial spirit—it can be a trip down a rocky road. And there don't seem to be any books on how to do it all right the first time. Just do the best you can. Figure out what went right, then don't worry—others will tell you what you did wrong. There's a lot of 20/20 hindsight out there, and you're going to get it. But don't ever lose that entrepreneurial spirit.

It's a wild ride on the entrepreneurial roller coaster, and I've had many weeks without paychecks myself. But I wouldn't trade what I've been through for a steady paycheck from living life, day after day, at a job I didn't like. Even if it fails, I know I had the guts to take a shot and risk it all for a chance, just a chance for my own self-made success. That's what business is about. And that's what entrepreneurship is about: not necessarily achieving success, but allowing yourself the chance to achieve success.

I'd feel pretty good if I were you; you had the courage to be on your own and cover new ground. You knew you'd be at great risk. Hey, if this one didn't work, maybe the next one will. Depression and anxiety are natural. But pull up from these problems before they make you sick. Like your sadness at the loss of a loved one, this grief is OK. But the sun is coming up tomorrow, and you have a new chance at...at...well, at whatever you want to do. You have 365 new chances every year to accomplish your goals.

How To Create
A Winning Direct
Mail Package

T HE SECRET TO NOT LOSING YOUR SHIRT in a direct mail campaign is to run a test. This is the beauty of direct mail—you never, ever need to lose big money. You can test the response to any package you mail simply by mailing your initial package in small numbers. That way, unsuccessful packages won't turn into costly mistakes. Before you mail any big numbers—with their associated big costs—you'll know if your package is going to draw a response, approximately to what extent, and if it will be successful—all BEFORE you spend big money to roll it out to every name on your list. Nice.

In traditional direct mail packages, there are four printed elements to consider: the letter—which contributes the personal soft sell of the benefits and the hard sell of the response; the brochure or data sheet—to show the features and photos and reemphasize the benefits; the reply vehicle—the order form via post card, envelope, or telephone call; and the envelope—written with teaser copy to get the package opened.

In a direct mail campaign, the product is generally not what you sell. What you sell are the benefits derived from the product. The hard sell is not of the product, either—the hard sell is to generate the response: get the call or send in the order form. In a direct mail package, soft-sell the product and sell the call hard. That is the secret of successful direct mail.

There are many nonprinted elements you should consider. The most important are the offer, the price, the creative format, and the list—but those elements are discussed in other chapters. This chapter is about just the printed material. Let's take a look at a traditional direct mail package.

How To Immediately Increase Your Response by 30% to 40%: The Letter

If you are sending any mail without a letter, you're probably missing about 30% to 40% of your orders. Maybe more. Of all the mistakes I see my clients make, this is the easiest to remedy, with the biggest immediate gain in revenues. A letter is the most important and most powerful part of a direct mail package. Its pulling power is so strong, there are times when a letter can work just by itself.

Have you ever noticed that when you receive a mailing from any of the giant direct marketers, there's a letter in it? That's because they know the value of the letter and how it increases their response.

But is it really a letter? No, it isn't. A letter is a personal correspondence you write to one or two people. When you send it to 10, 10,000 or 10 million people, and it's designed to sell your product, it's really an ad. It's a highly stylized ad designed to look like a letter. Any arguments?

But we'll call it a letter for short. The letter is the part of your mailing package that your potential customers read. They may look at your brochure, but they read the letter. After all, if it's good, it's perceived as a personal note from you to them. Only in direct mail can you write a personal note to 10,000 of your closest friends.

So make your letter a great one. Don't try to write it in half an hour—it's not like the letter you send to your great-aunt every Thanksgiving so she'll remember you at Christmas. It takes me five to eight hours to write a tight, crisp one-page letter. Sometimes more. Even then my work is usually not finished, it's merely abandoned for reasons of practicality and time. If you can do it in less time, let's exchange notes.

The letter is the place to sell the benefits of owning and using your product. This is where your powerful benefits generate the response—which is the objective of the letter. You do this by flaunting the benefits, then asking the reader for a response several times in the letter copy. "Send for this new...Call now to reserve your own...Just fill out the order form...Use the handy postpaid envelope...." Well, you get the idea.

While I usually don't recommend repeating yourself when writing advertising copy, asking for the response you are seeking is the exception. Throughout the storyline, weave explicit directions leading readers directly down the path to respond. If the reader doesn't respond in some fashion, your package didn't work. The proof of this follows shortly afterward: you lose money. If your readers don't respond, your package goes from the good side of your spreadsheet to the bad side, and it changes color along the way.

For maximum effectiveness and believability, your letter must look like a letter. The more it looks like a piece of personal business correspondence, the better your response will be. While people generally recognize that it's not the personal letter from Grandma, they'll overlook that fact if it's done well.

Begin with a letterhead on the top of the page. Add a few lines after that, set flush right, to give the reader an enticing glance at your offer.

The salutation should be warm and friendly and as tightly focused to your audience as you can make it without alienating readers on the rim. Don't take chances here, and don't get too cute. For example, to veterinarians say "Dear Doctor" or "Dear Animal Lover." To pharmacists, "Dear Pharmacist." Not too exciting, but it's safe. Don't overlook the obvious correct choice.

Several favorites of mine: To people in your area, "Dear Neighbor." To customers, "Dear Valued Customer." Better yet, place "and Friend" after the salutation for a warmer reception: "Dear Neighbor and Friend"; "Dear Valued Customer and Friend." To someone in your business or industry, "Dear Colleague and Friend." "Dear Reader" can always be used, but it is always my last choice. The more tightly you can focus your salutation, the more personal your letter will look, the more it will be read, and the more response you'll get. Direct mail is, after all, a game of numbers.

Write a letter filled with benefits. State your most powerful benefits early, and describe what's in it for the reader. The product has features that give the benefits to the reader. So the feature of a stereo speaker made with a stereophonic amalgam rubber won't do much for the reader (or your order box), but the fact that "You can't blow out these speakers. No matter how loud you like your music, these speakers always sound crisp and clear—and are guaranteed for life!" will have meaning to your readers (and your bank account).

Start out with your best stuff: state your strongest benefit **first,** then immediately expound on it—don't wait till later in your package! You'll lose readers soon enough without hiding your biggest benefits in the middle of a few pages of copy. If you have a lot of benefits, list in bulleted form those that are too numerous to describe fully—everyone likes to read a short list. Write all copy in terms of "you," so "I am going to send" becomes "You will receive...."

Exciting graphics can be incorporated into a well-designed letter, too. The opening paragraph: One line. Two at most. Short paragraphs and lots of white space around the typed copy will help get the reader interested. Make your letter look easy to read, even if it isn't. Indent all paragraphs four or five spaces. Flush left, rag right—never justify the body of the letter. Use typewriter-style type such as Courier or American Typewriter. No paragraph should run over six lines. Vary paragraph length. Make the top line of each paragraph shorter on the right-hand side than the rest of the paragraph.

Select a particular paragraph in the center and shorten its appearance with wide 2" margins, then reduce the type size in this paragraph one or two points. Use short, action-packed words. At the end of the letter, include your signature, written legibly. Then add a PS that reemphasizes your best offer and asks again for the response. Everyone reads the PS—make it an order clincher. Allow five to ten hours per page for writing, editing, and layout.

THE BROCHURE

Your brochure or data sheet shows the features of your product. But most people won't read your brochure anyhow, unless they're already pretty much ready to buy. Would you read a brochure about a Ford station wagon if you weren't going to buy one?

Heck, no. But people who are ready to buy will read almost everything: (1) for reassurance they made the right choice, and (2) to feel good about their purchase. Of course, lots of photos and four-color printing keep the initially uninterested in the brochure longer.

Your brochure becomes important in three separate ways. People who are serious about your product want more information and will read it. So here, it becomes the clincher in the sale—the last frontier to make that extra one person in 100 step over the line and call to place an order. Next, your brochure gives you added credibility. You can tell people in your letter that the hotel they will be staying in is beautiful, but how much more convincing it is to show them the pictures of the pool and the veranda in the brochure! Finally, with this additional and less personal selling space, you can show all the features of your product that you didn't have the space for in your letter, which is reserved for benefits and a more personal plea for orders.

If your product has a lot of great features, it's best to list them in bulleted fashion. This is faster to read, and most readers will stop to read a bulleted list. I usually follow each feature with smaller type that shows the benefit of that particular feature. For example:

> • The blade is made of Rockwell Hardness 440 Steel. *This knife will hold a keen edge longer, and you won't have to sharpen it frequently, like you do with cheaper knives.*

Don't forget to have your company name, phone number, address, and complete ordering information on your brochure in case it gets separated from the rest of the package. It probably will.

A Data Sheet

If you have no money for an expensive brochure, create a DATA SHEET. This sales tool looks just fine in black and white. Some industries, like the electronics industry, use a data sheet for all new products. Label yours DATA SHEET or NEW PRODUCT BULLETIN at the top. Include a line drawing or photo, and information about the features—but sneak in as many benefits as you can. Use a typeface other than the one you used in your letter, so it looks typeset. To encourage orders, don't forget to say "Order from..." before your name and address.

Direct mail is like professional wrestling: you can do anything you want to your opponent, but only for five seconds. In direct mail, you can say anything you want, but you only have about five seconds to get your envelope opened and get the recipient interested in your material. An electrifying data sheet will spark interest from those on the verge of tossing everything out. Black and white is still OK, but make sure it's electric. Really electric.

The longer readers stay in your package, the better your chances of having them order your product. Shrewd retailers have known this principle for years. The longer customers are in their store, the more likely they are to make a purchase. You can prove this by following my brother Dean: after precisely seven minutes in any store, his wallet and credit cards come out.

THE REPLY VEHICLE

Face it, the easiest response to generate is a phone call. It's instant gratification for the reader, and with a charge card, it's money in the bank for you. So throughout the copy, I ask the reader several times for a phone call to place an order. You should, too. This is always my first choice for the type of response I solicit.

To encourage the call-reluctant, I recommend you also enclose a reply envelope with an order form that slips into it. The reply envelope can be a postage-paid BRE, or you can have the customer place a stamp on it. If your mailing envelope has a window, the mailing label should be affixed to the order form and show through the window. This makes it even easier for the recipient to order by mail, which helps overcome the law of reader inertia: A body at rest tends to stay at rest unless everything is laid out to make it ultimately easy to order.

My old firm mailed about 25,000 pounds of mail each year. Did we send out reply envelopes? Yep! In every package. And every day we saw our cute little purple envelopes come back to us crammed with money. Reply envelopes are generally worth their expense.

If your initial test mailing is small, you can place a live stamp on the order envelope—which will ensure that even if your prospects don't order your product, your envelope will stick around on their desk for several days while they try to figure out how to get the live stamp off an envelope addressed to you.

I recommend a reply envelope and order form instead of a reply card so you can get paid up front. With a reply card, no one sends you a check, sure as heck not cash, and only a fool would send a credit card number on a post card. Make sure you say on the top of your order form what it is: "Rush Order Form."

Somewhere on the reply form, make sure you give your regular phone number preceded by, "To place your order immediately by phone, call...." Also include your fax number, a recap of what you are selling, what they are getting, and if the benefits fit, throw in the most important ones one last time. Again, include your name and address; if the card gets separated from the rest of the literature, this piece should stand alone. Make sure they know what they are ordering and where to order from. Additionally, this is a great place to flaunt your guarantee.

THE ENVELOPE

The function of the envelope is similar to a storefront: excite reluctant potential customers enough to come inside. Tempt them. Lure them. Tease them. In every way, the envelope is designed to make the prospect open it. This is the only objective of the envelope. Ideally, if you can get the prospect to start salivating early about what's inside, that's nice, too.

If the mailing package is your ad, the envelope is your headline. Teaser copy—the few lines written on the envelope—is your one chance to get it opened. Keeping within the guidelines of legality and good taste is the only requirement. After that, whatever works, use. Because if it didn't work, your great offer just got trashed without being opened.

If your envelope isn't opened as soon as it's seen, there's a good chance it'll wind up in the pile to be opened sometime between later and never, and most likely it will just be thrown out. Make your envelope copy crisp, strong, and sharp, to force the reader to open it first—before any other piece of mail.

Writing envelope copy is tough. It's got to be short, yet the strongest copy you can output. Lots of people sort their mail over a trash can, and if your envelope copy is less than fantastic...well, you don't want to read the rest of this sentence.

Teaser copy should be focused, but not narrowly enough to turn anyone away. The envelope copy needs to be more precisely targeted than your letter. It's at this instant that your whole package is at the crossroads of being opened and—the greatest danger point of all direct mail—falling into the trash. You need a great hook for your teaser copy. An unbelievably great hook. If you spend 100 hours writing your direct mail package, spend 10 of them on the two or three lines that go on your envelope. I do. They're that important. Then carry that theme inside, and start your letter with it.

For example: "Free Gift Enclosed!" is probably my all-time generic favorite. "New Prices Enclosed" appeals to price-sensitive products and markets. Other variations include "Free Gift Offer" and "Wholesale Prices Enclosed—Please Open Immediately!" If your mailpiece arrives with a first class stamp, a favorite trick of mine (with less commercial-type mailings) is to put your name (NOT your company name) and address in plain type in the left-hand corner. People will think it's a personal letter and will open it. If you ever get stuck for an idea, or don't know what to write—this is my all-time favorite option.

You can also ask a perplexing question—a question so great, everyone will need to know the answer. Promise to give them the answer if oh, they'll only open the envelope. Or make an incredible statement. Intrigue them. Drive them crazy with the need to open your mailing package right now! Why do you think they call it teaser copy? If it works, you'll find out when you get orders. If it doesn't, well, you'll know that, too.

THE REAL
ESTATE ACTION
MARKETING PLAN

E VER WONDER WHAT A WRITTEN marketing action plan from my firm is? Here's an actual sample. It was written to enhance the current advertising, marketing, and PR campaigns for the R. Curtis Real Estate firm. The goals are to increase overall visibility and sales.

OUR OBJECTIVES
1. To increase public awareness
   (thus to increase listings)
2. To increase number of calls
   (thus to increase potential buyers)
3. To initiate a long-term awareness program
4. To increase customer and prospect loyalty

SIGNS
The lowly sign plays a shockingly important part in our sales. Since it accounts for an incredible 25% of our sales, I recommend every possible step be taken to ensure maximum visibility. This includes complete repainting with an exceptionally attractive design and with reflective paint to increase our visibility into the night. To keep costs at a minimum, signs may be repainted with only one color of reflective paint.

Reflective paint will increase our evening visibility, especially to passing motorists whose headlights will illuminate the paint as they drive by. I would also like to see a larger sign, if possible, when signs are redone. Signs should be meticulously designed to create a memorable impression. Consideration should be given to the "R. Curtis," the "telephone number," and the "For Sale." The signs should be put up as early as possible, and left out as long as possible after the house is sold.

OPEN HOUSE

Strict records should be kept at all Open Houses. People with nothing to do on Sunday who are touring houses do us little good. On the other hand, names of people who are actively looking for houses are an <u>immediate source of our very best prospects</u> and should be captured and contacted again in the immediate future.

Names and addresses should be taken. All attendees should receive a letter following the Open House thanking them for visiting. In fact, all people visiting an Open House should receive additional mail: specification brochures for the house they saw, as well as for several other houses that we list in this particular price range. For best results and maximum goodwill, a letter should be included in each mailing. A postage-free reply card should also be included for people wishing to remain on our mailing list.

We should also send a "House Appraisal Guide" to all Open House attendees. This is a check sheet we create that will allow customers and potential customers to evaluate a house better. The value of this worksheet is: (1) immediate use—our most active customers and prospects will see our name repeatedly each time they refer to it; (2) people will keep it—over time, when they sell their house or evaluate or price other houses, they will find and use this sheet bearing our name and phone number. Hopefully, we can design the sheet to make them call us at that time (to update the sheet, for current prices, or for new copies). More specifics on this brochure in a moment.

REFERRALS

Referrals in the real estate trade, as in most other industries, are the lowest-cost and most credible marketing resource we can utilize. We should develop a plan to increase the number of individuals and firms making referrals and increase the number of referrals made by each individual or group.

A letter series should be drafted to thank people and firms for sending others to us. Letters should be hand-typed and signed before sending—a preprinted form (no matter how attractive) should not be used. A referral is a personal invitation of trust and should be treated with such respect.

A small token gift may be included in appreciation. A gift at this time works very hard. Very hard. A planned approach using letters and gifts should be initiated to people who often refer us to clients. My own recommendation is to give Cross pens engraved with the name of the person making the referral. A referral may be worth $3,000 to $10,000 to us. A $10 pen can work pretty hard as a thank-you gift to bring us goodwill—and even more business.

The use of ad specialties should be incorporated into our advertising campaign, and this is where they are used first. Since one of our goals is long-range retention of our name to increase listings when people are ready to sell their house (which may be years away from our initial contact), ad specialties, along with spec sheets, brochures, and worksheets, should be designed to be brought out at that time.

RESOURCE SHEETS

Along with the appraisal guide worksheet, we should create low-cost flyers or brochures (called resource sheets) with titles like "What to do before selling your house," "What to do before listing your house," "How to get the best offer for your house," "How to price your house," and "How to know if your house is priced right." These brochures are used to increase the value of doing business with our firm, increase calls, and increase listings. They're designed to make potential sellers bring the brochures out when they are thinking about selling their house, so they will list with us. This information can be printed with our copier on the back of our house specification sheets (data sheets) and distributed to potential purchasers when we send them specs.

In addition, each time we create a resource sheet with this informative copy platform, we should create a press release and send it to the local papers, offering the resource page free to anyone who writes or calls us. Since we place so much lineage with the papers (and as realtors we get so little press coverage), they will be glad to give us great coverage on these free information resource pages.

In our ad, we should generate calls from buyers by offering free brochures like "How to purchase a house at a fair price," "What traps to look out for when buying a house," "How to inspect a house before purchasing," and "What to expect when you're a first-time home buyer." Once the caller is on the phone, we can find out if he is actively looking for a house, which makes him our prime prospect.

BUYERS

People whom we take around looking at houses should get letters and specification brochures of our houses for sale for four to six months or until we can figure out if they have already made a purchase or are no longer looking—either of which removes them from our market. In the final mailing, a mailing list card qualifying them as still in the market should be sent. They may check a box if still interested in houses and in our added services.

SALES HELP

In our meeting you said you needed sales help. Since you have mentioned that ads with the title "FSBO" (pronounced "Fizzbo"—For Sale By Owner) are read by almost all real estate sales agents who call and hope to get the homeowner's house listing, we should title our help wanted ads "FSBO." The next line defines it: "For Salespeople Beyond Ordinary—we have immediate openings...."

NEWSPAPER CAMPAIGNS

Our ad should be removed from *The Daily Local* and *The News of Our County*, or if you don't wish to withdraw ads entirely, they may be inserted once (preferred) or twice a month. Early results from our recent study and phone call logging procedure from our present campaign have determined that this is our weakest placement, with <u>each</u> inquiry costing over *$400*.

This money should be divided among other media—i.e., small, well-defined ads in local papers, magazines, and once in a while, other local media. To this day, cable remains an excellent media buy: a focused target market right in our own backyard. I recommend it.

While ads in local magazines or on radio may not sell houses very often, they will increase public awareness of our firm and should increase our listings. Small, well-designed ads may feature a single listing, which will please our sellers, but the real objective is to design an ad that is so visually unique that it promotes unusually high memory retention with excellent visual recognition characteristics.

Advertising Objectives

Our advertising has a single primary objective: to get people to call. It is not to sell houses. No one sees our seven-line listings and sends in a down payment. If we are successful in our ad, people pick up the phone. Our ad should be drafted to this objective.

Since the primary thrust of our advertising is to bring in calls, it is important that the telephone be handled properly. Telephone-selling skill books should be read and a light script drafted to help ease the anxiety of the floor person and to ensure that each call is handled in a proper and consistent manner. Since we have talked about this, and have designed a program to log all calls and track them to the source, I won't elaborate.

Newspaper Strategy

To encourage people to call, we should offer a free specification brochure on any house. After each listing—in the main body copy—the ad should include copy in the style of: "For a free brochure on this house, call now: 876-5432!"; "A free specification brochure is available on this house. For your free copy, call R. Curtis Real Estate: 876-5432"; "Call R. Curtis Real Estate to have a free specification brochure about this property mailed to you: 876-5432"; "Call for spec sheets on all the houses we have in this price range: 876-5432." All our ads should say "call now," and give our phone number repeatedly. This will increase our phone calls—our primary objective.

Public Relations

The second part of our campaign is longer-term and stresses service after the sale—very unusual in the real estate market. I feel this long-term approach to marketing ourselves with public relations work will have a lasting impact on our community as a whole, and especially on potential clients, to increase listings.

To be considered for the listing of a house, we must be remembered—which shapes a different long-term approach than just showing houses in the newspaper. Current listing ads promote little name retention of the realtor.

Here's the approach: service after the sale. This campaign is to call anyone in our neighborhood (referred to as the Main Line) with a maintenance sign in front of their house (i.e., roofer, siding, etc.) and identify ourselves as R. Curtis Realtors, say we are keeping track as a service provider, and ask if they are satisfied with the services being performed on their house.

When our associate realtors are driving around neighborhoods, they can leave a "How was the service?" reply card on the door to be filled in by the house owner upon the completion of the work.

People can then call us and ask if we have any good or bad reports for particular contractors or tradesmen. This PR campaign will prove inexpensive and will also, hopefully, further unify our family of realtors. A book or index card filing system should be kept to log responses. Initially a headache, we will have to answer questions concerning service with a bit of tact (like the Better Business Bureau system). In six months or a year, our file should be complete enough to let associate realtors handle questioning calls. Our response platform should be modeled after Zagat's restaurant guide.

We may wish to start announcing this part of our campaign in six months, after we have received sufficient data from our associate realtors to answer questions thoroughly. The objective of this campaign is to make sure community residents think of us first when it comes to anything to do with houses, so they will think of us first when they list houses.

Newspaper Advertising

I recommend we use the local papers to test our copy approach (it's cheaper), then incorporate our successful results into *The Inquirer*. We should then expand our ad size in *The Inquirer* to increase our visibility.

Our ad space in the local papers can be used more effectively. Our ad is large enough to incorporate selling copy within our present ad space. *The Inquirer* is a different story: it's extremely expensive, and we should test.

As an alternative to committing to a large block of ad space in the local papers every week, we should test. On alternate weeks we should list houses individually in separate ads. Individual listings are a less expensive way to go. Each ad should contain our logo, even though it will run additional lineage. We should have a "selling the call" line like "Call Now: 876-5432" or "Call for instant information about this house: 876-5432!" This format would still cost considerably less than our current eight-column ad. The true answer will be determined by testing each ad and each ad format and tracking the response to its source.

Ad Content

Our ad objective is to sell the call (as opposed to selling a house). Ads should be drafted entirely with this objective.

Some of our ads have prices, and some don't. My own personal feeling is that the majority of ads should contain the price of the house. Besides the number of bedrooms and some glowing words, the house listing ads don't contain much beyond the basics of information useful to a prospective buyer. A price defines a narrower, more realistic caller net.

Home address. It seems inconsistent to have directions to some of our houses, and no addresses for others. As we tighten our controls at Open Houses, we can ascertain whether having an address in our ads is worth the lineage. As with other elements under scrutiny, we should test this.

I'd like to see the address in ads, on the assumption that if people don't see the house, for sure they won't buy it. I'd rather have the sale, even if assisted by another realtor. Let people come out and see our sign in front of the house—maybe they'll then call us directly. For what percentage of houses where the address is shown in the ad are we the sole broker? We should question our current clients.

Other recommendations: Our *Inquirer* classified ads should contain at least one line of white space on the top and bottom of our single-column format. The R. Curtis logo should be redesigned (which can be as simple as honing down the big distinctive C that we use) to give us a logo that is wider than it is tall. This design is more efficient to save lineage in newspapers, our primary site for logo placement.

A computer insert of this new expanded logo (sample has been provided) will gain us much greater visibility while costing less to place. The logo now appearing in the computer type of *The Inquirer* classified ads needs a higher impact. Since this section is very brutal (tight ads, tight columns, heavy, intensive copy without much white space on the page), our wider logo will be closer to a full column width in size for a more highly visible mark. White space—the often forgotten designing half of black and white—should be used more in our ads.

To help keep our name impressions high, we should keep our name at the beginning and end of each ad. This is not so much for our current clients, but to attract future listings for brand identity and reinforcement.

The R. Curtis name should be repeated as many times as practical in each listing in the body copy so that people reading each listing consistently read the R. Curtis name. This is to increase our brand identity, market positioning, and the likelihood of people remembering our name.

Another advantageous place to use our logo is in the Real Estate/Card section (i.e., Bulletin). We should insert a harder selling line in this placement—for instance, "Your instant access to any of over 2,500 homes for sale on the Main Line." We should also say, "Call us for a free spec sheet on any of them." Lots of folks do not know that we can provide information on ALL houses, or that they can use us as their realtor for ANY house. We should work to let them know we can be their realtor of choice for any house.

Lower-priced houses, $30,000 to $50,000, should be marketed in the Apartment section of newspapers with their monthly mortgage amounts shown.

Benchmarking

Since our advertising is a long-term commitment, a log should be kept of all ads. A copy of the ad should be placed on a scrapbook page along with a note outlining where it was placed, the date, and the response it drew. Placement costs should be recorded also. In a year we will have an exact readout of which ads are working best. At that time, we can fine-tune our ad program again. We should be able to do this in a computer database program.

Since advertising is mandatory in the real estate industry, we should test different types of ads for about a year—knowing it will pay off in the long run. We should experiment with direct mail copy, as well as with other copy platforms, to sell any Open Houses we are running.

Each listing should start with the town, followed by selling copy. If included at all, the term "Just Reduced" should be in regular type as in the body copy—not in the headline copy, as it is currently used. Although a necessary evil performed by an owner, "Reduced" says to me that the house was priced too high to start with and that we wasted time, effort, and clients in showing it priced too high to sell.

When a price is reduced, we may wish to send "post cards" or have our associate realtors write personal notes to people who have looked at the house, alerting them to the reduced price.

We should incorporate our hours into ads, and give a 24-hour phone number as well. Our larger ads should also give all of our office locations.

Data Sheets

The house specification brochures we currently use should be entirely revamped. Our name, address, phone, etc., should be preprinted in our corporate color, then listing information of individual houses should be photocopied on these with a high-quality copy machine. This format gives us two-color brochures, with information we can change readily right on our copier.

Since we have both talked about this at some length, I won't elaborate, but rather note that we may additionally wish to list dishwasher, outlets per room, school district (elementary, junior high, and high school), closest store, closest market, and mileage to market and post office.

The back of each sheet should be printed (with our copier) as described earlier, with information-rich articles such as "How to price your house," "Pricing guidelines," "What to look for in a house," "What to look for in a mortgage," "How to figure your expenses," etc. These sheets are used immediately with a high value to our perfect market—people shopping for houses right now—and then the form is kept and brought out at the appropriate time later to increase our listings even further.

We should increase Main Line newspaper ads to contain six listings instead of four. Same space commitment can be used.

We should place "For Sale" cards and listings in the neighborhood supermarkets. We should mail post cards of houses for sale to our prospective client list, noting them as "preferred" customers. Personalized letters should also be employed as sales vehicles.

The secretary answering the phone should log all calls and where they came from. A log book should be kept by her phone, and she should be briefed on how to log calls correctly.

It certainly was a pleasure working with you. I look forward to discussing these ideas with you in depth, and to answering any questions you may have concerning any of the programs. I trust this letter and plan will meet with your approval, and that I will be speaking with you shortly.

MAGAZINE PUBLISHERS HATE ME

How To Buy Magazine Ad Space at a Discount

YOU CAN NOW GET A DISCOUNT on your magazine ads. You just have to know how to ask. It's easy, once you know the secret to successfully negotiating with publishers. Here's a short course on magazine advertising and how to get the most magazine exposure for the least cost.

First a question: How do you think magazine publishers come up with their rates? Answer: They make them up.

That's right—they make them up. The cheaper magazine publishers who aren't too profitable meet in their basement offices and figure out the cost of paper, typesetting, and layout; then they have a juice and smoke session and talk about their circulation, what a reasonable price for ad space is, and what the traffic will bear. Then they make the prices up. How else did you think they do it?

The more profitable magazine publishers go out for a nice dinner and then do the same thing. As far as I can tell, most prices for magazine advertisement space are based roughly on what's reasonable for their circulation and audience. Accommodations are then factored in for charging what the client will bear.

No sense charging less—they lose profits. No sense charging more—no one buys. So the magazine publishers' constant high wire dancing act is to get as much as they can without leaving any pages blank.

But you say you never see blank pages. Oh, yeah—white holes. It happens more than you think: magazine publishers fail to sell the space. Blank pages. Blank half-pages. Why do you think you see so many house ads—ads for United Way, the American Heart Association, and so on? Filler. Filllller.

If you talk to the publishers, they'll tell you they plug in a price formula. Sure, any of the two or three dozen formulas available to them for price per page. This gives them a range of between, oh, $0 per page and $80,000 per page. Nice spread, huh? With so many formulas to choose from, they choose the one that creates the price, uh, of what the client will bear, of course loosely based on their circulation and their audience.

All magazines have a CPM, or Cost Per Thousand, which means the cost to the advertiser to reach 1,000 people. This figure is published in some reference directories, and it has more meaning for the less specialized consumer magazines. The big advertisers like General Motors and Tropicana use this figure to measure their reach in different markets. But to us direct marketing mortals with limited budgets, these figures are much less important. Advertising to precisely the correct audience is more important. Accuracy over breadth. I'd rather reach 100 people who will buy than 1,000 who won't.

Enough chatter. Here's how to negotiate. First, get the publication's rate card by calling and asking for a media kit and a few recent copies. They're free. Ask if they publish a directory or annual reference issue and get that, too. Some magazines charge a pretty penny for their directory issue, but they always send one to potential advertisers at no charge.

When you get their media kit, note the agency discount. As an advertiser who sends in camera-ready art, you already get a 15% agency commission by mentioning you have an in-house ad agency. No question about this—everyone but the novices gets this discount. Don't let the rep offer you this and claim he's a nice guy. If he tries this, tell him to get serious.

Now we're ready to negotiate. Note that on the rate sheet there are several rate columns—the longer you run your ad, the cheaper it is. This should tell you that most publishers will deal. Exception: the bigger magazines—the really big ones—won't deal (at least with us smaller accounts). They don't have to. They're fat cats.

With small and medium-size publishers, ask for the 12-time ad insertion rate before placing your confirmed insertion order for ad space. Heck, it never hurts to ask, and this is a good opening position. If no dice, fall back to the six-time rate. Take my word for it, most publishers don't want you—and your money—to get away. If you start out at the six-time rate, your fallback position crumbles fast to my last choice: the lesser position of the three-time rate. If you have to, reluctantly give in to the three-time rate, and mention that this is the very least they should do for you, or that you think you can get a nice price and a good ad position with their competitor, which you've been considering.

Still nothing doing? Hrumph. Thank them and hang up. Call back later. We'll now create our own modified rate card. Ask for the test rate. If you're a first-time advertiser to this industry or publication, this makes sense to both parties. If your test ad pays off, you'll place more advertising—so it's a win-win situation. This is a reasonable request.

No discount yet? Insist on the mail order rate. Some publishers even have a mail order rate printed on their rate card, and it's usually a 25% discount. You do sell by mail, don't you? Tell them that while institutional advertising is nice for getting your name out there, as a direct marketing company your ads have to bring in enough cash to make the ad pay for itself, fulfill the order of the product to the customer, and earn some profit. This is true, and in a reality check for a small firm, nothing else makes sense. If your ad loses money, you won't be back with more ads.

In truth, some magazine publishers won't budge on a discount, but that doesn't mean they won't negotiate. If your magazine ad salesperson won't budge (even after he or she has been into the publisher's office several times on your behalf) and you're still determined to place an ad, go for an upgrade in ad size. "Gee," I always say—cause it makes me sound kinda backward and sooo innocent—"I'd like to place that ad, but one-quarter of a page is just not big enough to be effective for a product like ours. If I could get a slightly larger space—like one-third of a page for the same cost...." Lots of magazines that won't give you a cash discount will free up additional space for a larger ad. If they're still holding out, thank them kindly, let them know you'd be interested in that as a deal, and hang up. See if they call you back.

Almost all magazines will give you a second color free with any decent-sized ad. Once in a while a publisher can be tough on this, but most—like 80% of them—give in without too much being said. When I have a client who asks me to contract for one-third of a page, I always express my request for a second color like this: "My client wants a quarter of a page, but I think I can get him to move up to a third of a page if you'll throw in a second color at no charge." This can also be followed by, "We need to be in the first 20 pages, too—or I know he'll cancel." This statement works for increasing ad size, too.

Let's talk about positioning. Where your ad appears in the magazine is ALWAYS negotiated. Don't take "I don't know where they'll place it," for an answer when it comes to where your ad is positioned in the magazine. The advertising salesperson absolutely does have a say in where your ad runs. Don't take "I guarantee you good position," for an answer, either. Reason: once the magazine comes out and your ad is on page 80, and your salesperson says, "Hey, I got you into the first half of the book—pretty good, huh?" it's too late to get a refund, or even a free reprint.

The best you can get at this point, if you complain loudly enough, is that the magazine will usually reluctantly run another ad at half price. This costs you more money, and it is not much consolation if your first ad didn't draw. Your idea of good position—in the front of the book, upper right-hand page (expressed as Far Forward Right Hand or FFRH)—may be different from your salesperson's definition of good position. You may be thinking first 20 pages, he may be thinking page 60. Better to specify exactly what good position means to you. Be explicit.

Now here's a warning. Your space rep will tell you to run your ad three times and get the three-time rate, which all magazines have. In truth, some magazines just stick to their rate card, and you may have to do this. If you actually need to purchase space for more than one insertion to get a better rate, do it. Only payment for the first ad is due at this time, and that's at the three-time rate. Consider this discount as an interest-free loan.

If you're placing an ad in an untested magazine, absolutely do not purchase space in three consecutive months. Reason: if the first insertion fails miserably, it'll be too late to cancel the other ads.

You need to see the response to the first ad before committing another nickel. And I don't care for the crap about how an ad has to be seen three times to work. It's BS. If it fails the first time by a wide margin, it's not going to work with the next two exposures, either. Period. And I'll guaran-damn-tee you that.

I also don't care what special issues are coming up (barring overpowering seasonal necessities). If you have to schedule three ads, schedule the first as planned, then schedule the next ad three or four months after the first one appears. This way you'll have time to see what draw your ad has—or doesn't have—and if the ad fails, you'll have time to cancel the next ads.

If you have any doubts about the publication's reputation, send the cancellation notice certified, so there won't be any question about whether they received it. If you cancel the rest of your ad schedule, you'll get the "short" rate—which means you'll pay the difference in price between the one-time rate and the three-time rate for the ad you ran. This is a legitimate bill, and you'll have to pay it. Sorry, too late to negotiate this out. Fair is fair.

GET 50% OFF—AND MORE!

Good news! I've saved the best for last. You can sometimes get ad space for 50% and 60% off. Maybe even 70% off. Sometimes even more of a discount. It's called remnant space, and all magazines have it once in a while, although I've never really had one admit it until I got the call.

Here's how it works. Remember the white hole I addressed earlier? Besides the magazine failing to sell the entire page, a white hole occurs when an advertiser pulls out an ad at the last second. It happens. Arguments. Bankruptcy. Nonpayment. Whatever. Call the magazine and ask if they ever have remnant space available and at what discount. Tell them you have a full-page ad, a half-page ad, and a third-page ad ready to go if they have a last-second cancellation. There are no guarantees you'll be in any particular issue, if any at all. Keep in mind the discount they just gave you is a starting figure for negotiating.

You take your chances with buying remnant space, but if you get the call, it's a chance to have a full- or half-page ad at an incredible savings. Third-page ads are more rare—magazines always have current advertisers whom they can plug in with a one-third-page ad if they give them a big discount. When they do this, they look like heroes to their regular clients.

The biggest drawback to purchasing remnant space, besides not knowing if your ad will run, is that your position in the magazine will always be poor—toward the back (and no, not that many people really read the magazine from the back to the front, regardless of what the rep tells you). Poor placement is almost guaranteed unless you negotiate this when they call you. Reason: they'll move an ad from a full-paying regular advertiser up if the free space is in the front. This way they look great to their full-price advertiser. Full-price advertiser? Not likely if they read this article. Geez. All my magazine publisher friends are gonna hate me now....Hey, fellas—I was just kidding. Really...

12 STEPS TO CHANGE YOUR ATTITUDE AT WORK

WORK GOT YOU DOWN? Layoffs all around? Boss sneering at you? Well, chin up—you can make an attitude adjustment that takes effect immediately. If you need a change, you can make it happen anytime you want. You have 365 days each year to get a fresh start.

Recognize you have to think about things differently, make small changes to lead up to the big changes, and make changes in your daily routine by breaking old habits. No problem—it's as simple as following these 12 steps.

1. Put your other sock on first. Yes, you know what I mean—you always put your right sock on first, so the first change of the day is to break that old habit. Go hog wild—put your left sock on first. This will start you thinking about change. Leave yourself a note in your shoe the night before: The one thing I would like to change today is: _____.

2. Eat breakfast. If you already eat breakfast, change what you usually eat. If you eat corn flakes, try raisin bran. If you already eat raisin bran, whoa, why the heck would you eat that? Eat something with a little taste and texture, like Rice Krispies. Change is the order of the day.

3. Talk to yourself—out loud—in your car on the way in. If you're not comfortable with you, and can't talk to yourself out loud and be comfortable with that—better learn. You should be your own best friend. Make a joke. Spring forth with a dialogue. Do it out loud. Plan the day. Say what you're going to say to someone who's on your mind. Yell if you want. Make noise. Above all, get comfortable with yourself.

4. Set a single goal you would like to accomplish that day. Whether it's cleaning your desk, keeping your to-do list up to date, making that phone call you've been dreading, catching up with an old friend, straightening files, or whatever—write it down at the beginning of the day. Carry that paper with you. Stare at it all day until you do it. If you don't do it, so what? At least you'll know it should have been done, and you'll have a record of it, and something you can do tomorrow.

Save those daily goal sheets and look at them once in a while. Prioritize them. They're a great back-end list and should tell you a lot about yourself over time—like your goals and your ability to achieve them in a timely fashion.

5. When you get out of your car or off the train, smile. Not that insincere smile you use when you see your Aunt Millie. Really smile. OK, so it'll start out as a grin, but as you get more comfortable with smiling, it'll become a natural act. It'll make people wonder what you're up to. Good, let them wonder. Soon, you'll learn to talk with a smile. Know who likes people who smile when they talk? Everyone.

6. Get exercise at work. When you are standing by the copier, do twenty toe lifts (roll your weight to the balls of your foot, full extension to stand on your toes, making yourself as high as you can, come down slowly) while waiting for the machine to produce. Simple—and after a week, you'll notice more spring in your step. Develops calf muscles, too. Others will notice that.

7. Before each break, and before lunch, do isometric stomach crunches at your desk. Tighten your stomach muscles as tight as you can for five seconds, then relax. Three times—three sets.

8. Start a change list and keep it with you. Before you can create the new you, you've got to know what you want to be. Start with a list. Write down five to ten changes you'd like to see, however irrelevant or difficult they may be. You don't necessarily have to do them, but you should have an idea of where you want to go, so you know which road you have to take to get there. Don't be afraid to change these—just once a week, or even daily. Mark up the list, cross out old ones, enter new ones—just having this list with you shows you know where you want to be. It's better than 98% of everyone else.

9. I'd like to say, "Be nice to someone you don't like," but— don't. That's right, don't be nice to them. Recognize it's not your responsibility to have to like everyone, and besides, some people are just jerks. Be comfortable—and happy—with the fact that you don't have to like everyone.

10. Treat yourself to a nice lunch one day a week. If possible, make it the same day of the week every week. Go out, and take a friend with you. Pretty soon you'll look forward to that treat on that special day.

11. Eat with the fork in your other hand. Not when you go out—you don't want to spoil your nice lunch day. But for regular lunches, eat with the fork in your other hand to symbolize that things are changing—and you are making them change.

12. At 4:30, make a to-do list for tomorrow, and then prioritize it. Spending five minutes now will save about an hour of fumbling time of reorganization in the morning.

Hope these have helped! Every day is a brand-new chance to make whatever you want to happen, happen. Every day is a new chance—365 fresh, new chances a year. Start now, or jump in anytime.

How Much Does It Cost to Market a Product?

It's the most common question I receive when I pick up the phone: "How much would it cost to market this?" The answer is the same as when asking such questions as "How much does it cost to buy a car?" or "How much does it cost to buy a house?" Might as well ask, "How high is up?"

The answer is dependent on the caller's own set of parameters. The first is, what size is your company? Are you just working out of your home? Are you a small firm with 3 or 4 people? Are you a small firm with 20 or 30 people? Different-sized companies have different ideas of a budget range. A half-million dollars to Green Giant isn't much for a product introduction. A half-million to me sounds like, "See you in Mexico—on the beach!"

The next question is, "What level of sales do you wish to achieve?" Is your first-year sales goal $10,000, $100,000, or $1 million? The amount you need to spend on marketing depends to a large degree on your financial goals. The more money you put into your marketing budget, the more revenues a bigger budget will generate. In theory, anyhow.

Don't forget: A part of determining your sales level is figuring out if—and how—you are going to grow. Are you prepared to create the infrastructure of a larger company with a crew of 100?

Another key question: How many markets are you selling to, and are there cost barriers associated with any of them? The more markets you introduce your product to, the more it will cost. Going to 25 cities and through three levels of distribution...well, you get the point.

Finally, you need to know how fast you'd like to achieve these sales goals. Prudent growth can come from 1/6-page ads, but if you have an aggressive plan, full-page ads may be necessary to attract the attention of bigger customers. So how aggressive did you say your plan was?

So "how much" depends on the size of your firm, what level of sales you're targeting, and how fast you'd like to get there. Also on the industry, your product, and the markets you are serving. Dial in your aggression and the amount you can afford with the rest of these parameters, and let's talk again soon.

THE BEST
CAMPAIGN
I EVER WROTE

T HIS CAMPAIGN PRESENTS YOUR COMPANY in a unique style and favorable light. Please feel free to use the ideas presented here for your own personal use just as they appear, or as a springboard—so you can tailor the letters to your specific needs. I hope this brings you additional business and proves to be of great value.

THE PEN CAMPAIGN

By now you know the beauty of direct mail—it's focused, targeted, and very inexpensive when aimed at only your best prospects. You've read "The $500 Campaign" in *How To Market a Product for Under $500*, and while you may not have done it yet, if you are anxious to improve the campaign by adding a little more money—this is it.

Still have those best prospects in mind? Thinking about writing to them once a month, but you're not sure what to say? Here's an idea, and an actual series of letters that forms an enhanced $500 campaign. It's so simple to initiate; the work is done for you—just retype and mail. If you ordered it on disk ($25), you don't even have to retype it.

Caution: copyrighted material. This is your copyright permission to use these letters, as I wrote them, for your own personal campaign. This permission is specific to you, and does not extend to anyone else in your firm or any other person, party, or friend. But you may use the letters all you like.

The campaign pointedly centers around a series of letters. With each letter you are going to send a gift. The letters will talk about the gift and compare the gift to you and your firm.

It can take up to a year to complete this campaign as written, but feel free to shorten the time between sending each letter from a month to two or three weeks, reducing the complete campaign to a few, six, or nine months—modified to whatever time frame you require.

After the first three or four letters, you can call your customers and chat with them. If you wish to follow the outline of the letters in your calls, tell your customers you hope they are enjoying the campaign, and you hope they are considering purchasing your products or services. It's a soft sell on the phone, if you like, at your own discretion.

Since the program runs over several months, the letter series is written in an initial soft selling style—allowing you the luxury of time until completion. As the program gets closer to the end, you can remind your customers that the purpose of your campaign is to show them how it is to work with your firm, and that you'd like their business. But don't forget: The objective of the entire campaign, even the first few letters, is to get their business. If you don't get their business, there is no point in continuing the campaign. To bow out nicely upon hearing that your target will definitely not be using your product or service, go directly to the last letter.

Here's how the program works. Each month you send your best customers a writing instrument.

Yes, you're right, lots of people have sent pens to prospective customers.

The value is not in the pen.

The value is in your letters, which go with them.

This is the difference between sending a pen and following this campaign.

Additionally, the value is in your diligence in sending the gift each month and in the content of the letter. Your customers will be starting to look forward to receiving a pen every month. So this is "The Pen Campaign."

MULTIPLE EXPOSURE MARKETING

The real value is in creating consistent, frequent, friendly contact and staying in the front of the customer's mind. I call it Multiple Exposure Marketing. The value is in having the customer think of you at the moment he needs a service or product like the one you offer. Whatever you want to call it—frequent friendly contact, relationship marketing, frequency marketing, whatever buzz words you like—it's having your best prospects think of you each month.

Some brief clarifications: This campaign will work to market either a product or a service. I just say "product," but if you offer a service, insert "service" there instead. When I say "him," please acknowledge that no slight is intended to our female counterparts; please insert "him or her." While it is called a monthly campaign, if you wish to send a pen every two or three weeks, you may do so.

Writing instruments aren't all going to be pens, even though the campaign is referred to as "The Pen Campaign." If you can afford a campaign that costs about $100 a person, by all means send all pens (if your prospective customers are worth it). Give me a call, and I'll write that campaign for you. If you can't, welcome to the club; this campaign is for small businesses on a budget. You'll be sending one of the cheapest pens you can buy, some crayons, a pencil, and...well, you'll see how they all fit into the picture.

In a moment I'll prove to you that the value is not in the pen, and the value of the pen is not really all that important. What's really important are your diligence in sending the letters, and their content. But first, let's discuss the tone of the campaign and the content of the letters.

As with all campaigns, you start by writing your objectives at the top of a blank page. Call, write, come in, respond, purchase, get noticed, set up for later transaction, be remembered. Bring your firm to the forefront of the customer's mind, stay in the front of the customer's mind, set up for phone call, set up for sales call—what is your objective? Every time you pick up a pencil or sit down at your computer to write any advertising or marketing material, it always starts the same way—with a written objective.

Since I wrote this letter series, I'll state my objectives. I start out with the early letters to increase the visibility and perceived goodwill of your firm. The next objective is to retain that visibility and stay in the front of the prospect's mind.

While fulfilling the initial objectives, as the campaign proceeds I shift the objective toward a call to action from the prospect: to make a phone call or send in the post card. Toward the end of the campaign I request the prospect to call, and the sell becomes increasingly harder. Then, finally, the objective is to set up an attractive and receptive atmosphere for a sales call—for you to call the prospect.

The initial letter introduces you and your firm and alerts the prospective purchaser of your intentions—so "Introduction" is a big part of the first objective. It goes along with the secondary objective: to get noticed and remembered. Then to generate an early response. That's all you hope to do with the first letter. Introduce yourself, get noticed and remembered at the forefront of the recipient's mind, include the chance for an early response— then get out. If you can make an early sale, that's fine—and that would be the ultimate objective of the entire campaign.

The tone of the campaign is: "Each month I am going to send you a pen, and I hope you enjoy the campaign." The tone continues: "Although there are no strings or obligations, I hope you will think of my firm when you need a product like ours, and ultimately, I hope you will purchase our products."

The letters begin by discussing the pen. At the end of each letter, your firm is correlated to the merits of the pen and its selection.

The first letter is sent with a Cross Pen. Cross Pens are widely available and can be purchased at a steep discount if you shop around. So we'll say your first investment is about $10. Is your best prospect worth $10? Sending a Cross Pen will ensure that he reads your entire letter, remembers it, and remembers your firm.

To enhance the campaign further, if you can have the pen engraved with THEIR name, do it. They'll like the pen better—everyone likes something engraved with their own name. No one will ever throw away the pen if their name is engraved on it. And don't worry, they'll remember who sent it. If you engrave it with your name, it'll have less value—and get tossed in an obscure part of their desk. With THEIR name engraved on it, it'll stay on top of their desk, and your firm will stay in the front of their mind, meeting one of the objectives of the letter.

Well, without further ado, I hope you enjoy the best campaign I ever wrote: The Pen Campaign.

THE PEN CAMPAIGN

Dear _____

Of all the companies in the world, we'd like the privilege of doing business with your firm. You'll like working with us, because I'll *personally* make sure it's always a pleasure.

Enclosed is a small gift, in the form of a pen, to show our desire to do business with you.

The selection is a Cross Pen. A. T. Cross manufactures a fine pen - it writes exceptionally well and has a smooth, responsive feel. It's a pleasure to hold and a joy to use.

The A. T. Cross Corporation, formed in 1846, is a story of success of American ingenuity. They have been manufacturing fine writing instruments all these years - through thick and thin, good times and bad - and have a reputation for quality and fine service.

Everyone knows the name and look of a Cross Pen. It's a product that gives good value; I'm proud to send it to you as an expression of our interest in doing business with your firm.

The Cross Pen is a lot like our own firm. We, too, offer exceptionally good value. Over time, you will see we have a reputation of fine service. The quality of our work is our tradition of excellence. We are a pleasure to do business with, and we remain responsive to your needs.

Our gift to you in this letter is not only the enclosed pen, but the opportunity for you to work with an exceptional company. We'd like your business, and we hope - as a test of your new pen - you'll fill out and return the postage-paid card. Like the enclosed pen, we look forward to being of service to you. Thank you.

Kindest regards,

Jeffrey Dobkin

P.S. - Something else to make you smile: A new writing instrument will be arriving at your office about the first of next month. If you'd like to see the next selection sooner, just give me a call, or mail the postage-free card today. Thanks.

Dear _____

I hope this letter finds you in the best of spirits, and your firm doing well.

Our business is quite good, thanks. But we can always use more. We'd like the pleasure of serving your firm.

You may have noticed this month's selection of a writing instrument is quite different from last month's Cross Pen. This month's selection is a BIC pen. It is, shall we say, inexpensive.

OK, it was cheap.

I can call a cheap pen a cheap pen, can't I? It's just being honest, and I always am. After all, if we are to work together I have to be able to say to you, "This is cheap." It should always be followed by, "Here's why."

So here's why: Not everything has to be expensive to be good. Some things are just as good - or better - if they are not expensive. Like this pen.

The BIC pen has a strong place in the industrial marketplace. You wouldn't give your shipping dock foreman a Mont Blanc, would you? It would sit out on the loading dock all day and get trashed by the rough handling of a multitude of truck drivers. It would get lost or lifted in the high-traffic area of a shipping desk. So the BIC pen fits in just fine right there. Sometimes cheap really is better.

While I don't like to think of our firm as cheap, there are times to purchase costly goods, and times to buy goods that are lower in price. We think it's of more value to recommend products in the best price range to fit within our customer's job specifications and budget. If we can come in below budget - and pass these savings on to you - we do. Not all jobs call for top-shelf products.

Next page, please...

Page Two

Our firm is neither the most expensive nor necessarily always the cheapest. But we always strive to submit
a competitive bid. A competitive bid is not always the
lowest cost estimate.

A competitive bid is a balance between cost and
quality. A successful bid should demonstrate good value
for the amount paid, while still delivering superior
results. The results are the bottom line.

Our own vendors know that to keep our business,
they must consistently give us good value. We prefer to
purchase our material and services from firms that have
their eye on long-term relationships; and we hope our
customers do, too. Maybe we are not always the cheapest,
but we offer reliability and consistent good pricing.

When our customers need quality goods, we purchase
quality goods. But when a lower price is called for, or
a lesser product is all that is necessary to get the job
done well, we offer that option to our customers, too. As
your specifications dictate, we'll submit an appropriate
bid.

We can be as cheap as this month's pen. But above
all, we offer uniformly good value and superior results,
whatever your budget. And that is our real gift to you
this month. Consistently good value from a firm you can
trust.

I hope you will use the enclosed pen to send in a
request for more information. Enclosed is a postage-paid
card for your convenience. Why don't you do it now, while
it's handy. Please always feel free to call me directly
at 610-642-1000. Your call is always welcome.

                    Yours very truly,

                    Jeffrey Dobkin
                    President

P.S. More good news. Next month you can look forward to
receiving a new selection of writing instruments.

Dear _____

OK, so it's not exactly the nice pen you thought you were going to get.

But as writing instruments, you have to admit they're colorful and fun.

I hope you mark up your office papers with the green. And give your secretary red stars when s/he does something right, or brown x's when s/he does something wrong. And highlight your favorite parts in pink or yellow.

Not everything in business is in black and white. When selecting suppliers for your company, there are lots of firms that fall into a gray area. We hope we will fall into a more colorful zone. We like to think we're pretty bright.

Some things you just have to have fun with. This month's selection of writing instruments is crayons (colored pens, pencils), because even in big business, not everything is a matter of life and death.

In any trusting business relationship sustained over time, you have to maintain a good nature, a sense of humor, and good feelings about the firm you work with. That's why we encourage our suppliers to call us whenever they need good, friendly help. Special problems, areas that require new services, special quotes, and emergency requests are handled with good nature, prompt service, and a pleasant disposition.

If we couldn't smile with our clients, we'd get out of the business. We'd like the opportunity to serve your company with a smile. A postpaid card is included for your convenience. Always feel free to call me personally at any time - heck, I usually wind up answering the phone anyhow. Thanks again.

                    Kindest regards,

                    Jeffrey Dobkin

P.S. - More good news: Next month we will return to a serious side of business - and send you a most favored writing pen.

Dear _____

It isn't the most expensive pen you can buy.

It doesn't have the distinctive Mont Blanc crown top. It hasn't got the smooth lines or the silky feel of a fancy Waterman tortoiseshell lacquer finish. But oh, how well it writes.

Not everything can be assessed by its looks.

This pen has the nicest writing feel of any pen I have ever had the pleasure of using. It lays a line of ink smoothly in a tireless, effortless glide across a sheet of paper. In short, it is a pleasure to use. It is one of my very favorite pens.

Because of its functionality and unique writing feel, I have enclosed this pen for your own personal enjoyment.

This letter accompanying it is short. Unlike all my other correspondence, the use of the enclosed pen is a valuable part of the gift. It comes along with the opportunity for me to be of service by sharing with you an item that gives me great personal pleasure. I hope you enjoy it, with my compliments and sincerest best wishes.

Of course, the best test of your new acquisition is still to fill out the enclosed card and send it back - even if it's just to let me know that you're enjoying this campaign and the writing instruments that arrive on such a regular basis. I'd enjoy hearing from you, with any comments you'd care to make. Thank you.

Yours very truly,

Jeffrey Dobkin

P.S. - Next month: Return to an excellent business opportunity.

Dear _____

Not everything in business is cast in stone. And
not everything should be written in ink. Over time, some
things change. When this happens, we'd like to think we
can roll with the punches, and we can change, too.

Sometimes meetings are just penciled in for the
convenience of our busy clients' schedules. Sometimes
orders change, perhaps from smaller to larger as customers
grow. Delivery dates can move forward and back. Sometimes
contracts just need to be struck out and rewritten.

It's our policy to accommodate our clients in every
possible way we can. When things change, we change. So
when you're not sure about something, just write it in
with the pencil I've included with this letter. If it
changes, we'll do everything in our power to help with the
change. We're that kind of company to do business with.
I think you are beginning to see that now.

The pencil is a reminder that we understand the
process of doing business in today's volatile economy.
We're willing to stand by you when things change. We'll
take the good times and the bad.

In our own business, our vendors who stay with us
through changing times, through thick and thin, are as
valuable to us as our customers. Loyalty is a trait that
can be found on both sides of the buying table.

You are invited to test out your pencil by filling in
the enclosed reply card for more information. Or call me
personally for an immediate answer to any question about
our services. I'm here to assist you in any way I can.

I hope by now you can see we will be a good firm
to work with. We are diligent and thoughtful, and we
understand that a good business relationship needs both
stability and growth - and sometimes, when things change
in the process, it needs to change with them. We are a
service company; it is our privilege to serve, something
we strive never to forget. Please call at any time.

                    Kindest regards,

                    Jeffrey Dobkin

P.S. - Next month, you will receive something different,
but of greater value.

Dear _____

   If you're looking for the gift, my gift to you is in
this letter. It is the gift of opportunity.

   Over the last several months I've written you letters
and have enclosed small gifts as a way of introducing our firm.

   I hope you have appreciated not only the gifts, but the
letters that were sent with them. They were part of an overall
campaign to show you the way we do business. With forethought
and fortitude. This is the way our firm works: We create an
intelligent plan, and we follow it with timely diligence. Is this
what you would like in a supplier?

   It is my pleasure to think you have been enjoying our
campaign to win you over as a customer and friend. It isn't over
yet. You still have the balance of the campaign to view, and I
hope one day you will extend our relationship beyond this, and we
will work more closely together.

   This letter offers you the opportunity to do business
with a company that has shown its worth and value over time.
The opportunity to work with a firm that you know you can trust.

   The true value of my correspondence is not in the gifts I
enclose, but in the opportunity to work with a firm dedicated to
fairness, quality work, prompt service, and a guarantee of
complete customer satisfaction. I hope you can see that.

   But now I do need a little of your help. I don't want you
to receive my letters if you don't enjoy them — and I never know
this until I ask. So I'm asking for the kindness of your reply.
Just fill out the postpaid card - or drop me a note. Just to let
me know you'd like to remain on our mailing list. No salesman
will call, no obligation, of course. Thank you for this courtesy.

   With the return of this card, I'd be pleased to send next
month's writing instrument a little early. You'll remain on our
preferred mailing list. I hope you will allow me the privilege of
continuing to correspond.

   Most of all, I'd like your consideration to do business with
us. But until then, just send in the enclosed card, or give me a
call. Your call is always welcome.

                    Yours very truly,

                    Jeffrey Dobkin

P.S. Next month...well, that's up to you now.

Dear_____

This month's writing instrument just goes to
prove a point.

There are erasers on pencils for a good reason: To
correct mistakes. Try as we may, once in a while we make
mistakes, too. I wish every mistake we made was as simple
and fast to correct.

But do you know what? Everyone makes a mistake once
in a while. We try to keep ours to a minimum, but no one
bats 1,000.

It would be foolish for us to think that over the
long haul we'd never mess anything up. In the course of
doing business, something is bound to happen, and once in
a while it may just be our fault. Just being honest. We
always are.

Since every firm makes mistakes, what separates us
from other companies is that we recognize up front that
mistakes will happen. And we have a policy for them: We
admit it. And apologize. Then we go right about fixing
our mistake to our customer's satisfaction.

> *If we have to stay late to get the job*
> *done, we stay late to get the job done.*
> *If we need to work three shifts, we work*
> *three shifts.*
> *And if we run into additional costs, well,*
> *we pay them.*

I'll tell you right up front, we don't believe in
giving a discount for a job done poorly. We wouldn't want
to do any job poorly or release a job with a mistake in
it. I don't think that's what our customers want, either.
It's correct, or it's unfinished. If it isn't right, we do
it again. We get it right. There are plenty of other
vendors who sell seconds. We are of a different nature.

But no one goes through life, or through business,
without ever making a mistake. So while it takes a boss
like me to let an error slip out (all those typos and
spelling errors in these letters, ouch!), our quality
assurance department makes sure our finished goods are as
perfect as you can get.

Continued on next page...

Our services and our products offer consistently high quality, time after time - month after month, and year after year. A myriad of product inspections. Tough quality checks throughout our manufacturing process. Tests and retests. And a final inspection even our best product engineers dread.

Mistakes will happen, but we try not to give them too much help. The enclosed pencil and eraser can make short work of a misspelled word. We take any error on our part much more seriously. Even the little ones.

Consistently excellent products, shipped on time. That's our policy. We may not be perfect, but we're close. And the proof: We're willing to stand behind any product we sell with strong guarantees.

If you are looking for this in a supplier, please use the pointed end of the pencil to fill out the postpaid card. I'd be glad to give you a call upon its receipt.

Good pricing, solid quality controls, and a firm that stands behind its products with strong guarantees. If you like the way we do business, why don't you give me a call? No one can truthfully promise they'll never make a mistake. Our promise: We'll make sure we get it right before we consider any job finished. And that's a personal guarantee.

Very truly yours,

Jeffrey Dobkin

P.S. If you need a quick quote, as good as our pricing is, we're always looking for ways to sharpen our pencil a little more and make things a little less costly for our clients. Just give me a call - or use the postage-paid reply card enclosed. Thanks.

Next month: An innovation takes businesses by storm.

Dear _____

    When I was a kid, there were pens, pencils, and
crayons.

    When the writing instrument revolution came along in
the mid-'60s, felt-tipped pens took the industry by storm.

    You see, until then, innovation in the writing
industry was lacking. The manufacturers who made the
writing instruments of the day were blocked by their own
vision of their limited market.

    Sure, you could purchase writing instruments.
A variety of pens, pencils, and crayons. But there were
still only pens, pencils, and crayons.

    The revolution changed all that forever.

    The innovative porous-point pen suddenly struck,
and it grabbed a strong market share. It was something
different. Bright colors were introduced. Pens that
could offer a writing style that showed the personality
of the holder were now available.

    And this single innovation opened up the marketplace
to new and different variations. Other brand-new ideas
about pens emerged. Soon smooth-writing roller balls were
introduced. Felt-tip pens. Plastic nib pens. The
revolution in writing instruments started from one new
concept: A pen could have a different point.

    Perhaps your firm is looking for an innovation.
Something simple that may change the way you do business
forever. A single idea that can be used to start a
revolution. We can help with that idea.

    Sometimes it's tough to get a fresh new perspective
from your singular point of view. An outside agency - if
selected with care - may readily bring innovations to the
table. And change your marketing forever.

                        Next page, please...

If you're looking for some fresh perspectives, for an idea or two that may change your firm for the better, and for innovation that perhaps may be the springboard to give your firm a creative advantage that your competition is missing, I've enclosed a postage-paid card. I'd like to think we have already proved our point.

As always, your call is also most welcome. And a discussion of your needs with us is no cost, certainly no obligation. The ideas we generate in our first meeting are yours to keep forever.

We tend to keep our accounts over the years by presenting consistently fresh ideas and an extraordinary level of service. Please call us when you're ready.

Kindest regards,

Jeffrey Dobkin

P.S. Next month - finally, the highlight of this campaign.

Dear _____

   Perhaps you've already noticed, I've taken the liberty
of filling in your name on the postage-paid reply card.

   This month we've enclosed a highlighter - to highlight
our best offer. Please take a moment to drop the postage-
paid card in the mail.

   I'll make sure you receive a call promptly. We
are a very good firm to do business with, and we take
each response we receive seriously.

   Our firm is completely dedicated to excellence in
customer service. Even though we manufacture a product,
we know we are in a service business. It is our privilege
to serve - something we strive never to forget.

   But now we have a request: We request the honor
of your business. You must now respond to remain on our
mailing list.

   Over the past months we've tried to show you an
innovative campaign to win your heart and your business.
A campaign that you'll never forget. I hope we've done
just that. But now, without your response, we'll devote
our time and energy to others who may be more in need of
innovative partners in their marketing.

   Of course, we hope it doesn't end here. Just call,
or highlight your name and drop the enclosed postage-paid
card in the mail - we'll take it from there. You'll remain
on our mailing list, I'll see to it personally.

   I hope you have enjoyed this campaign and will
continue to think of us each month, even without these
reminders. Thank you for your time and for any referrals
you may have given us over these past months. As always,
I appreciate your consideration to do business with us at
any time - now or in the future.

                         Kindest regards,

                         Jeffrey Dobkin

THE MOST
VALUABLE LETTER
YOU CAN WRITE

S IMPLE: IT'S A THANK-YOU LETTER. So the cat's out of the bag right up front. But there's a very special place you should ALWAYS send a thank-you letter. Reason: because it pays so well. Let's take a deeper look.

The first reason a thank-you letter is so valuable is obvious— it makes the recipient feel good. This elevates you from the pack of not necessarily ingrates, but from the silent majority who never expressed their appreciation in a letter.

I know, you called them and thanked them. Did I say this is the most valuable call you could make? Nope. It has to be a letter. In this instance, a call just doesn't have the impact of a letter. It's not even a close second. A call is nice, don't get me wrong, and better than 80% of the other folks who left their sentiments unspoken. But to get the most leverage, it has to be a personal, one-to-one letter. (And I can't tell you how many hundreds of people received our own personal one-to-one letter.)

You see, a letter, well, that's a permanent record of your special thanks. It took time to write it. You cared enough to find an envelope and stamp. And you went that extra mile to put it all together and mail it. Now your effort will sit on the recipient's desk as a lasting memento of your appreciation. A phone call just doesn't compare to the lasting goodwill generated by an appreciative letter. No way.

A letter is an enduring note of special thanks. It's a personal and permanent expression that lets the recipient know how kind it was of them to give you their business. It shows your deep appreciation. Their kind thoughts didn't go unnoticed. You can say this on the phone, but it never has this striking impact. And in a day, whatever you said on the phone fades into the horizon like the sun. But not a letter. A letter has time to sink in. It can also sit on their desk or be posted on a wall for a month. Or a year.

THE MOST VALUABLE LETTER

So the most valuable letter is written to thank someone; and the time you ALWAYS write it is when you receive a business referral. *"Thank you for the opportunity and the privilege to be of service to your colleagues."* A business referral is not to be taken lightly or casually. It's the utmost show of trust a client or friend can display in you. It's the leap of faith that you'll perform exceptionally well. *"Thank you so much for your referral and your trust."* The person who recommends you puts their own name and reputation on the line for you. Does it deserve a letter? You bet. Here's why:

I don't have to make money every time I pick up a pen, but face it, sitting here at a computer writing isn't as much fun as watching TV. And I do need to make money to eat and live, so most of the time I need to stay focused on earning an income with my writing/computer time.

A "Thanks for your kind referral" letter, well, that IS about making money. Without a doubt, this letter is the least costly AND most effective piece of advertising I can write, bar none. Least costly? AND most effective? Hmmm...

Did you notice how casually the "Thanks for your kind referral" letter has now become the most effective piece of advertising you can write? It's no longer in the "I'll just dash off this thank-you letter" category. Now it's in the "I can write this incredibly effective and low-cost advertisement that will get me more business!" range of tools. It has become a prime weapon in your marketing arsenal.

Back to basics: Is it really a letter? No, it isn't. A letter is a personal piece of correspondence you send to one or two people. When you send it to a dozen (or a hundred) people, and it's designed to get you more business, it's an ad. It's a highly stylized ad designed to look like a letter. Any arguments? To perpetuate the myth, we'll continue to call it a letter.

Why is it so effective? And what can you do with a "Thanks for your referral!" letter that makes it so effective? For one thing, you can make the person feel comfortable with their recommendation of you, because you're going to do the very best job you possibly can for their friend. You'll be on your toes 100% of the time. You're going to bend over backward to look good, and to make them look good for giving a referral of someone so conscientious. You can't make them feel like this with an ad, but it's easy to do with a letter.

Your letter can convince them that you appreciate the trust they've placed in your products or services, and that their trust in you is worth more to you than anything else in the entire world. You can make them feel, well, like they should refer more people to you all the time. And therein lies the beauty, the value, and the monetary worth of the most valuable letter you can write: The receiver will remember it, and when the opportunity comes up again, they will continue to refer people to you.

You've heard of word-of-mouth advertising as the best (and the cheapest) form of advertising? Well, this is how you make it happen, again and again.

Sending a Hardworking Gift

Of course, it never hurts to dress it up a bit. "I would have sent money, but oh, I'm sure this letter shows my deep appreciation in a more sincere and heartfelt way," only works with relatives.

What does my office do for people who refer direct marketing consulting or copywriting clients to us? We send them a Cross Pen. Wow, you say? A Cross Pen. Yep. And we have THEIR name engraved on it, too. By the time we ship it to them with the nice box it comes in, and of course our own personal letter of thanks, it costs us about $25. Is it worth it? You tell me: The prospect already trusts us from receiving the recommendation from a friend. If we do any work for the client, our copywriting and consulting fees range from...well, we get our $25 back pretty soon. Many clients stay with us for years.

We don't convert all the prospects referred to us into actual rent-paying customers. Some don't need our high-powered direct marketing or response-driven sales material. Some aren't ready to launch products just yet, and some are just fishing. But we always seem to get more referrals from the referral source. Which we really do appreciate.

If you'd like to get more business, write an exceptional "Thank you for your referral!" letter and keep it at-the-ready in your computer. If you've got ten bucks, send a Cross Pen with a thank-you letter. If not, a letter by itself will do nicely. If you have $25, send an engraved Cross Pen with your letter of thanks. If you engrave your name on it, they'll keep it in a top drawer. Engraved with *their* name, the pen will stay in their shirt pocket or ON TOP of their desk. Don't worry, they'll remember where they got it. You can't buy that kind of advertising—that goodwill or trust, or those kind referrals—at any price. Or can you?

SUCCESSFUL KITCHEN TABLE MARKETING

YOU'VE HEARD SUCCESS STORIES about people like Lillian Vernon who started on their kitchen table and made fortunes. Any truth to this? Yep. Can you do it, too? Yep.

It isn't even that tough, although you do need to stick with it, as there's a little bit of trial and error in the beginning. There are only two necessities to create success in any business: sales and profits. That's all you need for any successful business.

The formula is quite simple. First, figure out what you're going to sell. Then create a direct mail package offering your product. Ouch, you say—how can I do that? This, my friend, is the easy part. No need for a slick, glossy brochure. No fancy four-color double-fold sheet, either. Nope, not even a single-color sheet...and you may not even need a brochure.

You will need a letter. The most valuable tool you can use in direct marketing is a letter.

Can you really sell from just a letter? Absolutely. Is it easy? Incredibly easy. From your kitchen table? Yes, even in your underwear. It happens every day. Some of my most profitable clients work from their homes. The only reason I have an office is that it was too challenging to dodge the toys my kids were throwing at me and write at the same time.

Here's how to start.

Find a product you're comfortable with, that you can buy at a steep wholesale discount. Then price it fairly, but with a good profit built in for you. The item should not sell for less than $15 to $20, and it's better if it sells for $35 to $50. It can be anything that is of good value to the recipient.

Write a tight direct mail letter. I'm not going to spend the next 10 pages telling you how to do this—it's easy once you know the rules, and you can find them in the several articles in this book about writing effective direct mail letters or in my first book, *How To Market a Product for Under $500*. There's an entire chapter on direct mail, demonstrating in simple yet exhaustive detail how to create an intense and powerful direct mail letter.

Is it hard to write a letter—even with no experience and not much skill? No, it isn't. It just takes more time. If you've never tried writing before, it may take you two or three days, maybe more. But the secret to successful kitchen-table marketing is, once you have a successful product, letter, and price, just keep mailing the exact same package out. Some successful letters and offers run for years. All you need is one winning package to set you up for life. I can't tell you how many millionaires started this way.

Now the hard part.

The hardest part is finding the correct list of people who are most likely to buy your product. Fortunately, there's free help. Besides the explicit explanation in *How To Market a Product for Under $500* of how to find, negotiate, and buy a list, you can go to any list broker. There's one in every large city. And a good number of list houses will send you their free 40- and 50-page catalogs and do business by mail. Their toll-free phone numbers are shown in the reference section at the back of this book.

A list broker gets his commission from the list owner, so it doesn't cost you anything to talk or have him make a buy for you. For an extraordinarily fast ramp up on lists, read "How To Buy a

Great Mailing List!" in this book or the section on selecting and buying lists in the first book; these will help quite a bit and will immediately give you a deep understanding.

The key to not losing money in direct mail is to test small. You never, ever have to lose a lot of money in direct mail. You can start out with a couple hundred dollars or less and, in your FIRST MAILING, be able to predict with reasonable accuracy if your letter, product, offer, and list will make you money. Test by mailing out 100 packages: costs are $32 postage, $5 stationery, $6 list = $43. Now do the math. If your product costs you $10, plus $3 to ship, and you sell it for $34.95, you need to sell 2 pieces to break even, and 3 sales to make a profit.

Is it really that simple? Yes, it really is. Write a convincing and powerful sales letter. Buy a unique product at wholesale, then sell it at a good profit margin. Buy a list, test small, and continue mailing your successful packages to your successful lists. Direct mail and marketing. It's really that simple. What are you waiting for?

THE DANIELLE ADAMS PUBLISHING COMPANY
——————————☆——————————
~ Office of the President ~
Box 100 ☆ Merion Station, PA 19066
610/642-1000 ☆ Fax 610/642-6832

Mr. Steven Dash
513 Glen Arbor Drive
Wynnewood, PA   19096

Dear Steve:

Thank you very much for your kind referral of me to _____ at _____. I appreciate it.

I don't take referrals lightly, or for granted. A referral means that you thought enough of my skills to recommend me as a professional, and thought enough of me as a person to recommend me to a friend.

I appreciate your trust – and assure you I will always act well within the framework of fairness and good taste, and will strive at all times to provide exceptional value.

Thank you again for the privilege of your referral, the opportunity to be of service to your associate, and your trust.

Kindest regards,

Jeffrey Dobkin

Enclosure

THE 13 FASTEST & BEST WAYS TO GET BUSINESS

MAIL TO YOUR HOUSE LIST

Names and addresses of people who have bought from you, shopped at your store, sent for your merchandise through the mail, or have given you business in some way are all members of an elite group: your house file of customers. These people are your most likely prospects for doing business with again, if you'd only entice them with a nice offer.

Especially great prospects are those that have purchased from you two or more times. They like your products or services; they've proven that by coming back. You don't have to sell them on anything—they already know where your store is, as well as the quality of your merchandise or workmanship. Why don't you drop them a nice note?

"Just going through my files and I saw your name. I wanted to thank you for all the business you've given me in the past. I appreciate it, and I thought you'd like to know." They'll get the idea. "By the way, our new extended hours are...."

SEND CUSTOMERS A GIFT CERTIFICATE

Gift certificates are cheap to print, inexpensive to send through the mail, and always a delight to receive. Don't give away the store, but make sure it's of good and significant value. Include a letter of thanks for past business.

WRITE A PRESS RELEASE

The most effective you can be in marketing is with a single sheet of paper. Yes, you've read that correctly: most effective with a single sheet of paper. Write a press release and send it. If you don't know how to write a release, see the first chapter of my first book, *How To Market a Product for Under $500*, for almost 50 pages of explicit details on how to write a targeted, effective release designed to generate maximum response (from only your best prospects) and exactly how to submit it for the best possibility of getting it published. Also, reread the article "Getting Your Press Release into Print" in this book.

GO TO NETWORKING EVENTS

As much as I hate it too, networking can be a viable source of immediate business. Section out events where your products or services are most likely to be needed—and go. Business events are held every month by most local chambers of commerce. Don't forget civic groups like Lion's Clubs, Optimists and Rotarians.

Take lots of business cards. When you're there, don't get bogged down speaking to one person for a long time, even if they seem interested in what you're selling. Your function at a networking event is to meet as many qualified prospects as you can. When you speak with someone, first (and fast) qualify their interest and their candidacy, then get their business card, then move on to the next person. Would you rather go back to the office with one good lead that may or may not pan out, or a dozen?

Follow up every single lead you get at a meeting with a letter. New prospects may not need your services *right now,* and if your business card is one of a pack of two dozen, it'll get tossed out. But they'll file a letter for future reference.

GO TO THE LIBRARY

Look up books specifically on your business. Take about ten or twelve books to a comfortable table and scan the better ones. Read the marketing section of each. The different books will provide you with a handful of new ideas that you can test immediately.

Look up books on marketing and sales, too. Same procedure: Scan the better ones for immediate and practical ideas you can put into practice right away. I've never been to the library without getting something great out of it.

CREATE AN IDEA SHEET

I hate lists. But if you need new business, you should create a list of the best ways to get it. This is your road map. Start with a blank sheet of paper. Write down "where to look for new business" in a short "key word" or one-sentence format. Write down the best ways you've made sales in the past. Write down every idea for getting business you can think of, no matter how silly it seems. Sorry, turn off the TV and radio when you're doing this.

Finally, write down your best prospects, how you found them, and where you can find others that are similar. Allow one hour to do this initial writing. Let it sit for a couple of hours, then go back and add more ideas. Repeat this entire procedure two times. Finally, prioritize this entire list from best to worst, and engage.

SEND A LETTER

The most effective direct marketing sales tool—and my personal favorite—is a letter. If you can send just one business letter a day, I guarantee you will increase your business. (If you can send two, so much the better.) And if you have a regular business or are fluent on the computer, make it a personal goal to send 5 business-building letters a day—25 a week—and your business will flourish and grow. Definitely.

PICK UP THE PHONE

Geez, I hate making phone calls. But if you want instant action, the phone is the first place to start. It's a necessity of business and of life.

The phone as a sales tool is a mixed blessing. It's immediate, fast, and powerful, and it's a much stronger medium for closing sales than a few sheets of paper. But it's time consuming. And you certainly can't contact 5,000 people a day like you can in a direct mail campaign. Not to mention call reluctance and burnout. Still in all, if you need immediate sales, call everyone you can think of "just to say hello."

Write a loose script, so you'll have a few interesting things to say leading up to your request for new business or a referral to someone who may need your service or products. The pecking order for calls is: First call all your old accounts—these are the most likely candidates for continued business. Then call your most likely prospects from your best house list. Then pick up the phone and call likely suspects from a new prospect list that you just bought or recently compiled. Keep all phone calls brief—under two minutes—until you smell a sale.

Join an Association

Whether you join the Possum Hunter's Club of North Jersey, The American Society of House Sitters, or the local Lion's Club, mixing with a fraternal bunch of guys (or ladies) who share the same interests and problems is always a good move. Ask successful people how they market. Co-op advertising space or direct mailings with other newcomers. Share ideas. Learn what works and, as importantly, what doesn't. Learn about your industry from the trade association bulletins, magazines, newsletters, and offers that are sent to members.

Go to Other Meetings

Need business immediately? What better way to get it than through an in-person presentation? Only one way to do that: show up. Attend events where you have a good chance of exposing yourself to potential prospects. Everyone likes doing business with people in their own neighborhood, so try school board meetings, library meetings, business presentations of other groups, civic meetings, and so forth. For example, I went to a meeting for small press publishers and sold several copies of my first book, *How To Market a Product for Under $500*. I doubt anyone in the room said to themselves that morning, "Hmmm, I think I'll go to that meeting and buy Jeff's book." It happened because I was there. Check the newspapers and business journals published close to your home.

Create a Sign

If you are in a service business and your market is homeowners, a sign can account for bringing in about 25% of your new business. Just as realtors and roofers place their signs in front of houses, you can, too. Have several signs made up at a sign shop. Don't be cheap; they're an immediate impression of you and your company, so make them outstanding! Clearly state what service you offer, and have a large telephone number. If you offer free estimates, state that, too. Use reflective paint and increase your visibility into the night.

Ask friends if you can place a sign in front of their house for a month. Place one in front of your house, too. At least until that neighbor that never liked you complains and the cops ask you to take it down.

If you can place about half a dozen signs, I guarantee you'll get more business—way more business—than the signs cost. The results are immediate.

Get Trade Magazines

And read them. There's usually a column in each on marketing or getting new business. If the writer is great, get old copies and read his column. You may even stumble on some of my writing. Ugh.

A subscription to most trade magazines is yours for the asking; you can subscribe free if you qualify. But a subscription may take six weeks to start, and in this chapter we're talking IMMEDI-ATE help. You can get a free sample of a magazine rushed to you first class (or priority mail) by calling the publisher and asking for a media kit (boy, my magazine publisher friends are going to hate me for saying this!).

A media kit is an advertising package about a magazine that its publishers send to potential advertisers. It includes their advertising rates, plus all the hype about why you should spend all your advertising money with them. When publishers get a call asking for a media kit, it gets sent right out—usually the same day! Make sure they include two recent copies of the magazine, and ask if they'll send you any directory issue they may publish.

Get the names, addresses, and phone numbers of ALL the trade journals for your specific industry (find them in the *Oxbridge Communications National Directory of Magazines, Burrelle's Media Directory/Magazines and Newsletters*, the *SRDS Business Publication Advertising Source*™, or *Bacon's Newspaper/Magazine Di-*

rectory) at the library. When you get the package of advertising material in the media kit, check out the magazine audit page to find out if the magazine is sent free to qualified individuals. Never mind the paid subscription cards in the magazines; if others get it free, you can qualify, too. (My publisher friends are really gonna hate me now.)

BUY THIS BOOK

As if you didn't know this: If you don't have it in your library already, buy a copy of my first book, *How To Market a Product for Under $500.* It contains the other 1,000 ways to bring in business fast. Thanks.

A SIMPLE RULE
TO CREATE THE
BEST HEADLINES:
THE
100 TO 1 RULE

NOBODY USES THEIR FIRST DRAFT IN COPYWRITING—at least none of my friends do. Heck, I can't even make the fifth draft come out right on some projects; this, of course, depends on my hangover. While I don't like to waste time writing copy that isn't going to be used, in writing it's just as important to edit severely as it is to write succinctly.

Too bad I never do. Proof of this? Take my first book (please), *How To Market a Product for Under $500*. It weighs in at over 21/2 pounds. I wasn't finished writing it, either—I merely abandoned it because of the element of time. I also stopped writing because, all things considered, I knew I wanted to sell a book people could actually lift without getting a hernia.

What does this have to do with creating the best headline? It's called **Jeff Dobkin's 100 to 1 Rule.** It's the rule all copywriters use but don't tell you about. It's the reason great copywriters get paid so much money. It's the writing you never see. It's also the way I came up with the book's title.

The 100 to 1 Rule states that for every line whose contribution is so crucial to making your writing successful, for each line that is so important it can make or break your entire piece, for any line that is so pivotal that you place your bet on this single line and you win or lose everything on its strength, say hallelujah; so significant that the success or failure of your entire direct marketing package, mailer, ad, or press release depends on its existence being close to perfection, say hallelujah again; so it is written ye must write that single line one hundred different ways, then go back and pick the best one. Amen. Yep, 100 times. That's the Jeff Dobkin 100 to 1 Rule.

Let's take a closer look at where the 100 to 1 Rule is used.

1. **Press release headline.** The headline determines the success or failure of your release. It starts by getting the editor's attention, then convinces the publisher to publish it, makes the correct segment of the audience read it, and helps make qualified prospects respond. In a press release, the headline is the single most important line you can write. Recommended formula: *New product offers benefit.* Examples: "New hammer is easier to grip"; "New motorcycle has incredible acceleration."

2. **The first line of your press release body copy.** After 25 years of writing press releases, I've developed my own system for sneaking benefits into a release without editors cutting them out. Since editors cut from the bottom, I place my two or three most powerful benefits in the first line or two of the body of the release—and they NEVER get cut. Recommended formula: *New product offers benefit, benefit, benefit.* Examples: "New lawnmower is easier to start, quieter, and still cuts lawns 40% faster"; "New jacket is lightweight, waterproof, and comfortable—at minus 30 degrees."

Where else does the 100 to 1 Rule rule?

3. **The headline of your ad.** A press release headline has to conform to the editor's need to fit in well with the rest of the editorial material. The headline for your ad is entirely up to you—so it can be more powerful and harder-selling. Yes, there is a great deal of crossover, and these recommendations may work for both press releases and ads.

Recommended formula: *Free booklet offers useful information.* Example: A roofing company offers, "Free booklet shows how to install a new roof."

Why is this a great formula? It attracts only the specific market segment the advertiser is looking for—saving you $$$ on literature and fulfillment. Then it generates excellent response from qualified prospects by offering something for free.

Would anyone want a brochure on installing a roof besides someone who needs a new roof? Not likely. Are they really going to install a new roof themselves? Nah—don't be silly. The percentage of people who are going to install their own roof from a free booklet is pretty darn small. And if they do, these are the people who are going to need even more professional help when they screw it up. Trust me on this one.

4. **The first sentence of the body copy of your ad.** The only function of this first line is to keep the reader reading. Your most interest-arousing line is needed to entice the reader to read the rest of the ad. The rest of the body copy then sells the product by showing the benefits and making a strong call to action. To hook the reader early, the first line must be electrifying. Write 100, pick one.

5. **The teaser copy on your envelope.** If this crucial selection of a great line isn't perfection, your mailpiece goes right into the basket over which most people sort their mail. The sole function of envelope teaser copy is to get recipients to open the mailpiece.

Unlike with an ad or press release, you've already invested money to get your message delivered right into your prospect's hands. Make a broader appeal with this teaser copy—you wouldn't want anyone to get turned off by focusing it too tightly.

Recommended formula: *Free Gift Certificate Enclosed.* Gift certificates are effective draws, and they're inexpensive to print on 1/3 or 1/4 of a sheet of paper. Since they're only good for the products and dates you select, they're cheap to redeem, and you can target them specifically toward merchandise you want to sell off. Nice promotion! Variations on this: "Discount Coupons Enclosed"; "Free Gift Enclosed!"

6. **The first paragraph of your letter.** 99% of my letters start with a first paragraph consisting of one or two lines. And most are only one or two words. The opening of a letter has to be the most electric it can be, because the reader makes the decision in a nanosecond to read, scan, or toss. Keep the opening paragraph short and electrifying. One line is best. Two lines are OK. Three lines only work if the entire second paragraph is shorter than five words.

Recommended opening lines: One of my favorite openings is, paragraph one: Cough. Paragraph two: Cough. Cough. Paragraph three: Now that the dust is settling from the (name holiday) holiday, let me....Another favorite: Paragraph one: You're invited. Paragraph Two: You're invited to our biggest...

Any way around the 100 to 1 Rule? Not to any great extent. If you're good, you may be able to get away with writing 50 or 80 lines, then picking the best one. But the 100 to 1 formula is a sure-fire winning solution to finding that single explosive line. The all-out winner may be number 100, the 100th line you wrote. Of course, it may be the very first line you wrote, too—but you'll never know this...until you finish.

THE 10 WORST MISTAKES IN DIRECT MAIL

I MADE ALL THESE MISTAKES, SO...you don't have to! Yes, I made plenty more, too. You can learn from my mistakes—and increase your chances of success. It's just as easy to succeed as anything else—so follow these few simple guidelines of exactly what not to do. Don't worry, you'll find lots of other mistakes to make on your own, but at least you won't have to make these.

1. **Not knowing your audience.** All writing should be to a specific targeted group that you research until you know it intimately. Aim for your readers' personal hot spots, in a writing style and level they are comfortable with. Learn how the group feels, acts, what your audience likes or hates. Then craft your writing in style and content specifically to your readership.

2. **Mailing to the wrong list.** This is probably the most common—and most fatal—error made in direct mail. Spend as much time on researching your list as you do on the creative aspects of writing and layout, and on the research about your products, pricing, and offer. Unless the people on your mailing list have a desire or need for your product (or service), they're going to be tough to convince, and probably impossible to sell. Offering Buick mufflers to Chevy owners just won't work, no matter how great the copy or the price.

3. **Not writing to clear objectives.** Nothing muddies good writing like not having a specific goal. Make sure you know where you're going with each piece you write, then stay focused. Write your objective first, in the upper right-hand corner of your page, and refer to it often. Stay on target. My objectives are usually to have people call, write, or send in the business reply card. 99% of the time it's for a free brochure or booklet, offered so we can send a more qualified prospect a harder-hitting package.

4. **Price before offer.** "Only $49.95!" No matter what you're selling, a price has no meaning until readers know what they're getting. Make sure you tell them about your product first. If your number one sales point is your product's low price, you may introduce the price early on in the same sentence.

5. **Price before benefits.** "Just $89.95!" may sound like a great price to you for a stereo, but if you present it first—before showing exactly how great the radio is—most of your readers will go right past your ad, or toss your brochure out before they even see your product or offer. You need to tell readers what makes your price so great—in terms of benefits to the reader.

6. **Wrong price point.** There are thousands of theories on how to price your product correctly. Funny, each formula gives you a different answer. My formula is correct, and it works with every product, every time: Let the market set the price. You do this by testing each price point you feel will work, and seeing which one brings in not only the most orders, but the most overall profit. That's your price; simple, isn't it? This is the only way I know of to set the correct price for maximum profit in direct marketing. The only way.

7. **Inadequate testing.** There's no reason to lose big money in direct mail. Everything is testable, and you should test small mailings until one is clearly a winner. Then ramp up slowly: next time mail to a slightly larger test group. If that works, test still larger mailings. Until you know you're absolutely going to be profitable, just stick with smaller test mailings. So you'll never lose big money. How will you know you will be successful? As long as you mail the same package to the exact same list, your results should be the same.

8. **Wrong objective to your marketing piece.** Asking for the sale instead of selling the call can be a fatal mistake. The objective of a small or classified ad for any product over ten dollars is to get the prospect to call or write in. Unless you're sending a long, hard-selling direct mail piece (or have a full-page direct selling ad) your objective again should be to make the reader call for additional information or your free informational booklet. In an ad or short letter you generally do not ask for the sale, you ask for a call. Offer the product, show the benefits, and sell the call hard—that is the secret of success in direct marketing.

9. **Wrong headline.** *The headline is the single most important element of your ad.* Solely on the basis of this one line, your reader makes the decision to continue—or not continue—to read. Use the Jeff Dobkin 100 to 1 Rule to create both the headline of your ad or press release and the teaser line on your envelope: Write 100 headlines, then pick the best one. No, no TV on while you're doing this. Take several days for this task. If you can figure out a quicker and better way, please let me know.

10. **Not telling your readers exactly what you want them to do.** You should tell your readers several times exactly what you want them to do. Be specific. Let readers know exactly what action you want them to take; tell them, and tell them again. I wrote a sales letter for a printer and actually asked eighteen times for readers to call! Excessive? After mailing it, the printer had to hire two more people to answer the phones. If I can smoothly weave "please call" into the copy this many times, you can ask for the call at least three or four times without being obnoxious. To see how I did this, check out the printer's letter in this book.

SEASONAL VARIATIONS IN DIRECT MAIL

Which month is the best for mailing? Since direct mail may be tested so precisely, several book and magazine publishers mailed the same package month after month to determine which month drew the most response. With 100% as their average response, their results:

January .... 125 %

February 108

March 97

April 90

May 89

June 87

July 100

August 108

September 104

October 97

November 103

December 102

Many smaller direct mailers may find it more profitable to mail outside the peak response times of January and August; their mail has less chance of getting lost in the clutter of the giant direct response agencies' packages. These figures represent specific offers; your results may be very different from these magazine publishing industry giants'. Source: Direct Marketing Association

— Projecting Total Probable Returns —

Week	Average of Total Orders Received	Percentage Range of Orders Received	Median Percentage of Orders Received	Mode of Orders Received
1	3.9%	0.3- 24.7%	17.7%	1.3%
2	27.0	6.5- 77.3	39.5	31.4
3	54.6	13.6- 96.4	66.2	75.0
4	67.2	18.9- 100.0	74.9	68.9
5	77.8	36.5- 100.0	82.5	81.4
6	82.8	46.9- 100.0	87.8	100.0
7	85.8	58.1- 100.0	89.2	100.0
8	92.6	74.3- 100.0	92.2	100.0
9	95.3	87.5- 100.0	93.8	100.0
10	96.2	88.0- 100.0	96.8	100.0
12	99.4	92.0- 100.0	99.7	100.0
17	100.0	100.0- 100.0	100.0	100.0

Definitions: Time intervals are weeks from the day the first order was received. Percentage range of orders received indicates limit of tolerance one way or the other. Median column is a standard measurement indicating that 50% of all responses will be greater and 50% lesser.
Mode is the percentage figure of the total orders occurring most frequently.
Source: Direct Marketing Association

12 Rules for Increasing Your Response by Creating Better Direct Mail Letters

ALL DIRECT MAIL PACKAGES HAVE COMMON BASIC ELEMENTS: the creative, the list, the offer, and the price. Each adds its own catalyst to make your package a winner—or an expense. The primary result-driving component of all the mailing elements is the list. The wrong list will ensure you receive no sales at all. But that's discussed in another chapter. Right now we'll look inside your direct mail package. So the envelope, please...

Once inside a traditional DM package of letter, brochure, reply card, and envelope, it's the letter that's the primary driver to shift your mailings from the debit side of your books to the "we made money" side.

It's the letter that brings in the orders. A great letter can overcome a poor offer or an expensive price. If the rest of the package is only fair, the letter can still work—and sometimes work well. Sure, a nice brochure can build confidence and credibility in your firm, but people just look at the brochure, while they read the letter. Proof? A letter can work in direct mail even when it's mailed just by itself.

But is it really a letter? No, it isn't.

A letter is a personal correspondence you send to one or two people. When you send it to 10, 10,000, or 10 million people—it's an ad. It's a highly stylized ad designed to look like a letter. Any arguments?

Like a traditional ad, the letter has specific elements to increase response:

(A) Teaser copy is like the headline of your ad—and is meant to draw the readers in, force them to keep reading.

The teaser copy that entices the reader is set above the salutation and just under a shortened form of your letterhead. I prefer it to lean toward the right side of the page. This area is referred to as a Johnson Box, and its sole function is to capture your readers' attention, driving prospects to read the rest of the letter.

Here's the place to reuse the teaser copy found on your envelope, or state your best offer and biggest benefit here. Teaser copy at the top of the page is the ad for your letter.

This area is reserved for your hardest-hitting stuff—it's here that potential readers decide if the letter is worth further reading. You can make sure they decide it is—with just a few great words.

Copy may be typeset in a stylized typeface like Bookman or Avant Garde to separate it visually from the rest of the letter. It may look like a small ad, but don't put a border around it.

(B) The opening paragraph of your letter is like the subhead of an ad. It's designed to quickly pull the reader into the body by way of intrigue, interest, coercion, desire, and seduction. (Holy cow, this sounds like how I got married!) The opening paragraph is one, maybe two sentences long at most. My preference? A first paragraph of under seven words. It's still considered a teaser line in my book.

(C) The second paragraph is a transitional paragraph showing your biggest benefit and expanding on it. In comparison to an ad, it's the same as the lead-in sentence to the body copy.

(D) The body of the letter—like the body copy in an ad—expounds on the major reader benefits of your product or service while continuing to request the readers to call and place an order or ask for free additional information.

(E) The signature in your letter, like the logo in an ad, builds credibility. Here's your chance to create additional goodwill and trust in your firm. Give someone a name to call if they want action.

(F) The PS. Slightly different from the tag line in an ad ("At Ford, Quality Is Job One"), which endears readers to your firm, the PS is the place to make that final closing pitch in a way that no one can resist. You'll have to, because depending on how well you've done it here, your letter hits either their desk or their wastebasket. Unlike in an ad, you have about four or five lines (some writers create even longer PSs, or a PPS) to restate your best benefit, reconstruct your offer, and ask for action, again.

So the letter is really an ad. But to make it the most effective it can possibly be, it's got to look like a letter. We'll still call it a letter. It'll be our secret.

12 Rules To Make Your DM Letter More Effective

1. **Start by writing your letter exactly** as you would draft an ad—write your objective in the upper right-hand corner of a blank sheet of paper. Then write your letter to this objective. Is your objective to generate further interest? Generate a phone call? Have the customer place an order by mail? Fill in the BRC for a follow-up sales call? In-store visit? State it in writing.

2. **The salutation should be as personal as possible** without turning anyone off. My favorites are usually industry specific: "Dear Pharmacist"; "Dear Pet Lover"; "Dear Car Enthusiast." I also like to add "valued" and "friend": "Dear Valued Customer"; "Dear Neighbor and Friend." Remember, direct mail is a personal medium; the closer you can come to calling your perfect target by his or her name, the better.

3. **Write benefit-packed, action-oriented copy.** Show your best stuff first—why wait till you lose them? Then immediately expound on the biggest and best benefit. This is the central theme of your letter. Hammer home one, two, possibly three of your biggest benefits and have a strong call to action. If you have more benefits, show them in a list format.

4. Don't try to write your letter in a few minutes. Like an ad, a polished letter takes hours to create. You can't dash it off like the letter you write to Grandma every Thanksgiving so she remembers you at Christmas or Hanukkah. It takes me five to eight hours per page to write and design a clean, crisp letter; more if I'm hung over. If it takes you less, let's compare notes. No, no TV on, either—even if it is only in the background.

5. Make it look like a letter, the personal medium that it really is. Typewriter-style type. Salutation. Informal writing style. Short words—like you're writing to a friend, because you are.

6. Design it to look easy to read, even if it isn't. A well-designed letter increases readership—and, therefore, response. Use lots of white space. Short one- or two-line opening paragraph. Indent all paragraphs. No paragraph over seven lines. Vary paragraph length. Set type at flush left, rag right—never justify letter copy. I always like to make the top line of each paragraph shorter than the rest.

Add visual interest by placing a foreshortened paragraph in the middle of the body of the letter. This can be set in a different typestyle, or can be in a smaller typeface to get more copy in. This shortened paragraph may be justified.

7. A bulleted list of benefits gets high readership. Visually stimulating letters work best, and everyone reads a short bulleted list. If it's possible, make the last item in the list ask for the order, to call right now.

8. Accent what you want readers to read and what you want them to do. Use sparingly: bold, italics, underscore, caps, marginal words. Accent action words, always pointing at the order form or telephone number. You can use bold for up to three or four words, once in each paragraph. Caps only once or twice on a page. Marginal handwritten words can work, but they are my last choice—you can really make a letter look ugly fast when you hand write in the margins. But if you have a FREE OFFER, this is a great way to highlight it. Marginal words pop off the page.

9. Make a call to action early and often. Soft-sell the product, show the benefits, and sell the call hard—this is the secret for success in direct mail. Ask for the order and the phone call several times—if you don't get this, nothing else matters. Nothing.

Throughout the letter, pitch the response you are seeking with your call to action. "Call to get this free offer of a...." "Call right now before you forget." "This is a limited time offer, so send in your order right now." "We're waiting by the phone, your call is most welcome." "Call for free information!" I usually wind up weaving "call" into the copy about a dozen times over a two-page letter. I know this sounds like a lot; to see how smooth it can be, check out the printer's letter in this book. Count the word "Call."

10. **Sign legibly.** This adds credibility.

11. **Include a PS.** Busy business people now know the best parts of the offer are repeated in the PS—make this last shot an order clincher. Give the phone number again, so it's handy. Remind them to "Call now." Don't forget to say "Thanks" at the end.

Sure, people know it's not a personal letter. But if it's done well, they'll somehow overlook that part and let you into their hearts and minds. If you're really good, opening their wallets will follow. If your letter shows them some hard-hitting benefits that strike home in your own friendly, sincere personal style of offering them, people will order.

Now here's Number 12: **Jeff Dobkin's best copywriting trick** you've ever learned in your entire life. Having trouble starting? Just start writing anything, then go back and cross out your first sentence. Having a bad day? Go back and cross out your first paragraph. This trick immediately pulls you into the center of the copy, the exciting part. It's a great jump-start.

Better letters = greater response. Make yours a winner. Only in direct marketing can you send a personal note to 10,000 or 10 million of your closest friends (just ask Ed McMahon). Treat them to their own personal reasons why they should order from you, then ask them to call and place an order—and they will.

Direct Mail Profit Planner   Breakeven Analysis

Costs to get in the mail
Creating the Mailing Package
1. Creative Package
    Letter..$ _____
          Writing   First Draft, Second Draft....($____)
                    Edit, Final, Proofing............($____)
          Type   Specs, Typography..............($____)
          Design   Roughs, Final.....................($____)
          Artwork/Logo
    Brochure & Order Form...................................$ _____
          Writing   First Draft, Second Draft......($____)
          Edit   Final Edit, Proofing...............($____)
          Type   Specs, Typography...............($____)
          Design   Roughs, Final, Mechanical..............($____)
          Artwork Logo, Illustration, Photography........($____)
TOTAL COST OF CREATIVE (Letter & Brochure).........................$ _____
2. Printing (Quantity_____)
          Letter...................................($____)
          Brochure.............................($____)
          Order Form.........................($____)
          Business Reply Envelope....($____)
          Outer Envelope...................($____)
TOTAL COST OF PRINTING $____
3. LETTERSHOP $____
4. MAILING LISTS $____
5. POSTAGE $____
6. Total Costs of Preparation and Mailing (Mailing Package: Creative +
Printing + Lettershop + Mailing List + Postal Costs).$_____

7. COST PER THOUSAND pieces mailed..$_____

Product Costs
8. SELLING PRICE of your product or service.............................$_____

Costs to fulfill an order
9. Fulfillment Costs
          Product ....($____)
          Free Gift ....($____)
          Order Processing ....($____)
          Postal Reply Fees...........................($____)
          Shipping.......................................($____)
          Other (800#, Credit Card Cost, Etc.)..($____)
10. TOTAL FULFILLMENT COSTS...................................$____
11. Returned Merchandise, Cost per Order.......................$____
12. Cost per Bad Debts, Bad Checks, Credit Card...............$____
13. Overhead Costs per order...$____

Break even analysis
14. TOTAL EXPENSES (Fulfillment + Returns + Bad Debt + Overhead).........$_____

15. PROFIT PER ORDER (Selling Price – Total Expenses).........................$_____

16. BREAK EVEN:_____ Orders (Amount of orders needed per 1,000 pieces mailed
    to break even. COST PER THOUSAND divided by PROFIT PER ORDER.)

*This chart is reprinted with permission from the Hugo Dunhill Mailing List company. They publish some excellent mailing and marketing guides and reference materials, and are a quality list house. They can be reached at 800-223-6454 (in NY 212-213-9300). © 1988 Hugo Dunhill and Bruce Thaler

"WE TRIED DIRECT MAIL AND IT DIDN'T WORK!"

WHEN ANY OF MY CLIENTS TELL ME they've tried direct mail and it didn't work for them, I always ask, "What exactly was that campaign?"

The response I usually get: "We mailed to our top 25 prospects, and none of them bought anything! Damn, they were our best prospects, too."

I then make a left turn in the conversation and ask, "How many in-person sales calls does it take you to make a sale to a new customer?" The answers vary, but usually the number of sales calls ranges from two to five personal visits. Given that figure, here's what always amazes me: Why an otherwise intelligent person expects a sale will result faster or sooner from sending their prospect a sheet of paper in the mail.

Face it. Like it or not, the easiest and most persuasive way to sell a product or service to a customer is face to face. You can get immediate feedback. You can shift gears and change your pitch. Apply pressure—or back off, according to their immediate response. And when you see a closing signal, you can secure the sale right then and there with a smile and a handshake—and, of course, a goodwill deposit.

In direct mail, you not only have to convince someone that (1) you have what they want, (2) they should buy it, (3) they should buy it from you, (4) yours is a reputable company, and (5) you will send the customer what he orders in a timely fashion, but you have to do it in a way that will entice them to buy right off the bat. Further, you have to do it is such a way that they don't lose interest at any point in the sales process. On top of that, you have to convince them to put money in an envelope and wave to it as they drop it in the mailbox. Ugh. Very tough. But very possible.

THE DIRECT MAIL ADVANTAGE

In person, you can see five or six people in a day. In direct mail, you can reach thousands every day. Even hundreds of thousands. Mmmmmm. Hundreds of thousands in one day? There's the advantage of using direct mail. Just ask Publishers' Clearing House.

Direct mail is a game of numbers. Test small numbers. When you hit on a winner, mail large numbers of your successful packages. If you initiate a direct mail campaign with this knowledge from the get-go, you can create a realistic campaign where the odds definitely work in your favor. Direct mailers do it all the time, some with incredible profits. You can, too.

If you send out 25 letters and call it a direct mail campaign, we have different definitions. A one-time mailing of 25 pieces isn't a direct mail campaign. A mailing to 25 people? Sure, it's a mailing, but not a campaign.

A direct mail campaign needs to have more mail sent at one time, or sent with greater frequency if it's to a smaller list. If you need one sale (or one qualified inquiry) from every 100 pieces you send—a 1% response—the one person in 100 who was going to respond may not be in the first 25 pieces you mail. He may be the 99th person in your list of 100.

What does a successful campaign look like? Let's take a look. A client of mine spent $1,000 for a short direct response campaign selling boxes of taffy. He mailed to 2,000 mail order candy buyers at a final cost of 50¢ for each mailpiece ($1,000 total) which included everything, even postage. He received a little under a 2% response: 38 people ordered at $45 + $4 shipping or $49, totaling $1,862. He shipped the candy at an all-inclusive cost of $12 a box or $456, so he made $406 in profit.

"Whew," he said. "That was a lot of work, and I only made $406 dollars." And he left the direct mail business, saying it didn't work for him.

When he told me about his efforts in direct mail, I had only one question: "How long was the list of mail order buyers?" It was from a big direct mail merchant, he replied, and the list was a couple of million records.

I was excited! You see, once you have a winning package in direct mail, if you just keep mailing it (seasonal offers excepted), it should just keep on bringing in the same response. On the next page, you can see from the Probability Chart of Results of Test Mailings that his chances are better than 95% that his mailing would draw a response between 1.37% and 2.63% if we sent additional mailings.

I then told him I'd be his partner and we'd test the list further—we'd buy 20,000 names and mail to them. We'd mail the exact same package and, figuring the same response rate, we'd make $4,060. With this large of a mailing, the Probability Chart narrows its prediction on further mailings with greater accuracy: the response rate (95% accuracy) would be between 1.72% and 2.28% if we mailed to the rest of the list. If our response fell within these figures, then we'd mail to 200,000 names, and clear $40,600 profit. Then we'd mail to all 2 million names, and clear $406,000. And that's what we're doing now. With the economies of scale in buying candy and printing, we'll do even better next year.

That's how you make money, and how you make direct mail work for you. Test small but reasonable quantities—100 to 200 at the minimum. Then 500. Then 1,000 and 2,000. When you find a product, an offer, and a creative direct response package that works, figure out what it will earn if you increase your mailing size to run the entire list. Then go to dinner and celebrate.

Probability Chart of Results of Test Mailings

If the size of the test mailing is	And the return on the test mailing is	Then 95 chances out of 100, the return on the identical mailing to the whole list will be between			If the size of the test mailing is	And the return on the test mailing is	Then 95 chances out of 100, the return on the identical mailing to the whole list will be between		
100	1%	0	&	2.99%	250	1%	0	&	2.26%
100	2%	0	&	4.80%	250	2%	.23%	&	3.77%
100	3%	0	&	6.41%	250	3%	.84%	&	5.16%
100	4%	.08%	&	7.92%	250	4%	1.52%	&	6.48%
100	5%	.64%	&	9.36%	250	5%	2.24%	&	7.76%
100	10%	4%	&	16.00%	250	10%	6.20%	&	13.80%
100	20%	12%	&	28.00%	250	20%	14.94%	&	25.00%
500	1%	.11%	&	1.89%	1,000	1%	.37%	&	1.63%
500	2%	.75%	&	3.25%	1,000	2%	1.12%	&	2.88%
500	3%	1.48%	&	4.52%	1,000	3%	1.92%	&	4.08%
500	4%	2.25%	&	5.75%	1,000	4%	2.76%	&	5.24%
500	5%	3.05%	&	6.95%	1,000	5%	3.62%	&	6.38%
500	10%	7.32%	&	12.68%	1,000	10%	8.10%	&	11.90%
500	20%	16.42%	&	23.58%	1,000	20%	17.48%	&	22.52%
2,000	1%	.55%	&	1.45%	5,000	1%	.72%	&	1.28%
2,000	2%	1.37%	&	2.63%	5,000	2%	1.60%	&	2.40%
2,000	3%	2.24%	&	3.76%	5,000	3%	2.52%	&	3.48%
2,000	4%	3.12%	&	4.88%	5,000	4%	3.45%	&	4.55%
2,000	5%	4.03%	&	5.97%	5,000	5%	4.38%	&	5.62%
2,000	10%	8.66%	&	11.34%	5,000	10%	9.15%	&	10.85%
2,000	20%	18.21%	&	21.70%	5,000	20%	18.87%	&	21.13%
10,000	1%	.80%	&	1.20%	100,000	1%	.94%	&	1.06%
10,000	2%	1.72%	&	2.28%	100,000	2%	1.91%	&	2.09%
10,000	3%	2.66%	&	3.34%	100,000	3%	2.89%	&	3.11%
10,000	4%	3.61%	&	4.39%	100,000	4%	3.88%	&	4.12%
10,000	5%	4.56%	&	5.44%	100,000	5%	4.86%	&	5.14%
10,000	10%	9.40%	&	10.60%	100,000	10%	9.81%	&	10.19%
10,000	20%	19.20%	&	20.80%	100,000	20%	19.75%	&	20.25%

13 BEST MARKETING TIPS FOR SMALL BUSINESSES

I'VE BEEN INVOLVED IN MARKETING AND DIRECT MARKETING SINCE... my God! Am I that old already? Anyhow, over the years I've been asked to give tips on marketing, along with my specific advice. Here's a short list of some of my best tips of all time.

1. **The most valuable tool in marketing at the lowest cost** is a letter. In fact, the most valuable tool in marketing at any cost is a letter. You can catch and hold the attention of a busy magazine editor or the president of American Airlines. It's a powerful tool. Write one business-getting letter every day.

2. **The best formula in marketing is** "New product offers benefit, benefit, benefit." Use this to create the headline of your press releases and advertisements, for envelope teaser copy, and for the beginning lead of your brochure. Example: "New lightweight tennis racket makes your swing faster, more powerful, and more accurate." Or "New keyboard offers faster typing, greater accuracy, and is less tiring."

3. **The most valuable single sheet of paper you can create** in marketing is a press release. You should be sending press releases every month.

4. **The most effective trick I've learned in 25 years** of copywriting is this: When you are having a tough time writing, just start anywhere. Start writing anything, then go back and cross out your first sentence. On really bad days, go back and cross out your first paragraph. This immediately pulls you into the heart—and the electrifying part—of your copy.

5. **Send more than one piece of mail** to follow up serious inquiries and sales leads. Remember, a campaign is not a single letter or brochure, but a sustained effort over time.

6. **The 12 most valuable words** to get any press release published are, "Are you the person I should be sending this press release to?" Before sending any important press release, call the magazine or newspaper editor and say these 12 words. Even if you know darn well they ARE the correct person, you should still call and ask this question. Asking this positions your call as "Can you help me?" which invites most editors to do just that. Then send your release—they'll be looking for it, and will try to help you further by publishing it.

7. **Create a letter series—in advance**—to get new business. Mail the series to new prospects on a continual basis. I call this "multiple exposure marketing," and it's the basis of my first book, *How To Market a Product for Under $500.* By the fifth letter they receive, they'll be ready to receive your call as a friend—and buy your product. Make your letters look like traditional letters; make your prospect think he is the only one receiving them.

8. **Always use a *thank-you letter* to acknowledge** when something nice is done for you. No, a call is not the same. A thank-you call is forgotten in a day, but the impact of a written thank you can last a lifetime. A small gift works very hard if sent with this letter, but it's not necessary.

9. **Write your objective first.** When you start to write any business communication, always figure out and state in writing what you are trying to accomplish. For example, an ad objective may be to generate maximum direct orders, or to get as many leads as possible, or to generate retail store traffic. If this document works exactly as you wish, what would you like to have happen? Write this objective in the upper right-hand corner of your paper so you can refer to it often. Compose all of your

material specifically to fulfill your objective. Writing the objective first clarifies your writing, defines your purpose, and gives it more focus.

10. **If you'd really like a response** from a personal letter, include a return envelope in it with a live stamp on it. It's amazing what this does! Your recipient will either send it back right away or keep your stamped envelope on his desk for days trying to figure out what to do with a letter addressed to you with a live stamp on it. It'll increase your response or it'll drive them nuts.

11. **Test all the variables** anytime you run a successful long-term direct mail campaign. Test everything, although not all at once. Whether your mailings—and profits—are up to your expectations or not, as your campaign runs longer and longer, test higher and lower prices, copy style and approach, smaller, less expensive formats, lists, and list sources.

12. **Take your time writing.** No one will ever know that the one-page letter they received took you three weeks to write. Just make sure that when you send it, it's perfect. And if the letter is going to more than one or two people, have several people look at it, and get their opinions. Remember, there's a big difference between a friend saying he would buy your product and a stranger reading the mailpiece and sending you a check.

13. **Don't be afraid to ask for the order—several times**—in a direct mail solicitation. While I usually don't repeat myself unless well juiced, I make an exception to this rule when it comes to asking prospects to call and to send in their order. If the recipient doesn't call or send an order, the piece fails. For best results, be very explicit and tell the reader exactly what you want him to do—twice in the body copy, and again in the PS.

If you can think of any more great marketing tips other readers would appreciate, please let me know. Thanks. I hope these are great for you.

Summary: To Create a Press Release

1.   On a blank sheet of paper write who your audience will be, then write in a style your audience can comfortably read.

2.   Type "FOR IMMEDIATE RELEASE" on the top of a blank page of white paper or on your letterhead.

3.   On the right-hand side, type "For Additional Information Call," then your name and phone number.

4.   Directly under this, type the release number—which can be the date, your product's initials, plus T for trade publication or C for consumer publication releases.

5.   Write a catchy headline and type it in caps and center it. This should include your product, and make everyone want to read the rest of the release.

6.   Double space the rest of the release, with wide margins. Write your product description in a concise, newspaper style of writing. Include what, where, when, and if possible, how and why. Write in a few user benefits if possible, but be brief. Do not make it sound like an ad or it won't be used.

7.   Include the important parts of the information in the beginning; editors cut from the bottom.

8.   Try to stay within one page in length, and end with the marks ### or *** centered on the page.

9.   If it runs longer, type "MORE" on the bottom of the first page and continue with a new paragraph on a second sheet of paper.

10. Include a sharp 5" x 7" black-and-white photo of your product, preferably in use. Don't clip anything onto, or write on, the photo. Identify the photo by writing product name, company name, and phone on a piece of tape, then taping it to the photo.

11. Send release copy, photo, and "Thanks for publishing our release!" letter in one envelope to editor.

12. When published, send editor thank-you letter.

SELF-HELP FOR SELF-PUBLISHERS

THE BEST BUSINESS IN THE WORLD IS SELLING INFORMATION. There's nothing to inventory, it's fine to be a one-person shop, and short informational blocks—a.k.a. special reports—can be sent inexpensively through the mail. This includes how-to reports, magazine articles, and news and instructional features on anything.

The worst business in the world is book publishing. If you self-publish, you'll find your print run quantities never match your needs, short print runs are very expensive, and distributors in the bookstore industry buy on consignment, then pay verrrrry slowly—only after your book sells.

In addition, if your book doesn't sell through the bookstore after 3 or 4 months, it gets sent back to the distributor, and if damaged in the process continues on to you, who must also incur the shipping. A fact you should know: you're not alone while you're eating your returned books for lunch—the average return rate for most books is 25% to 30%. Remember Newt Gingrich's book? The publisher printed a million copies, got 900,000 back. Yum.

If you're lucky enough to get your books to a distributor, then into bookstores, expect to give the distributor a discount of 65% off the cover price. Yes, you read that right, sixty-five percent. Our first title sells at retail for $30; we sell it to our distributor for $10.48. Ouch.

Finally, for those who persist in self-publishing books, two or three major wholesalers dominate the industry and if your book doesn't land in their hands by hook or by crook, bookstore sales will be nonexistent—because the national chain bookstore market is very hard to break into. With 200,000 titles in print, imagine if chains had to cut a check for each title.

The real reason for returns? The large chains, which now dominate the industry, use returns as a way to pay off current debt to the wholesalers. They send books back for credit, buy other titles, and use the new 120-day payment float from the books just shipped to them. If they continue this cycle to the end, they never have to pay a bill until all the books sell through.

Even if you entice a large publisher to take on your title, don't expect ANY promotional money to sell your book until your book is selling well on its own. Catch-22. The promotion is up to you, the author. And don't expect any free copies for you to send around to increase your sales—you BUY all your books from the publisher, and you negotiate the price. Standard is 40% off the cover price. Yep. You buy your own book at 40% off list. No free copies. Man, they're cruel.

But all is not lost. There's hope for writers, self-publishers, and other masochists, except in fiction. Fiction is a different animal.

First, the bookstore market is only a fraction of the market for most books. Other markets include libraries, book clubs, discount clubs, catalogs, retail stores in your particular market niche, and direct mail. In addition, don't forget individual sales to local shops and organizations, use of your book as a premium or giveaway, and the Internet.

The best books to publish on your own are industry-specific books that will find a ready market of industry personnel. Business books encompass a wide market, and we market to a niche within this broad base. Our first title, *How To Market a Product for Under $500*, is sold to entrepreneurs, small business owners, and home office pioneers. One-quarter of our books are sold to marketing professionals who want fresh new low-cost campaigns for their clients and want to beef up their in-depth marketing skills.

As you can imagine, industrial titles like *Steel Rule Die Making* (for the paper cutting industry) or *Designing with Type* (for the graphic art industry) sell in limited numbers within their industries, but these titles usually enjoy better press relations with the industry publications. Editors know and respect books that are marketed only to their industry, and they favor them in reviews. The very best way to promote books like these is to write columns and articles for the trade journals on a regular and recurring basis. Next best is a planned press release program, sending press releases every month. Yes, every month.

Fiction. Ahhh, fiction. Ugh, fiction. Better get an agent. No big publishing house will touch a fiction manuscript over the transom—it has to come in from an agent. And the smaller houses may not be enough for good market penetration and super-wide distribution—they're best looked at as a stepping stone to the mass market, so keep your reprint rights close at hand and your fingers crossed for a buy-up at a later date.

Beware of agents—talk to several to find the best deal. All agent deals are negotiated, no matter what they tell you. Shop around. There are some honest, knowledgeable agents, and some who just charge up-front fees and kill any possibility of a deal. Don't forget to negotiate subsidiary rights, foreign rights, TV rights, movie rights, audio rights, serial rights, CD-ROM, and the Internet. When you have an agent, you are buying who they know, as well as the best deals—so ask about deals they negotiated for their other clients and exactly whom they have dealt with in each firm.

If you were thinking about writing a bestseller, don't bother—mass market books are submitted with just an outline and the first three chapters. When your agent pitches to large publishing houses, go for the biggest up-front advance you can get. It's the only way the publishing company will invest marketing money—so it can get back its advance.

Whatever you do, don't stop writing, and don't ever stop promoting your work. The markets are out there.

THE DANIELLE ADAMS PUBLISHING COMPANY

~ Office of the President ~
Box 100 ☆ Merion Station, PA 19066
610/642-1000 ☆ Fax 610/642-6832

The Value of a Logo

I ADMIT IT. MY FIRM, THE DANIELLE ADAMS PUBLISHING COMPANY, doesn't have a logo. And you know what? I don't think we need one, either. I admit that, too.

Yet I've seen hundreds of companies pour money into a logo they don't need; and countless companies stopped in the midst of important matters - like making money - to create or reproduce a logo. Here's when you need a logo, and when you don't.

The only value of a logo is in its repetitive use. Once in a great while a logo will be so outstanding, and so memorable, it'll get some great attention when it's seen for the first time, but so what? If it's never seen again, it had little value.

You need a logo when you're starting your advertising or marketing campaign and your ad or marketing material will be appearing week after week, month after month, to the same audience. Then your logo creates a recognizable mark for your company. This adds credibility to your firm. Customers who may not remember what your last 4 ads said should certainly remember your logo after seeing it the last 4 times.

Since the Danielle Adams Publishing Company doesn't run any coherent type of consumer advertising schedule in the same publications, I haven't spent forty hours or so creating a logo that isn't necessary.

Sure, it's nice to have a slick logo on your letterhead—and something that can make that corner of your envelope sizzle in a blaze of high-quality graphics. But for us, I simply set our name in small caps in a pleasant Bookman typeface and noted that this would suffice for now. It's been a year and a half, no one has complained, and I haven't missed it, either.

Famous logos make their mark by repetition. I'm sure a definite image comes to your mind when I say RCA, Coca-Cola, IBM, or NBC. These specific logo images, measured in number of impressions per year, are pressed into your brain over and over again, millions of times a year. But for us smaller guys? It may not be all that important. Don't let it slow you down.

212

How To
Buy a Great
Mailing List!

THANK GOD, THE WORST THAT CAN HAPPEN to you in direct mail is you lose money. I mean, considering the grand scheme of things—like major sicknesses, car wrecks, or that occasional bad bottle of wine—it's not too bad. But still, it stinks.

Kindly remember, the only reason you're in the mail is to make a profit. No, don't give me that "I just want to get this on the market! I'll make money on the next one" crap. How many marketers have told me that? If you don't make money, you won't be in the mail again.

Without profit, there isn't any next mailing. It's a necessary part of running any business. In fact, profit is why you are in business. Any arguments?

You can make lots of mistakes in direct mail. You can create a terrible mailing package that no one will open. You can set your price too high—or too low—and people won't buy. You can offer your products at the wrong time—heck yes, we always celebrate Christmas this late in January. But nothing is as bad as mailing to the wrong list. Poor list selection is the worst mistake you can make in direct mail. Yep.

When you mail to the wrong list, you get experience—which is what you get when you don't make any money. No one orders at all. Chevy hubcaps to Buick owners. Radios to the deaf. Bottle caps to a tuna factory. A simple mistake in the list changes all the hard work you put into your mailing from the "we made money" side of your spreadsheet to the "we got experience" side. So here's how to correct it.

The first consideration in any—and every—marketing campaign is to define your audience. Precisely who is your market? The more precisely you can define your perfect target audience, the better you'll be able to aim your mailing, and the better your response will be. And the name of the game in direct mail is to maximize response per thousand—to make that one extra person in 1,000 stop, look, pick up the phone, and call.

Anyone can put a direct mail piece together and drop it off at the post office (barring disgruntled post office workers wielding semi-automatics). But without knowing who your target market is, you certainly won't score any sales.

You know, direct mail really is like shooting fish in a barrel. First, you've got to find the right barrels. After defining your markets, this is selecting the right lists. Then you've got to figure out which barrel has the most fish. That's buying the list with the most prospects. Narrowing the size of the list even further with the proper list selection overlays—such as recency, frequency, and monetary purchase criteria—is like reducing the size of the barrel even more, then making sure the fish are big. Now you have a better chance of shooting the most fish with each shot—er, getting the most response from each mailing. Well, you know what I mean.

In direct mail, the more closely you identify your perfect prospect, the more tightly you specify your list, the better your response. The better your response = the more money you make per 1,000 packages mailed. Simple as that.

An example: Suppose you're selling a pilot's bag to airplane pilots. You mail to a list of owners of small airplanes that was compiled from airplane registrations. Your response is 1%, and you break even. But ugh, all that work and you didn't make any profit.

Take the same scenario, but this time you mail to a list of airplane pilots that was compiled from a list of flying instructors. These pilots are airplane enthusiasts, and they practically live, eat, and sleep airplanes. Since your bag has a cool picture of a plane on it, they love it. Your mailing draws 2%, and you make a little money. OK, you're warming up.

Now you try a different tack: You mail to a list of mail order buyers who have recently made a purchase from an airplane specialty catalog such as Sporty's Aviation Catalog. This time your mailing brings in a 6% response. Wow. You laugh all the way to the bank thinking how easy it is to make money in direct mail; you buy that new car you were looking at, and on the way home that cheerleader you were always eyeing in high school sees you in your new car and gives you a whirl. You're having that nice day everyone keeps telling you to have. Old relatives drop by unexpectedly to swim in your pool.

Now you're getting smart. You buy a list of (1) flying instructors who (2) own (3) planes and who have recently made a purchase (4) specifically from a catalog of airplane specialty items such as Sporty's. Bingo. Your mailing draws 9%. You purchase the bank, you drop that cute little blond cheerleader, and you marry one of your depositors—the rich and beautiful sole daughter of a wealthy Texas billionaire who has just celebrated his 94th birthday. All from the correct selection of a better list. Now you see the value of specifying and purchasing the correct mailing list. Hey, if this really happens, send me a nice bottle of champagne. Hmmm. If this really, really happens, wrap that bottle in hundreds.

Granted, list research and selection is not glamorous work. It's the behind-the-scenes grind to figure out and specify the best list parameters. It's not like creating a slick, eye-catching brochure. But you can see your mailing go from no response to profitable in a hurry, just in the extra attention to and correct selection of your mailing list.

Here's how the list industry works. Lists are big business. No, I mean lists are really big business. All of the big-name direct marketing magazines like *Target Marketing*, *Catalog Age*, *Direct*, and *DM News* have full-page ads for lists. Ads costing $4,000, $5,000, $6,000 an issue—issue after issue. Lists are big, big business.

Where to start: Get all these magazines for free by following the directions on page 262 of my first book, *How To Market a Product for Under $500*, or in this book, in the chapter "Magazine Publishers Hate Me." Call the list management companies (a.k.a. list brokers) that run these ads and inquire. Just remember, even though you are the purchaser, the brokers work for the LIST OWNER. So make sure you get tough with them about answering your questions.

Questions to ask? Precisely who is the list audience made up of? Does the list include actual purchasers or merely inquirers (who are of less value)? How old are the names on the list? How often is it updated? How often—and how recently—has it been cleaned? Cleaning a list means the list owner passed it through the postal service NCOA (National Change Of Address) file and most of the old, outdated nondeliverables have been removed. If a list is clean, you won't get a lot of your mailpieces back. Ask brokers for a data card, which shows list specifications.

When purchasing names to sell products to, ask how recently the people on the list have made a purchase. Recency is a key factor in mailing lists, and most lists have "Hot Name" selects—buyers who have purchased within the past month or two or three. Ask if you can get a select of multi-buyers—and ask how often they have purchased (frequency is another key factor in mailing lists, along with how much money has been spent on each purchase). The formula "recency, frequency, monetary" is the standard for measuring the quality of most mail order purchaser lists.

Ask how often the list has been rented. You don't want to get a list that has been rented toooo often and may suffer from list fatigue. Or a list that is never rented, because there's probably a reason no one is using it—no one is getting a response from that particular market or that list.

Ask how many other mailers have tested the list. Tests in direct mail are usually 5,000 names, and only a few list owners will rent you a lesser number of records. This doesn't mean you have to mail to all 5,000 names, but you may have to purchase them. Ask how many people continued after their test—meaning their test mailing drew a response and they mailed to it again. Ask how many ordered names for another continuation, meaning they absolutely did make money and it was worth the effort. Then ask how many people rolled out—mailed to the rest of the entire list.

Ask the origin of the list. A common source of names is records that have been compiled in some fashion. Compilers may acquire their names through public records such as vehicle registrations or state records of high school teachers. Directories, such as a directory of plant maintenance engineers, are usually compiled lists. Many lists are compiled from listings in the phone books across the U.S. Examples would be all the veterinarians or all the luggage dealers in the United States. Or all the plumbing supply dealers. Don't forget that you can specify an overlay for these lists, like a demographic overlay of plumbers located in a few selected states such as New Jersey, Pennsylvania, and New York, or a business-specific overlay such as small-animal-only veterinarians.

Keep in mind that compiled information—like fish—gets old rather quickly and doesn't age particularly well. Even though some firms pay for postage on returns, that won't be of much help when you are staring at a couple of mail sacks full of crushed, mutilated returned mail. Some compiled lists are excellent, but some are horrible—and compiled lists are usually my least favorite way to purchase records, but sometimes a necessary evil.

Guaranteed delivery of 93% may sound good up front, but it is actually pretty mediocre. In reality, a minimum of 10% of your mail is going awry; more likely, 20%. Guaranteed deliverability of 95% is still just fair. 98% is good, 99% better. These lists are out there.

Another common source of names is magazine subscribers. These lists are usually very good—when a subscriber moves and the publisher gets the magazine back, it costs him money, so most publishers are extremely prompt with their name and address corrections. Call a magazine publisher and ask if his subscriber list is for sale, then ask for the name of his list broker.

Trade associations are usually an excellent source of mailing lists. Better associations always contain the major industry players. Local associations like the Chamber of Commerce are good for local business names. You can select by business size, number of employees, SIC code (the government's industry classification of each business), or any of a multitude of other selection parameters.

Two excellent resources for investigating lists at the library are the *SRDS Direct Marketing List Source*™ and the *Oxbridge Communications National Directory of Mailing Lists*. We use the Oxbridge directory in our own office—it's thorough and exceptionally easy to use.

List brokers are found in the phone book in every major city. They can be heaven, supplying incredible information, or hell—looking for that fast buck. Make sure you ask tons of questions before handing over any money.

Lists are sold for a single use (unless you pay a premium for multiple uses) and usually cost between $65 and $85 per 1,000 records. They're available on disk, tape, and printed out on paper or pressure-sensitive labels. Residential lists are low in cost at $20 per thousand, and may or may not come with a name in the name field. If there is no name, I always have the computer house imprint "To our Friends at" or "To our Neighbors at" on the top line.

New for the '90s: Several companies now offer lists of every business or every person in the U.S. on CD-ROM. These products allow you to create your own list criteria and generate your own mailing lists. Some of the better programs make it easy and fast to use their CD-ROM products. Whatever you do, don't settle for a mediocre list, unless you want mediocre (or worse) results. Spend some extra time in this most important arena to tighten your criteria, and search out the best lists you can. Then test several. It's worth the extra time and money to target your audience with precision and come up a winner at the post office.

Cross-Index To Subjects

-A-

Abrasives - See Manufacturing

Abstracts & Abstracting Services- See Bibliography, Library, and specific field of interest

Accident Prevention-See Safety

Accounting-See also Computers & Automation, Banking & Finance, Business & Industry, Management, Office Methods & Equipment, Public Management & Planning, Taxes

Accoustics-See Architecture, Construction & Building, Physics, Sound Engineering & Reproduction

Actuarial Sciences-See Insurance, Mathematics

Adhesives-See Manufacturing

Adult Education-See Education, and field of specific interest

Adventure-See Fiction, Science Fiction & Fantasy, Mystery & Horror

Advertising & Marketing-See also Broadcasting, Economics, Journalism, Newspaper Industry, Periodical Industry, Salesmanship & Selling, Television & Video, and field of specific interest

Aerodynamics-See Aeronautics & Astronautics, Engineering, Physics

Aeronautics & Astronautics-See also Military & Naval, Traffic & Transportation

Aesthetics-See Art & Sculpture, Philosophy

African American History-See African American Interest, Ethnic, Genealogy, History

African American Interest-See also Ethnic, and field of specific interest

African History-See Anthropology, Archaeology, African American Interest, Ethnic, History, Sociology

Agricultural Aviation-See Agricultural Supplies, Agriculture, Aeronautics & Astronautics

Agricultural Chemicals-See Agricultural Supplies, Agriculture, Chemicals, Engineering/Chemical

Agricultural Conservation-See Agriculture, Environment & Ecology, Forestry

Agricultural Supplies-See also Agriculture, Hardware, Machinery

Agriculture-See also Agricultural Supplies, Dairy, Feed, Food, Forestry, Fur, Horses, Livestock, Oils & Fats, Poultry & Poultry Products, Produce, Sugar, Tobacco

Air Conditioning-See Heating/Plumbing /Air Conditioning & Refrigeration

Air Pollution-See Environment & Ecology, Public Management & Planning, Sanitation

Air Purification-See Environment & Ecology, Heating/Plumbing/Air Conditioning & Refrigeration, Sanitation

Air Transportation-See Aeronautics & Astronautics, Traffic & Transportation, Travel

Airplanes-See Aeronautics & Astronautics, Hobby

Airports-See Aeronautics & Astronautics, Traffic & Transportation

Alarm Systems(Burglar, Fire)-See Fire Protection, Law Enforcement & Penology, Safety, Security & Surveillance

Alchoholism-See Health, Social Services & Welfare

Algae-See Biology, Botany

Allergies-See Health, Medicine

Ambulance-See Hospitals

American Indian-See Anthropology, Ethnic(Native American), History, Sociology

Amusement Guides-See Entertainment

Anaethesiology-See Medicine

Analytical Chemistry-See Chemicals, Engineering/Chemical

Ancient History-See Archaeology, History

Animals-See Agriculture,Cats, Dairy, Dogs, Horses, Livestock, Veterinary, Zoology

Antarctic Studies-See Geography, Science

Anthropology-See also Ethnic, History, Literature & Linguistics, Museum Publications, Sociology

Antibiotics-See Drugs & Pharmaceuticals, Medicine

Antiques & Art Goods-See also Arts & Sculpture, Museum Publications

Apartment Buildings-See Real Estate

Apparel & Accessories- See also Children, Department Store & Retail, Textiles, Men's Women's

Appliances- See also Broadcasting, Electric & Electronic Equipment, Furniture & Home Furnishing

Applied Mechanics-See Engineering, Chemical, Engineering, Mechanical

Appraising-See Real Estate

Apprenticeship-See Employment, Industrial Relations, Labor, Labor Union

Archaeology- See also Art & Sculpture, History, Museum Publications

Archery-See Gifts, Games, Toys, Sports, & Sporting Goods

Architecture-See also Art & Sculpture, Construction & Building, Gardening & Horticulture, Home & Home Entertainment.

Artic Studies See Geography, Science

Area Planning-See Chamber of Commerce, Public Management & Planning

Army-See Military & Naval

Art & Sculpture- See also Antiques & Art Goods, Literary Reviews, Literature & Liguistics, Museum Publications

Art Exhibition Catalogues-See Art & Sculpture, Museum Publications

Art Galleries-See Art & Sculpture, Museum Publications

Art Goods & Supplies-See Antiques & Art Goods, Gifts, Games & Toys

Art History-See Art & Sculpture, Museum Publications

Arts & Crafts-See Art & Sculpture, Hobby

Asbestos-See Glass/Stone & Clay

Asian History-See Anthropology, Archaeology, History, Politics

Asian Interest-See Ethnic, International Affairs, and specific area of interest

NATIONAL DIRECTORY OF MAILING LISTS

Market Analysis *Association*

List Owner: MEMA-Motor & Equipment Manufacturers Assn., PO Box 13966, Rtp, NC 27709-3966 Tel # (919) 549-4800 Fax # (919) 549-4824
Description: Items & interest on the automotive products market: Consumers, distribution channels, Etc. Most taken from more extensive market Studies. *Newsl.*
List Rental Information: Inquire for rates.

Midwest Automotive & Autobody News *Business*

List Owner: Automotive Publishing, 2900 W. Peterson Ave., Chicago, IL 60659 Tel # (312) 764-1640
Description: Merchandising of automotive products for wholesalers, retailer, service stations, garages, & body shops. *Magazine*
Circulation Management: Publisher-Warren B. Daemicke
Circulation:
(PSS, 100% controlled)
Total: 12,000
List Rental Information:
Base Rental Price: $45/M

Mile Post
See: HOBBY

Miss Information's Automotive Calender of Events *Business, Consumer*

List Owner: Bobbie'dine Rodda, 1232 Highland Ave, Glendale, CA 91202-2027 Tel # (818) 887-1646
Description: Calendar od events plus articles on the automotive industry. *Newsl.*
Circulation Management: Publisher-Bobbie'dine Rodda, Circ. Mgr.-John Meyer
Circulation:
Total: 33,000
List Rental Information:
Base Rental Price: $70/M
List Management: MSC Lists, 450 Los Verdes Dr, Santa Barbara, CA 93111-1506 Tel # (805) 967-5394

Mobile Electronics Monitor *Business, Association*

List Owner: Electronic Industries Association, 2500 Wilson Blvd., Washington, DC 20006-1813 Tel # (703) 907-7782 Fax # (703) 907-7767
Description: Magazine about trends in vehicle electronics and automobile engineering that affect the manufacture, sale and installation of aftermarket mobile electronics. Includes business operating ideas, installation tips, industry government and Association news. *Magazine*
Circulation:
Total: 1,000
Readership: 1,500
List Rental Information: Inquire for rates.

Modern Tire Dealer *Business*

List Owner: Bill Communications, Inc., 355 Park Ave S., New York, NY 10010-1789 Tel # (212) 592-6200 Fax # (212) 592-6499
Description: For independent tire dealers, with emphasis on merchandising & automotive service. Subscription includes annual directory. *Tab.*
Circulation Management: Publisher-Greg Smith, Circ. Mgr.-Virginia Caswell
Circulation:
(BPA)
Total: 31,414
List Rental Information:
Base Rental Price: $95/M Quantity: 30,683
List Management: Aggressive List Management, 18-2 E Dundee Rd Ste 101, Barrington, IL 60010-5273 Tel # (708) 304-4030 Fax # (708) 304-4032; Manager @ List Company-Larissa Galjan

Mopar Muscle Magazine *Consumer*

List Owner: Dobbs Publishing Group, 3816 Industry Blvd, Lakeland, FL 33811-1340 Tel # (813) 646-5743 Fax # (813) 648-1187
Description: Provides how-to and technical information on the restoration, repair and maintenance of high performance automobiles. *Magazine*
Circulation Management: Publisher-Larry Dobbs, Circ. Mgr.-Kathy Willis
Circulation:
Total: 50,000
Single Copy/Newsstand: 35,000
Subscriptions: 15,000
List Rental Information:
Base Rental Price: $75/M Quantity: 23,220
Expires: $65/M Quantity: 8,194
List Management: Media Management Group, 666 Plainsboro Rd Ste 340, Plainsboro, NJ 08536-3026 Tel # (609) 275-0050 Fax # (609) 275-6606

Motor Age *Business*

List Owner: Chilton Publications, One Chilton Way, Radnor, PA 19089-0001 Tel # (610) 964-4000 Fax # (610) 964-2915
Description: Features developments and information for the automotive service industry. *Magazine*
Circulation:
Total: 133,385
List Rental Information:
Base Rental Price: $65/M
List Management: Stevens-Knox List Management, 304 Park Ave S, New York, NY 10010-5312 Tel # (212) 388-8800 Fax # (212) 388-8890

Motor Crash Estimating Guide *Business*

List Owner: Motor Pub., 5600 Crooks Rd # 200, Troy, MI 48098-1705 Tel # (313) 828-0000 Fax # (313) 828-0215
Description: Collision estimating and parts pricing information. *Magazine*
List Rental Information:
Base Rental Price: $80/M Quantity: 18,000

Motor Magazine *Business*

List Owner: Hearst Business Communications, 645 Stewart Ave., Garden City, NY 11530-4709 Tel # (516) 227-1300
Description: Emphasis on repair and service end of automobile business for owners and managers. *Magazine*
Circulation Management: Publisher-Michael Bernstein, Circ. Mgr.-Ed Martin, VP Circ.-Barry J. Green
Circulation:
(ABC, 63% controlled
As of 12/31/94)
Total: 138,941
Subscriptions: 50,544
List Rental Information: Inquire for rates.

Motor News Analysis *Business*

List Owner: United Communications Group, 11300 Rockville Pike Ste 1100, Rockville, MD 20852-3030 Tel # (301) 816-8950 (800) 929-4824 Fax # (301) 816-8945
Description: Newsletter interpreting automotive marketing and product developments U.S. and worldwide. *Newsl.*
Circulation Management: Publisher-David Rhode, Circ. Mgr.-Sharon Welch
Circulation:
Total: 3,000
List Rental Information: Inquire for rates.

Motor Service *Business*

List Owner: Adams/Hunter Publishing Co., 2101 S. Arlington Hts Rd., Suite #150, Arlington Hts., IL 60005 Tel # (708) 427-9512 Fax # (708) 427-2006
Description: Published exclusively for independent repair shops, new car/truck dealer, service depts. & self serviced fleet shops. *Magazine*
Circulation Management: Publisher-Larry M. Greenberger, Circ. Mgr.-Patricia A. Kaminski
Circulation:
(BPA, 100% controlled
As of 06/30/95)
Total: 170,239
List Rental Information:
Base Rental Price: $85/M Quantity: 134,304
List Management: Mail Marketing, Inc., 171 Terrace St., Haworth, NJ 07641-1899 Tel # (201) 387-1023 Fax # (201) 387-2976

Motor Trend *Consumer*

List Owner: Petersen Publishing Company Inc., 6420 Wilshire Blvd, Los Angeles, CA 90048 Tel # (310) 854-2222 Fax # (310) 854-2718
Description: Contains information on new cars, driving impression, road tests, overseas news, motor racing, nostalgic looks at the past, design and engineering trends, shopper's guides and service tips. *Magazine*
Circulation Management: Publisher-Doug Hamlin, Circ. Dir.-Gus Alonzo, Circ. Mgr.-Nigel Heaton
Circulation:
(ABC, As of 06/30/95)
Total: 932,281
Single Copy/Newsstand: 158,388
Subscriptions: 773,893
List Rental Information:
Base Rental Price: $70/M Quantity: 791,355
Hotline Buyers: $75/M Quantity: 92,851
Expires: $65/M Quantity: 127,350
List Management: The Lake Group, 411 Theodore Freund Ave., Rye, NY 10580-1497 Tel # (914) 925-2400 Fax # (914) 925-2499

Classification Numbers and Titles

BUSINESS LISTS

3	Advertising & Marketing
5	Air Conditioning, Heating, Plumbing, Sheet Metal & Ventilation
7	Amusements
9	Appliances
11	Architecture
13	Arts
15	Automatic Data Processing - Computers
17	Automotive, Automobiles, Tires, Batteries, Accessories, Service Stations, Garages
19	Aviation & Aerospace
21	Baking
23	Banking & Financial
25	Barbers
27	Beauty & Hairdressing
29	Boating
31	Books & Book Trade
33	Bottling
35	Brewing, Distilling & Beverages
37	Brick, Tile, Building Materials
39	Brushes
41	Building
43	Building Management & Real Estate
45	Business Executives
46	Business Firms
47	Camps & Camping
49	Cemetery, Monuments & Funeral Suppliers
51	Ceramics
52	Certified Public Accountants & Accountants
53	Chain Stores
55	Chemical & Chemical Process Industries
57	China & Glassware
61	Clothing & Furnishing Goods (Men's)
63	Clothing & Furnishing Goods (Women's)
65	Coal Merchandising
67	Coin-Operated and Vending Machines
69	Confectionery
71	Control & Instrumentation Systems
73	Corsets, Brassieres & Undergarments
75	Cosmetics
77	Dairy Products
79	Dental
81	Department, General Merchandise & Specialty Stores
83	Discount Marketing
85	Display
87	Draperies & Curtains
89	Drugs, Pharmaceutics
91	Educational
93	Electrical
95	Electronic Engineering
97	Engineering & Construction
99	Engineers
101	Farm Implements & Suppliers
107	Feed, Grain & Milling
109	Fertilizer and Agricultural Chemicals
113	Fire Protection
115	Fishing Commercial
117	Floor Coverings
119	Florists & Floriculture
121	Food Processing & Distribution
123	Funeral Directors
125	Fur Trade, Fur Farming, Trapping, Etc.
127	Furniture & Upholstery
129	Gas
133	Giftware, Antiques, Art Goods, Decorative Accessories, Greeting Cards, Etc.
135	Glass
137	Golf
139	Government Administrative Services & Public Works – Municipal, Township, County, State, Federal
141	Grocery
143	Hardware & Housewares
145	Home Economics
147	Home Furnishings
149	Hospital & Hospital Administration
151	Hotels, Motels, Clubs & Resorts
156	Human Resources
161	Industrial Distribution
163	Industrial Purchasing
165	Infants', Childrens' & Teen Age Goods
167	Institutions
169	Insurance
171	Interior Design/Space Planning
173	International Trade
175	Jewelry & Watchmaking
177	Journalism
179	Landscape, Garden Supplies, Seed & Nursery Trade
181	Laundry & Dry Cleaning
183	Leather, Boots & Shoes
185	Legal
187	Lighting & Lighting Fixtures
191	Luggage & Leather Goods
193	Lumber & Forest Industries
195	Maintenance
197	Maritime, Marine, Shipbuilding, Repair & Operating
201	Materials Handling & Distribution
203	Meats & Provisions
205	Medical & Surgical
207	Metal, Metalworking & Machinery
213	Mining (Coal, Metal & Non-Metallic)
215	Motion, Talk, Sound, Commercial Pictures, Etc.
217	Motor Trucks & Accessories
219	Motorcycle & Bicycle
221	Moving & Storage
223	Music & Music Trades
225	Notions & Fancy Goods
229	Nursing & Health
233	Ocean Science and Engineering
235	Office Equipment & Stationery
236	Office Equipment Mail Order Buyers
237	Office Methods & Management
241	Optical & Optometric
245	Packaging (Mfrs.) Paperboard
247	Packaging (Users)
249	Paint, Painting & Decorating
251	Paper
253	Parks, Public
255	Petroleum & Oil
257	Pets & Pet Supplies
259	Photographic
261	Plant & Manufacturing Executives
263	Plastics & Composition Products
265	Plumbing
267	Police, Detective & Security
269	Pollution Control, Environment, Ecology, Energy
271	Poultry & Poultry Products
273	Power & Power Plants
275	Printing & Printing Processes
277	Produce (Fruits & Vegetables)
279	Product Design Engineering
281	Public Transportation
283	Radio & Television
285	Railroad
289	Religious
291	Rental & Leasing Equipment
295	Restaurants & Food Service
297	Roads, Streets, Etc.
299	Roofing
301	Rubber
303	Safety, Accident Prevention
305	Sales Management
309	Schools & School Administration
311	Science, Research & Development
315	Selling and Salesmanship
317	Sporting Goods
319	Stone Products, Etc.
323	Swimming Pools
327	Telephone & Communications
329	Textiles & Knit Goods
331	Tobacco
333	Toys, Hobbies and Novelties
335	Trailers & Accessories
337	Transportation, Traffic, Shipping & Shipping Room Supplies
339	Travel
341	Venetian Blinds/Storm Windows
343	Veterinary
345	Water Supply & Sewage Disposal
347	Welding
349	Wire & Wire Products
351	Woodworking

CONSUMER LISTS

502	Almanacs & Directories
506	Art & Antiques
508	Automotive
510	Aviation
512	Babies
514	Boating & Yachting
515	Book Buyers - Consumer
516	Brides
518	Business Leaders
520	Children
520A	Collectibles
521	College & Alumni
521A	Consumer Electronics, Video & Video Games
522	Contributors (Philanthropic)
524	Crafts, Hobbies & Models
525	Credit Card Holders
527	Disabilities
528	Dogs & Pets
530	Dressmaking & Needlework
532	Education & Self-Improvement
534	Entertainment
536	Epicurean & Specialty Foods
538	Ethnic
544	Fashions - Clothing
546	Fishing & Hunting
548	Fraternal, Professional Groups, Service Clubs & Associations
549	Game Buyers, Contest & Puzzle Participants
550	Gardening (Home)
551	Gay & Lesbian
552	General
553	General Merchandise Mail Order Buyers
554	Gifts - Gift Buyers
556	Health
558	Home & Family Service
558A	Home Computers & Software
559	Horses, Riding & Breeding
560	Insurance Buyers
561	Investors
562	Labor - Trade Unions
563	Land & Real Estate Investors
564	Magazines
566	Mechanics & Science
568	Men's
572	Military, Naval & Veterans
578	Music & Record Buyers
584	Occult, Astrological & Metaphysical
586	Occupant & Resident
588	Opportunity Seekers
590	Photography
592	Political & Social Topics
593	Premium & Catalog Buyers
594	Professional
596	Religious & Denominational
598	Senior Citizens
600	Society
602	Sports
604	Teenagers
606	Travel
612	Women's

FARM LISTS

700	Dairy & Dairy Breeds
702	Diversified Farming & Farm Home
704	Farm Education & Vocations
710	Field Crops & Soil Management
714	Land Use & Conservation
716	Livestock & Breed
718	Poultry

Direct Marketing List Source

April, 1997

2. DESCRIPTION
Desktop computer graphics and desktop video software buyers.
3. LIST SOURCE
Direct mail.
4. QUANTITY AND RENTAL RATES
Rec'd Mar. 10, 1997.

Total list 56,523 105.00
Selections: state, SCF, business/home, ZIP Coding, gender, recency, one per company, title slug, 5.00/M extra; keyword-ing, 3.00/M extra; run charges, 10.00/M extra. Splits, 25.00 flat fee.
Minimum order, 5,000.
6. METHOD OF ADDRESSING
4-up Cheshire labels. Pressure-sensitive labels, 7.00/M extra. Magnetic tape, 25.00 flat fee.
7. DELIVERY SCHEDULE
Five days.
8. RESTRICTIONS
Sample mailing piece required.

COMPUTER GRAPHICS WORLD

PennWell Lists

Location ID: 13 ICLS 15   Mid 025829-000
PennWell Publishing Co., Advanced Technology Group.
P.O. Box 1260, Tulsa, OK 74101. Phone 918-831-9551. Fax 918-831-9497.
1. PERSONNEL
List Rental Mgr—Deanna Rebro.
Broker and/or Authorized Agent
All recognized brokers.
2. DESCRIPTION
Subscribers are users, vendors and manufacturers of computer graphics systems, equipment and technology.
ZIP Coded in numerical sequence.
List is computerized.
Selections available: Purchase influences.
3. LIST SOURCE
Direct request from qualified or paid recipient.
4. QUANTITY AND RENTAL RATES
Rec'd Jan. 16, 1997.

	Total Number	Price per/M
Total list	64,127	125.00
With Phone Numbers	47,453	200.00
U.S.	53,876	"
Canada	1,836	"
Foreign	8,415	"
Type of Business:		
Software/Software Develop.	6,361	+10.00
Consulting	4,861	"
Computers/periph mfg./System building	3,344	"
VAR's/VAD's/Systems Integrators&Systems Houses	2,738	"
Automotive/aerospace/industrial mfg.	10,352	"
Arch./engineers/const.	5,037	"
Financial/brokerage/insurance/real estate	773	"
Distribution: wholesale/retail/restaurant; transportation	708	"
Utilities/common carriers/communications	1,274	"
Personal/business svc: medical/legal/acct.	826	"
Bus. svcs: print/pub/adv/tv/motion pictures	4,732	"
Scientific/educational research	1,899	"
Video Production	5,566	"
Government/military	3,249	"
Non-mfg. ind: explor/mining/agri.	366	"
Educational institutions.	3,075	"
Job functions:		
Corporate management	13,522	+10.00
DP management & staff	4,271	"
Design/Engineering Management & staff	22,607	"
Production/operations management	1,754	"
Marketing	1,714	"
Consulting	3,496	"
Creative/Graphic Design/Animator	8,358	"
Applications in use:		
Mechanical CAD/CAE/CAM	19,873	+15.00
Electronic CAD/CAE	15,052	"
A-E-C CAD	11,398	"
Mapping	9,023	"
Medical/scientific imaging	7,617	"
Business/presentation graphics	25,672	"
Video/film/animation	19,156	"
Video/tv/interactive video	3,885	"
Training/Simulation	15,499	"
Graphic Arts/advertising	20,959	"
Electronic publishing/Pre-Press	15,070	"
Image processing	19,038	"
Technical Documentation	20,394	"
PC's/Workstations in use:		
Macintosh/Apple	20,759	"
IBM/IBM Compatible	42,440	"
HP/Apollo	12,903	"
DEC	7,409	"
SUN	11,690	"
Silicon Graphics	12,494	"
Operating Systems in use:		
DOS	37,998	"
Windows	43,911	"
Windows/NT	20,542	"
Macintosh	20,499	"
Unix	23,183+	"
Selections: state, SCF, 6.00/M; job function, business/industry,applications, purchase influence, pc's/workstations, 10.00/M extra; operating systems, 15.00/M extra; key coding, 2.00/M extra; splits 35.00 each.
Minimum order. 625.00.
5. COMMISSION, CREDIT POLICY
20% commission to all recognized brokers. Prepayment with first order.
6. METHOD OF ADDRESSING
4-up Cheshire labels. Pressure sensitive labels, 9.00/M extra. Magnetic tape, 25.00 flat fee.
7. DELIVERY SCHEDULE
Five working days. 48 hour processing available at extra charge.
8. RESTRICTIONS
Sample mailing piece required for approval. Guarantee of one-time use required. Owner reserves right to refuse rental. No competitive offers.

---

11. MAINTENANCE
Updated daily. Requalified annually. 99% deliverability guaranteed. Postage refunded for non-deliverable material in excess of 1% if returned within 45 days of mail date.

COMPUTER HARDWARE REPAIR & MAINTENANCE COMPANIES

Location ID: 13 ICLS 15   Mid 108956-000
1. PERSONNEL
List Manager
L.I.S.T Inc., 320 Northern Blvd., Great Neck, NY 11021.
Phone 516-482-2345. FAX 516-487-7721.
2. DESCRIPTION
Independent computer service and repair throughout the United States that maintain pc's, mini-computer, work stations, peripherals, complete systems, etc.
4. QUANTITY AND RENTAL RATES
Rec'd Jan. 17, 1997.

	Total Number	Price per/M
Total list	12,438	120.00
Selections: state, SCF, ZIP Code, 10.00/M extra; key code, 2.00/M extra.
Minimum order 5,000.
6. METHOD OF ADDRESSING
4-up Cheshire labels. Pressure sensitive labels, 10.00/M extra. Magnetic tape, 25.00 fee.
8. RESTRICTIONS
Sample mailing piece required for approval.
11. MAINTENANCE
Updated quarterly.

COMPUTER HOTLINE

Location ID: 13 ICLS 15   Mid 105935-000
1. PERSONNEL
List Manager
AllMedia, Inc., 4965 Preston Park Blvd., Suite 300, Plano, TX 75093-0014. Phone 972-612-4060. FAX 972-612-4061.
2. DESCRIPTION
Subscribers to a trading publication for computer products, supplies and services.
Selections available: Mth.
4. QUANTITY AND RENTAL RATES
Rec'd Feb. 19, 1997.

	Total Number	Price per/M
Total list	99,856	110.00
Industry:		
End user	16,631	+10.00
Manufacturer-computer	2,822	"
Secondary equip/dealer	2,856	"
Distribution	2,392	"
Repair/service	6,990	"
Consultant	4,828	"
OEM	1,123	"
VAR/VAD	3,268	"
Government	2,949	"
Mfg-other	8,945	"
Installation	1,136	"
Software	3,294	"
Communications	1,372	"
Computer retailer	3,489	"
Education/school	9,275	"
Hospital/medical	4,555	"
Banking/financial	7,143	"
Insurance	3,561	"
Energy/utilities	2,476	"
Publishing	3,848	"
Other	6,903	"
Title:		
Pres/owner/gen mgr	41,199	+10.00
Treas/controller/finance	1,697	"
Sales mgr	1,582	"
Customer srvc	930	"
Operations/engineer	5,470	"
Purchasing/buyer	4,754	"
Office/bus mgr	5,507	"
MIS/data proc mgr	26,308	"
VP/officer	4,482	"
Field tech.	969	"
Mktg mgr	900	"
Sales person	781	"
Teacher/instructor	1,778	"
Other	3,701	"
Number of employees:		
1-10	30,607	+10.00
11-25	12,205	"
26-50	10,746	"
51-75	5,442	"
76-100	2,441	"
Over 100	34,799	"
Unknown	3,716	"
Selections: state, SCF, 10.00/M extra; key coding, 2.00/M extra.
Minimum order 5,000.
6. METHOD OF ADDRESSING
4-up Cheshire labels. Pressure sensitive labels, 10.00/M extra. Magnetic tape (9T 1600/6250 BPI), 25.00 nonrefundable fee.
7. DELIVERY SCHEDULE
5-7 working days.
8. RESTRICTIONS
Sample mailing piece and list rental agreement required for approval.
11. MAINTENANCE
Updated quarterly.

COMPUTER INTEGRATED MANUFACTURING AND CAD/CAM

Location ID: 13 ICLS 15   Mid 048468-000
Fairmont Press.
1. PERSONNEL
List Manager
W.I. Mail Marketing, 470 Main St., Suite 317, Ridgefield, CT 06877-4516. Phone 203-438-6822. FAX 203-438-7756.
2. DESCRIPTION
Buyers of Strategic Planning for Computer Integrated Manufacturing report.
Average unit of sale 495.00.

---

4. QUANTITY AND RENTAL RATES
Rec'd June 20, 1996.

	Total Number	Price per/M
Total list	16,975	125.00
Selections: geographic, state, SCF, A/B split, 10.00/M extra; keying, 5.00/M extra.
Minimum order 5,000.
5. COMMISSION, CREDIT POLICY
Commission to recognized brokers at standard industry rates. List manager reserves right to require prepayment on any order. Payment in full required within 30 days of invoice date. Cancellations in writing received before mail date required to pay a 50.00 cancellation fee plus running charge of 12.00/M, any selects and shipping. Mailer is responsible for payment in full if order cancelled after mail date.
6. METHOD OF ADDRESSING
4-up Cheshire labels. Pressure sensitive labels, 12.00/M extra. Magnetic tape, 25.00 nonreturnable fee.
8. RESTRICTIONS
Sample mailing piece required for approval.

ComputerLife

Location ID: 13 ICLS 15   Mid 106456-000
1. PERSONNEL
List Manager
Direct Media , Inc., Business List Management Div., 200 Pemberwick Rd., P.O. Box 4565 New York, NY 06830.
Phone 203-532-1000. FAX 203-531-1452.
2. DESCRIPTION
Subscribers to Computer Life who are home computer users buying faster more powerful new hardware, software and peripherals; 26% women, 59% men, average age 43.
Average unit of sale 24.97.
Selections available: state, SCF, Zip.
3. LIST SOURCE
Direct mail.
4. QUANTITY AND RENTAL RATES
Rec'd Dec. 17, 1996.

	Total Number	Comp. Offers	Non-Comp. Offers
Subscribers	339,310	*125.00	*85.00
Hotline (1 month)	54,899	"	"
(*) Advertisers rate, 125.00/M; fundraisers rate, 60.00/M.
Selections: home or business address, sex, 5.00/M extra; direct-to-publisher, 10.00/M extra; expires, 90.00/M extra.
Minimum order 5,000.
6. METHOD OF ADDRESSING
4-up Cheshire labels. Pressure sensitive labels, 8.00/M extra. Magnetic tape, 25.00 nonrefundable fee.
8. RESTRICTIONS
Sample mailing piece required for approval.
11. MAINTENANCE
Updated biweekly.

COMPUTER MANUFACTURERS AND RETAILERS

Location ID: 13 ICLS 15   Mid 108588-086
Compiled Solutions.
666 Plainsboro Rd., Suite 540, Plainsboro, NJ 08536. Phone 609-275-6452, 800-585-5720. Fax 609-936-1918.
NOTE: For basic information on the following numbered listing segments 1, 3, 5, 6, see Compiled Solutions listing in Mailing List Compilers section under Mailing List Compilers.
2. DESCRIPTION
Computer manufacturers, retail software stores and companies providing programming services.
4. QUANTITY AND RENTAL RATES
Rec'd Feb. 21, 1997.

	Total Number	Price per/M
Computer mfg's/ srvcs	146,709	50.00
Contact names	112,529	+25.00
Female names	16,950	+00.00
Male names	96,111	"
Phone numbers	146,709	+12.00
Industry/SIC:		
Electronic computer manufacturers	2,583	50.00
Storage device mfgr	140	"
Terminals mfgrs	117	"
Peripheral equip NEC mfgrs	1,225	"
Peripheral equip whlsalers	7,242	"
Retail software stores	78,392	"
Computer prgrmg srvcs	27,996	"
Prepackaged sftwr srvcs	925	"
Computer integrated systems design	1,795	"
Data prcsng srvcs	7,867	"
Computer leasing	2,155	"
Computer mntnce & repair	8,375	"
Computer related srvcs NEC	3,519	"
Computer training	4,378	"
Employee size:		
1-4	74,342	+12.00
5-9	37,180	"
10-19	15,317	"
20-49	11,273	"
50-99	4,119	"
100-249	2,390	"
250+	1,682	"
Sales volume:		
Under 499,999	57,167	+12.00
500,000-999,999	30,376	"
1,000,000-2,499,999	32,899	"
2,500,000-4,999,999	12,148	"
5,000,000-9,999,999	5,928	"
10,000,000-19,999,999	3,312	"
20,000,000-49,999,999	1,189	"
50,000,000-99,999,999	536	"
100,000,000+	768	"
Computer manufacturer:		
Apple	568	50.00
Altos	13	"
AT&T	111	"
Atari	22	"
Compaq	2,151	"
Commodore (CBM)	50	"
Digital (DEC)	324	"

continued

I Can Make You Famous

I USUALLY WRITE ABOUT PRINT ADVERTISING, but not today. You see, you never hear about most of the marketing that goes on in the United States. You only hear about the splashy retail products. Products you find in department stores, catalogs, five and dime stores, drugstores, and so forth. And the hot products that make the news, like Tickle Me Elmo.

But most of the products in the U.S. are marketed to specific industries. You never see an ad for gears or bearings on TV, but if you're an automotive engineer, you see ads for them in your trade journals all the time. If your firm manufactures ovens, you see a plethora of ads for oven controls, high-temperature resin coatings, high-temperature glass, and stamped metal hinges with and without springs. Suit manufacturers see ads for buttons, lining material, and thread; computer manufacturers see ads for CRTs, electronic chips, and keyboards; keyboard manufacturers see ads for injection molders for keys, and hot stamping houses and silk screeners for lettering.

Industrial marketing is very big. There are over 15,000 trade magazines serving fields as big as the automotive industry and niches as small as ferret-raising. Each industry has its own trade journals.

But today I'd like to introduce you to a different marketing method. There are some excellent buys in marketing, and right now, one of these is cable TV.

You can buy an ad on TV for $20. Yep, you heard that right, twenty bucks. It's on cable. But not on that local programming channel that no one watches. You can get your ad on prestigious stations like ESPN, The Discovery Channel, or USA. Yep, $20, for a 30-second spot that airs one time. The local cable companies offer this every day.

Call your local cable company. Our local company distributes its programming to almost 19,000 area residents. So while buying time on a local cable TV show can make you famous, it can only make you famous within a limited area. This may be all you need.

The cost of actually creating a 30-second spot can be under $500. Chances are the cable company will recommend a few good video companies that have produced ads for insertion into their networks. Prices for shooting are negotiable, but $500 is realistic for a local video company to write a script for a 30-second segment, send a professional camera crew of two with a high-quality camera to your location, and schedule between one and two hours for the shoot. It also includes about an hour of editing, and the result will be a pretty tight 30-second spot.

Cable TV ads can be incredibly effective, but you must select your time slot with care, as the viewer profile changes abruptly with time and station. Homemaker-oriented products do well on daytime TV. Business products mid-evening. Business-oriented services do better on news stations like CNN or CNBC. Male-oriented products have ESPN and shows like boxing, car racing, and golf. Wow, if it weren't for ESPN, I'd have a lot of free time!

You can buy time on most national stations—like ESPN, TBS, Discovery, and USA—as well as the other national-but-not-quite-as-popular stations like the Golf Network, Court TV, and so on. Prices for time on these offbeat channels are lower, and viewership is lower, too. Viewership can be nonexistent on some channels, on some shows, or in some time slots. Buying time when no one is watching is not worth it, no matter how little the cost.

Most stations will try to sell you a run of schedule (ROS) for the morning, afternoon, or evening time blocks. Air times may be a little cheaper than airing your ad on specific shows, but you may miss your targets and get very little response—especially if your services or products are geared to a specific target audience or group. It's the first package cable companies try to sell because they can fit your ad in at THEIR convenience, not necessarily in time slots in your best interest. Your ad gets bumped around as other advertisers demand better positioning and times.

If you schedule ROS air times, make sure you know about a week before each ad airs exactly WHEN it will run so you can nix any dead air time. Offers abound at some cable companies and you may hear offers of 2-for-the-price-of-1 specials, but the second ad will air after midnight. Man, talk about dead air time.

Negotiation is the law of the land when buying local cable time, so get tough. Negotiate costs, air times, and channel. And make sure your contract can be canceled if the first week or two don't produce results. While it's important to have your ad be seen more than once, if it doesn't draw anything from the first few airings, better rethink your strategy—or change the copy. It's likely it won't get better with age. TV is an immediate medium without much longevity.

Each cable company has its own unique customer demographics. Some cable companies serve mostly upscale neighborhoods. Some serve urban customers. Some companies serve markets that are predominantly Black or Hispanic. So if you have a product or service that is best directed to a specific market segment, call several cable companies and get their customer profiles. A little homework here will pay off handsomely in the long run.

Everyone likes to shop in their own back yard, so any firm that markets its products or services locally can be successful in this arena. And local cable is especially good for local service companies like printers, roofers, auto body shops, and athletic clubs. Restaurants and retail stores can also do well, if focused on a particular market. If your business serves a geographic marketplace, there's a good possibility it can do well on cable TV. Obviously, more than one ad is necessary to achieve any penetration; to be noticed, you'll probably need about 50 insertions. But you can still be famous, in your own back yard, for well under the price of a new sofa and love seat.

5-Mile Marketing

MOST MARKETING QUESTIONS I RECEIVE from retailers and service providers are based on selling their goods and services to prospects located in specific areas. Here are some local marketing options.

Coupon mailings—packs of coupons you receive in the mail. Coupon packages are purchased in quantities of 10,000 households in selected zips. Costs are around $450 (slightly negotiable) per 10,000 households, and the mailing company will do all of the art and graphics. Most advertisers seem to recoup the cost of the ad, although some advertisers complain about customers being too price conscious, er, cheap.

Post card mailings can be incredibly effective. While a single post card may or may not work, a series of post cards is among the most consistently hardest-working promotional vehicles on the planet. It's so easy to read a post card. You don't have to open anything, it's just...there. Everyone reads post cards.

Yellow pages. My favorite yellow pages ad is called a "logo ad," which is a small in-line ad that has your logo in it. To see an example of this, look at the airlines section of any yellow pages book. A logo ad always appears alphabetized within the regular listings. BUT—here's the secret: don't use your logo unless it's very well known. Instead, sneak in your town name in a very bold face. You see, everyone likes to shop in their own back yard. When customers are skimming down the listings and see your town name, if it's close to their home, they'll call.

Other sources of unconventional advertising are airport advertising, high school/college campus advertising, advertising in hotels, movie theater trailers, shopping mall ads, sports and fitness facilities, stadium/arena/sports team advertising, truck and truckstop advertising, and event marketing. Don't forget Entertainment coupon books (810/637-8400), supermarket register tape ads, supermarket entrance advertising (community bulletin boards), church and synagogue programs (and yearbooks), advertising specialties, package insert programs, Internet ads and Web sites, orchestra program books, professional and local theater program books, high school newspapers and yearbooks, local team sponsorships, college sports programs, motor racing event programs, town festival programs, messages on hold, and ATM messages—to name a few.

How To
Find a Product
to Market

ANY PRODUCT YOU BRING TO MARKET is going to be the direction of your life force for the next four or five years—maybe longer. So the first rule of thumb in the selection of a product is to make sure you love the product, the industry it serves, the prospects, and the purchasers—because you're going to be immersed in their bathwater for quite a while. Better make sure you like the scent.

If you have no product in particular you're thinking about bringing to market, how do you select one? Well...do you have a hobby? Do you have a passion? For example, do you love computers? How about plastics? Are you interested in metals? Or in manufacturing? Can you sit and talk endlessly about antiques with your friends? Does the conversation always turn to airplanes? Or to food? All of these passions are great pursuits that become industries you can get involved in. The industries become markets to sell your products to.

Or...do you have an industry that you're familiar with? Have you been on the distribution end of a particular field? Are you in retail (ouch, those long retail hours!)? Are you familiar with direct mail? Do you enjoy catalogs?

What are you good at? Are you a good writer? A great chef? Do you enjoy working with your hands? Are you creative? Are you good at design? Are you good at art? Are you skilled at creating mechanical objects? Are you a great negotiator? Are you detail oriented? Do you have a special gift in any one area? These are all considerations in product selection.

Once you figure out some product ideas and the industry you'd like to be involved in, ask yourself if, somewhere down the road, there are other products you can market to the same audience. Keep in mind that some products can't be marketed profitably by themselves. To make a profit, you may need to have additional depth in your product line and companion sales. For example, if you sell a book, can you sell your purchasers additional books by the same author or by other authors in the same field? A person who buys one book on computer programming is likely to purchase a second on the same topic.

Throw the above mix into a hat, swish it around with a few beers, and these are your considerations for product selection. Stay with product fields in which you have a great interest. If you decide that you can stick it out, selling the same products to the same group without getting bored or tired of it, here's where to find the products.

The U.S. Patent Office holds a wealth of stimulating ideas for products in every field. There are 81 patent depositories located in libraries around the United States where you can look up patents to find hundreds of thousands of both great and poor ideas in any particular field. Since patents are only good for 17 years, any patent issued before 1981 is fair game for you to duplicate, improve, or borrow from. Take a look at the product; if you can improve it—all the better! Voilà—your product concept is ready to go.

If you see a product with a patent issued after 1981, call the patent holder and ask if you can license the product. Don't offer—or pay—any money up front, and only offer a very small percentage—2% to 5% of any net income—"if and when" your marketing of the product is successful. Most patent holders never market their inventions and will be happy to grant you permission to sell their products. Most inventors are just that—inventors; they invent a product, then move on to the next invention. Most aren't marketers, which is a profession far removed from inventing.

By the way, one of the most fun government publications to read is the *Patent Gazette*. It's the weekly publication of the Patent Office, and it shows all the patents issued for that particular week— usually 1,500 to 2,000. The booklet shows a line drawing of the invention and a one-paragraph description of the device. A single copy costs $50, but you can find it at the patent depositories.

No luck at the Patent Office? Go to the library and ask to see their copy of the *Thomas Register of American Companies*. This set of reference books weighs in at an incredible 270 pounds and contains products and their manufacturers in EVERY field. There are about 30 books in the *Thomas Register* set, each containing well over 1,000 pages. Just imagine all those manufacturers and distributors, all referenced in this one huge directory for only one reason: just to increase their sales. Can you find products and manufacturers to help you? Heck, yes. And in great depth.

So look up the industries you're interested in, and get a look at all of the manufacturers and the multitude of products each produces. Call any of them and see if they have any inventory—or tooling—of products they've tried to market and haven't been successful with. Remember, most manufacturers are good at...well, manufacturing. They may be horrible at marketing, and as a result, they may have had little success in launching new products. These may be great products. Of course, they may be terrible products, too. But you never know until you ask and explore.

One thing is for sure—if you're an OK negotiator, the price will be right. Products sitting in their basements for a couple of years have little value to manufacturers—and have already cost them time, and still cost them space. They may just want to get rid of them. They may take 5¢ on the dollar. Plastics houses, like injection molders, are a good source of overstock and unsold inventory. Toy manufacturers, too!

If a manufacturer already offers a product you'd like to market, the price goes up. Naturally, as a "special marketing licensee" of their products, you'll want their best pricing structure. But if you have to go through their set of distributors and retailers, there won't be enough profit for your nontraditional marketing efforts. You may ask to license their products only for select industries, or through special avenues where they have no presence, such as only marketing through the mail or through TV ads. Make an offer.

Can't find a ready-made product? If you need to develop a product, the *Thomas Register*, again, is the ultimate source for products, component parts, and their manufacturers. The set can be found in most libraries or purchased for $240 + $15.80 shipping (800/699-9822, ext. 444, 5 Penn Plaza, NY, NY 10001). Although I haven't read every page, I believe it contains listings of manufacturers of every product ever made. Yep. Every product and every industry are represented. As you get familiar with the *Register*'s contents, you can learn which players are in any particular field and which manufacturer makes each part of any component. It's an incredible resource tool for ideas, products, parts, components, and manufacturers.

For example, suppose you invent something electrical, and you need electrical wire and a plug for each device. *Thomas Register*: hundreds of wire manufacturers, electrical plug makers, specialty distributors of electrical anything. Call, get a price for 1,000—and 10,000—units, and ask for a sample. When you get quantity prices, the samples are usually free and are shipped right out. Nice trick.

Still need creative stimulation and more resources? Get the trade magazines for the industries you would like to be involved in. In the reference section of the library, get the names of the various trade magazines from directories such as *Burrelle's Media Directory/Magazines and Newsletters*, the *Oxbridge Communications National Directory of Magazines*, or *Bacon's Newspaper/Magazine Directory*. These reference books are easy to use from the start, and in a single evening, you can get the names of every magazine serving any industry.

Call the magazine publishers and ask for a media kit. This is what potential advertisers ask for—and you were thinking about running an ad in their magazine, weren't you? The media kit contains sample magazines with the publisher's current advertising price schedule; it's sent right out to you first class. Ask them to include any directory issue they may publish, too. It'll probably be free if you request it at this time.

When the magazines arrive, look at the ads. Any ideas for better products? Look at the new product sections. Anything you can improve upon? Circle the bingo numbers on the reader service card for free information. If you fall in love with a product, call the manufacturer and ask for special licensing and marketing rights—and special pricing—so you can start marketing their products.

Trade shows are another incredible source of products. There are almost 20,000 trade shows staged annually in the United States. Some shows, like the Premium Incentive Shows held each May in New York and again each October in Chicago, span every conceivable product category and every industry. The gift show and the variety merchandise show are other huge broad-based product shows. The annual New York toy show is also pretty incredible.

Other shows are more industry specific. Some are product oriented—and are hard-selling, order-taking shows. Others only demonstrate products and supply information for further follow-up. But one thing is certain: every company that takes a booth has it for only one reason—to increase sales. You can learn an incredible amount of information about products, product needs, or even an entire industry in a single afternoon at a trade show.

Finally, if you see a product you like on any retailer's shelf, call the manufacturer and ask about a special licensing arrangement. If the manufacturer is big, they may not allow it—they'll have distributors and retailers all over the country who would get mad if they sold to you directly. But lots of smaller manufacturers will be eager to talk.

You see, no one knows what you have in mind. What kind of campaign you're thinking about, or how much money you're going to invest. You may just be the home run a manufacturer is looking for. You may be the one who takes out an ad on a cable show (ads can cost as little as $20 to place on such prestigious networks as ESPN or USA), and you may sell tons of their products.

Still stuck? There are nonprofit inventors' groups all over the United States that will help you. No, I'm not talking about the rip-off inventors' hot lines or invention marketing scam firms that seem to abound in the inventing industry (never pay anyone whom you haven't checked out first to evaluate your idea, and never, ever pay any invention marketing firm over $300 for any reason!). Most big cities have inventors' groups. In Philadelphia, we have the nonprofit American Society for Inventors, of which I am privileged to serve on the Board of Directors. *Inventors' Digest* is a great magazine of help for inventors (800/838-8808, just $22 per year—and worth it!). *Dream Merchant* is another exceptional inventor's magazine (310/328-1925, $15.95 per year). Now you just have to do the hardest part: start.

As always, dear reader, I am privileged to be able to share with you my ideas and philosophies about business and marketing, I am honored you have elected to read and study my material, and I appreciate the trust you have placed in me by using these concepts to increase your own business. Thank you.

I couldn't help but include this theory I have about saving lives. You see, the rest of the book may save you money, but this may save your life, or the life of your child or a friend. If you remember only one detail from this entire book, I hope this is it. As with all my writing, your comments and questions are most welcome. If you ever employ this technique, please call me and let me know that my life's work has been successful in saving a human life. Thank you. For the longer version of this technique, along with its history, please see the book How To Market a Product for Under $500. *Thanks.* THEORY BY JEFFREY DOBKIN • © 1986, 1993, 1997

A TECHNIQUE FOR DELAYING BRAIN DEATH IN HEART ATTACK VICTIMS

WHILE CURRENT MEDICAL METHODS cannot entirely prevent heart attacks, there is an emergency procedure that can save lives. A simple technique can reduce or delay the possibility of brain damage and brain death to a heart attack victim for up to an hour—or more.

If this procedure saves one life, it is fully worth all the time and effort I have spent in research.

The Technique seeks to prevent or delay the irreversible brain damage thought to occur when no oxygen reaches the brain for four minutes.[1] It is used as a time-buying procedure to save the lives of heart attack victims and victims of suffocation, drowning, respiratory failure, and drug overdose. Perhaps it will even help SIDS (crib death) or stroke victims until proper medical equipment and personnel are summoned and arrive.

The Technique can be applied by a child or may be self-administered in almost any home. It takes less than 30 seconds to initiate and the results are as immediate.[2] It works on both conscious and unconscious victims. It can be explained on the phone in under a minute.

Almost everyone has heard of a boy drowning in cold water—then, after half an hour of submersion, being resuscitated with no ill effects and no brain damage. The *Canadian Medical Association Journal* documented such a drowning: After half an hour of complete submersion, a boy was rescued from the icy waters where he fell.[3] He was resuscitated and, with proper medical treatment, had no lasting side effects. There was no cerebral damage, although his brain received no oxygen for over half an hour.

Research has provided additional case study after case study of extended cold water submersion with no brain damage to resuscitated victims. Article after article, story after story, of people deprived of oxygen for up to an hour—with no ill effects or brain damage. What is it that protects the brain from damage in cases of oxygen deprivation over the four-minute limit? And can this be applied as a lifesaving technique to heart attack victims?

In all vertebrates, there is an automatic reflex called the Mammalian Diving Reflex. It occurs naturally as a life-preserving mechanism during cold water submersion. More commonly called the "Diving Reflex," it is a protective oxygen-conserving reflex to keep brain and body alive during submergence and possible drowning in cold water. The body prepares itself to sustain life. It is a totally natural protective mechanism serving Homo sapiens, originating from hundreds of thousands of years of evolvement.

Natural engagement of the diving reflex is what has enabled drowning victims to be revived successfully after cold water submersion for as long as an hour, with few or no ill effects. The Technique seeks to trigger this reflex in a crisis. The Technique may never replace CPR. The purpose of this article is not to compete with CPR, but to help sustain the life of the hundreds of thousands of victims of heart attacks or suffocation, thrust into a life-and-death situation, who may not be near people trained in CPR.

If you are not skilled in CPR, and you live in the country where an ambulance is 20 minutes away, and someone close to you has a heart attack—the options are frightening. Without the initiation of the Technique, a person whose heart stops has only four minutes until irreversible brain damage occurs. After you call for help, you can watch. If you think this is a horrifying alternative, I couldn't agree more. Or you can try this Technique.

The Technique may work to save lives in conjunction with CPR. There is also the possibility it may not work at all; this is, after all, a theory. But the fact that it just may work makes it worth closer study. When there is no other immediate remedy, this may be put into practice in an emergency. What would you have your spouse do if you lived in the country and you had a heart attack?

"The Technique for Delaying Brain Damage" is simple and easy to initiate. In natural surroundings, the diving reflex occurs when a mammal falls into water 58 degrees Fahrenheit—the mean temperature of the waters of the world—or colder. But this reflex may also be triggered by only a <u>facial</u> immersion in cold water (58 degrees or colder). **The Technique is to apply cold water, wet towels, or wet ice packs to the victim's face—especially the eyes—to trigger the diving reflex in the event of heart or respiratory failure.** This procedure starts the oxygen-conserving mammalian diving reflex. Here is what happens:

Bradycardia can start in as little as four seconds or can take up to thirty seconds, depending on what part of the breath cycle the person is in when cold water is applied to the face. In man, cold water facial immersion usually induces a 15% to 30% decrease in heart rate from normal resting values. The reflex is strong enough to override other seemingly vital reflexes; i.e., it can completely obliterate the tachycardia that accompanies moderately severe exercise on a bicycle ergometer and can abruptly reduce heart rate from 130–140 beats per minute to 80 or less, despite continuation of the exercise.[4] Bradycardia is initiated by parasympathetic vagal activity.

Skin and muscle blood flow decrease through a powerful constriction of peripheral arteries. Peripheral vaso-constriction brought about by sympathetic activity maintains blood pressure. At the same time, systemic arterial pressure, especially diastolic, is increased. This lower heart rate and redistribution of central blood flow supports more necessary life-preserving organs.

The reflex triggers anaerobic metabolism, shown by a fall in arterial pH. There is an increase in concentrations of lactic and other organic acids, and a rise in blood carbon dioxide and potassium. This indicates that the body's cells are using less oxygen.

In a study by Wolf, Schneider and Groover, arterial oxygen saturation fell very little during immersion when the reflex occured.[5]

Because arterial oxygen saturation falls very little, the term "oxygen conserving" is appropriate for the reflex—an animal is enabled to survive without breathing for a much longer period than its supply of oxygen would warrant under ordinary circumstances.[6]

In Diving Reflex experiments, Charles Richet tied off the tracheae of two groups of ducks, then held one group under cold water. The ducks held under water lived more than three times as long as their partners not immersed in cold water.

In further studies of nerve-cutting experiments, Harold Anderson of Oslo, Norway, documented that the Diving Reflex, as manifested by slowing of the heart, depended on the integrity of the ophthalmic branch of the trigeminal nerve. With the nerve intact, a duck would trigger the diving reflex and survive under water for 20 minutes. When the ophthalmic branch of the trigeminal nerve was severed (bilaterally), immersed ducks failed to slow their heart rates when cold water was applied to their faces and survived only six or seven minutes.[7]

Accentuation of the reflex to the greatest degree occurs when the facial immersion in cold water is accompanied by fear. The more fearful the condition, the stronger the trigger to bring about the reflex and the greater the chance a strong oxygen-conserving reflex will take place.

In patients resuscitated by the team of a special ambulance service run by the Department of Anesthesia at Ulleval Hospital (from an article entitled "Resuscitation of Drowning Victims"), the most successful outcome was observed in those with cardiac arrest following drowning.

In an article in *Newsweek*, drowning specialist Dr. Martin J. Nemiroff (Michigan University Medical Center) suggests that the involuntary diving reflex saves lives of drowning victims by <u>delaying suffocation</u>—by shunting oxygen from extremities and sending it toward the heart, brain, and lungs—<u>and reduces the possibility of brain damage and death.</u>[8] A photo in the *Newsweek* article shows Dr. Nemiroff with Brian Cunningham, who was revived after 38 minutes under water.

Dr. Nemiroff has successfully revived numerous victims of cold water drowning who were submerged for 30 minutes or more and were pronounced dead. He says that what saved the victims was the automatic activation of the Mammalian Diving Reflex and the coldness of the water.[9]

It is my conclusion that if the diving reflex can save the lives of drowning victims by delaying brain damage, then triggering the reflex should also delay brain damage in heart attack victims.

A discussion in a *Scientific American* study of the human body's ability to resist drowning states that the Diving Reflex and cold water reduce the oxygen demand of tissues, extending the period of survival <u>without external oxygen</u> to as long as one hour. Previously, irreversible brain damage was thought to occur after four minutes without oxygen.[10]

The Diving Reflex is currently used by the medical profession in conversion of paroxysmal atrial tachycardia.[11,12,13] The Technique is to immerse the face of a person in a tub or basin of water 50 degrees or cooler. Since the technique produces an almost instant conversion to normal sinus rhythm and is not invasive, the use of the Diving Reflex is recommended by many authors and cited as a safe, effective treatment. In one study, nine out of 10 patients converted in 15–38 seconds, with an average of 23 seconds.[14] Its use is also the treatment of choice for converting a supraventricular tachycardia in children and infants, in whom the Diving Reflex effect is most pronounced.[15]

In a letter to Mr. Dobkin, Dr. Linus Pauling surmises there are two ways in which the damage to the brain might be delayed for some time when the oxygen to the blood is stopped.

"The brain can tolerate a certain amount of decrease in the partial pressure of oxygen supplied by the blood. If the circulation of the blood to the brain and to the tissues continues at its normal rate, the oxygen is used up rather fast, most of it (75%) by tissues other than the brain. Accordingly the induction of bradycardia, delaying the rate at which oxygen is brought to the tissues by the blood, would conserve the supply of oxygen and permit anoxic damage to be delayed by a considerable amount.

"There is a second way of delaying brain damage by anoxia. This way is to cool the brain. The biochemical reactions involved in anoxic damage have a high temperature coefficient, so that cooling the brain by a few degrees can slow down the rate at which anoxic damage occurs to perhaps one-tenth of its rate."[16] This letter suggests that ice or cold water also be applied to the neck, so that the blood is cooled and the brain itself is cooled in the region in which anoxic damage occurs. I concur with Dr. Pauling and recommend that after the face is immersed with ice packs or cold water, cold water be applied to the neck and the base of the hairline at the back of the head.

After countless hours of research, I am convinced that the Technique to delay brain damage will save lives. The technique of applying cold water to the face of conscious or unconscious heart attack or suffocation victims should be a known lifesaving procedure. It may be used in the event of any oxygen deprivation to the brain. Its procedure can be explained over the telephone, self-administered, or applied by a friend or child with no training. And while it will not stop heart attacks from happening, it will buy precious time until proper medical equipment and personnel arrive.

The Technique is quick and easy to apply. It is a time-buying procedure—when time is of the essence. It is nature's own way of protecting us—a non-invasive action that can be initiated immediately by someone with no training. This natural, life-conserving reflex is common enough to be found in all mammals and powerful enough to save someone's life in a traumatic moment.

Further investigation and clinical evaluation may be necessary, but from the empirical evidence I have uncovered, I recommend this reflex be initiated in time of emergent need. I hope this article is a catalyst to spur new research. My reward? I would like my name assigned to the Technique; after all, Heimlich has his maneuver. My goal? I hope at least one life is saved.

###

The Dobkin Technique triggers nature's own protective oxygen-saving mechanism to save lives. It is the same reflex that has saved children and adults from drowning even though they were completely submerged in cold water for up to an hour. Your comments are most welcome. If you know someone who has been revived from a cold water drowning, please write to me. Also, if this technique has been used, please let me know the details. Thank you.

Jeffrey Warren Dobkin • P.O. Box 100 • Merion Station, PA 19066

Abstract References:

CPR, Diving Reflex, Heart Attack, Brain Damage, SIDS, Suffocation, Respiratory Failure.

~ Abstract ~

Help for heart attack victims—when no one is around who knows CPR, initiate "The Dobkin Technique for Delaying Brain Death": Apply cold water or cold wet towels (58 degrees or colder) to the face and eyes of victim—leaving nose and mouth clear to breathe. After this, supplemental help may be to apply additional cold wet cloths to the base of the back of the head and to the back of the neck. This is an emergency time-buying procedure to delay brain death by triggering the Diving Reflex. The Diving Reflex is a natural oxygen-conserving reflex which can delay the irreversible brain damage thought to occur within four minutes of oxygen deprivation. Works on conscious and unconscious victims; may be applied by child or self-administered; technique may be described over the phone. Works in under 30 seconds. Works in victims of suffocation, SIDS, drownings, drug overdose, choking, electrocution, and other victims of respiratory failure or deprivation of oxygen for any reason.

Endnotes

1. *Scientific American*, August 1977, 57.

2. S. Wolf, R.A. Schneider, and M.E. Groover, "Further Studies on the Circulatory and Metabolic Alterations of the Oxygen-Conserving (Diving) Reflex in Man," (paper presented before the American Clinical and Climatological Association, Colorado Springs, Colo., 21 October 1964).

3. P.K. Hunt, "Effect and Treatment of the Diving Reflex," *Canadian Medical Association Journal* (21 December 1974).

4. J. Atkins, S. Leshin, C. Skelton, and K. Widenthal, "The Diving Reflex Used to Treat Paroxysmal Atrial Tachycardia," *Lancet* (4 January 1975): 12.

5. Wolf et al., "Further Studies."

6. Ibid.

7. Ibid.

8. *Newsweek*, 22 August 1977, 79.

9. *New York Times*, 7 August 1977, 20.

10. *Scientific American*, August 1977, 57.

11. Atkins et al., "Diving Reflex," 12.

12. *Newsweek*, 13 January 1975, 50.

13. P.G. Landsberg, "Bradycardia During Human Diving," *South African Medical Journal* (5 April 1975): 626-630.

14. M.A. Wayne, "Conversion of Paroxysmal Atrial Tachycardia by Facial Immersion in Ice Water," *Journal of the American College of Emergency Physicians* (6 May 1976).

15. V. Whitman, "The Diving Reflex in Termination of Supraventricular Tachycardia in Childhood," *Journal of the American College of Emergency Physicians*, letter to the editor (December 1976).

16. Letter to Jeffrey Dobkin from Dr. Linus Pauling, dated September 2, 1992.

Copyright Permission: Permission is hereby granted to use the writing of this technique to delay brain damage in whole or in part to save lives, or to increase the public awareness of this technique as a lifesaving emergency procedure—as long as credit is given to Jeffrey Dobkin and the technique referred to as "The Dobkin Technique for Delaying Brain Death."

How To Market a Product for Under $500

Just $29.95 + $4 shipping for a signed edition.

Uncommon Marketing Techniques

Just $17.95.   Please add $3 shipping. Signed.

Audio Cassette Series: Just $49 + $5 shipping.

3 Double-Sided Cassettes. Two studio-made cassettes are highlights of *How To Market a Product for Under $500*. One cassette is an AT&T tele-conference, 70 people on the line and only Jeffrey with an open mike. A brief question and answer period follows. Side two is a 1/2-hour radio interview (WMGK, Phila.) showing a more personal side of Jeffrey.

Two Video Cassettes: $69.95 + $4 shipping.

Watch Jeff as he presents a 40-minute information-rich speech to the members of the Highlander Club at their very first chapter meeting in Baltimore, MD.

Then see Jeffrey loosen up as he presents an hour and a half of solid Multi-Level Marketing information to a group of about 200 MLMers in California.

Finally, see Jeff sweat as viewers call in with the most unusual array of questions when he appears on a segment of CNBC's *The Money Wheel*.

_____Please keep me on your **Mailing List!** _____Send **NEWSLETTER** info!

Send Check, Money Order, or Call to Charge to Visa/MC, Discover, or AMEX.

Name_____

Address_____

City, St_____Zip_____

Telephone_____Fax_____

Products_____Quantity_____

If gift, endorsement should read:

Charging to Credit Card Number_____

Signature_____Expires_____

Amount_____Thank you! For additional orders, photocopy this form or just use a sheet of paper.

The Danielle Adams Publishing Co.

~ Satisfaction Always Guaranteed ~

Box 100 ☆ Merion Station, PA 19066

610/642-1000 ☆ FAX 610/642-6832

INQUIRIES: 610/642-1000
ORDERS: 800/234-IDEA

Notes... Comments, Or Questions.

If you have any, write them on this page, send or fax them to us, and Jeffrey will be happy to respond. We request the right to publish this material with your approval.

Please check here: ___ I approve. Signed _____Date_____

Print Name_____Phone_____

Address_____

Hope you have enjoyed this book and found it to be of good value!

~ Resources ~

Magazines, Newsletters, Reference Material

Public Relations Quarterly

Journal

44 West Market Street • P.O. Box 311

Rhinebeck, NY 12572

Phone: 800/572-3451; 914/876-2081 • Fax 914/876-2561

One year, 4 issues $49

Each journal is about 50 pages of industry-authored articles on PR. If you are serious about studying PR, this publication makes great reading. All authors are independent, so all articles are fresh and new. Two newsletters are also available: **Newsletter Design**, monthly, $99/year; and the **Newsletter on Newsletters**, 2 issues per month, $144/year. Recommended.

Public Relations Tactics

Association Newspaper

Public Relations Society of America

33 Irving Place

New York, NY 10003-2376

Phone: 212/460-1468 • Fax 212/995-0757

Monthly newspaper, $40/year

While this newspaper is geared towards larger companies, call these folks and get a sample issue anyway. It shows the nuts and bolts of the PR industry, how news is created, who is creating it—and what they're doing right, and what they're doing wrong. It also has lots of ads for PR services, but mostly from larger PR firms that are looking for big companies with big budgets. Still, if you are interested in taking a good look at the public relations field to see how it runs, how it ticks—this is a great initiation. (Of course, you do remember the part of this book that tells you how to get a free sample issue by requesting a media kit, don't you?)

PR News

Newsletter

Phillips Information, Inc.

1201 Seven Locks Road

Potomac, MD 20854

Phone: 800/777-5006; 301/424-3338 • Fax 301/309-3847

Weekly newsletter, $347/year

An industry insider's newsletter showing who did what to whom, and what company did it and how. Presents timely information on industry news and views. Ask for a sample copy.

PR Reporter

Newsletter

Dudley House

P.O. Box 600

Exeter, NH 03833-0600

Phone: 603/778-0514 • Fax 603/778-1741

Weekly newsletter, $225/year

One- and two-paragraph articles on PR: the campaigns, the results, and the impact they have on the marketplaces they serve. Industry news and campaigns, issues and trends, and significant news and research results. Gives tips and tactics on PR techniques; also reviews important PR books and articles. Ask for a sample copy.

Editor and Publisher

Magazine - Hard News; Business

11 West 19th Street

New York, NY 10011

Phone: 800/336-4380; 212/675-4380 • Fax 212/691-6939

Weekly, $65/year

Magazine for the newspaper trade. Newspaper media only, but very strong. Each issue is full of stories and articles about issues facing newspaper journalists. One of the best newspaper/PR industry trade publications. Big help wanted section for writers and editors. A good look at the inside of the newspaper business and how it relates to PR. This is the trade journal pulse of the industry. Their biggest help with press releases comes from their yearbook.

Editor and Publisher International Year Book

Yearbook - Hard News; Industry

Shows newspapers, syndicated services, and other organizations in the newspaper industry. Two volumes. Sections in Part 1 include:

I. U.S. Dailies

II. Weeklies & Special Newspapers

III. Canadian Newspapers

IV. Foreign Newspapers. Hard-fact information includes area population, circulations, subscription rates, advertising rates, and special sections and editions. Comprehensive lists of names, titles, areas of responsibility, addresses, phone and fax numbers.

V. News, Picture and Syndicated Services

VI. Newspaper Equipment

VII. Other Organizations and Industry Services. Names, titles, addresses, phone and fax numbers, membership directories, journalism schools and faculty, newspaper reps, foreign correspondents...and more.

Part 2. Who's Where: An alphabetical directory of newspaper personnel, title, newspaper, and phone number. Competitive with SRDS's and Bacon's newspaper directories, but cheaper. Also available on CD-ROM, $495 ($895 with listing capabilities). I have used this and personally recommend it. $125

The National PR Pitch Book

Directory

Infocom Group

1250 45th Street, Suite 200

Emeryville, CA 94608-2924

Phone: 800/959-1059 • Fax 510/596-9331

Business & Consumer Edition, $425

With 10 tabbed sections like "Wire Services," "Media Organization Index," "Regional TV," "Personnel Index," and "Syndicated Columnists," you almost forget that there are more traditional marketing sections on magazines, national TV and cable shows, and radio and newspapers. But the real beauty of this 700-plus-page book is that the editors and producers of most of the bigger media outlets (large-circulation magazines, major TV talk shows) were interviewed on how they like to be pitched, and on what topics. Their response is included. Nice insider stuff.

National PR Pitch Book, continued

Included in each listing are the editors' own recommendations for your best approach to reach them favorably, along with their personal interests in editorial coverage. Many write-ups contain best time of day to call, what to send (and what not to send), and their editorial mission. This book excels at supplying the contact dossiers and assignment beats of individual editors, writers, and producers; it also gives their direct-dial phone numbers, fax numbers, and e-mail addresses. Prices for the *National PR Pitch Book* series are: *The Business & Consumer Edition*, $425; *Issues, Policy & Politics*, $425; *Computers & Technology*, $225; *Health, Fitness, & Medicine*, $225; *Food, Hospitality & Travel*, $225; *Investment Banking & Financial Services*, $225; and the MediaPro CD, which includes all books on disk in a Windows platform, $995. Excellent, in-depth media guides, these marketing resources get my wholehearted A++ recommendation.

Bacon's Media Distribution Services
PR Distribution Service

Bacon's Media Directories
332 S. Michigan Avenue
Chicago, IL 60604
Phone: 800/621-0561; 312/922-2400 • Fax 312/922-3127

Helps in selecting your target publications and in distributing your release. Bacon's will reprint your release, duplicate your photos, and send your release to your target list. See the extensive write-up of Bacon's media directories and press release distribution service in the chapter "The One-Evening Marketing Plan" and in the book *How To Market a Product for Under $500*. Exceptionally strong in magazines, but also great for newspaper press releases. Reasonably priced. Recommended.

PR Newswire - 800/832-5522
PR Distribution Service

A <u>newspaper-only</u> wire service that transmits your release to selected newspapers and newsrooms, depending on the coverage you purchase. Offers both national and international broadcast bands. National newslines are offered at about $525 for releases up to 400 words, regional newslines (Northeast, Southeast, Midwest, or West/ Southwest) at around $220 for 400 words. State and local newslines, photo transmission, E-Wire, and fax and broadcast services are also offered. National headquarters are in New York, local offices in about twenty cities. Call for a complete listing of all the newspapers they serve; get a free copy of their 130-page distribution directory.

NAPS

PR Distribution Service

North American Precis Syndicate, Inc.

405 Lexington Avenue, 59th Floor

New York, NY 10174

Phone: 800/222-5551; 212/867-9000

NAPS offers a service to newspapers similar to the one Bacon's offers to magazines. While they aren't cheap, NAPS will take your rough draft and rewrite it to turn it into a winning press release. Then they fine-tune your release so it brings results. Just as this book suggests, they write to an objective: getting a response! Then they typeset the release to look like a newspaper story and send it to 10,000 newspapers. A publisher can just drop the already-typeset copy into an open section of the paper and it will look like the rest of the newspaper. With no further work to be done by the generally understaffed newspapers, this is a great option.

NAPS is used by large public relations firms and *Fortune* 500 companies. NAPS offers distribution of your one-column release to 10,000 newspapers for $2,950. They guarantee 100 to 400 placements when sent through their distribution system. If your release is presented in a typeset two-column by seven-inch-deep format, it costs $3,950. Besides a print media newspaper release, NAPS offers a television talk show release, which will give you 40 to 80 placements at a cost of $3,300. A radio news and talk show release costs $2,950 and will bring in 200 to 300 placements. A multimedia release of all of the above costs $6,500 and will generate 350 to 700 placements.

They're not cheap, and although I've never used them (I'm cheap), they appear to be a good resource for larger firms who need to get things done *now*, and who can afford to pay for the privilege of using a minimum of their own staff, time, and effort. Contact NAPS offices in Washington, D.C. 202/347-5000, Chicago 312/856-9000, Los Angeles 310/552-8000, San Francisco 415/837-0500, Atlanta 404/888-0400, or their headquarters in New York.

Bradley Communications Corp.
Media Communications Service

135 E. Plumstead Avenue • P.O. Box 1206
Lansdowne, PA 19050-8206
Phone: 800/989-1400; 610/259-1070 • Fax 610/284-3704

Bradley Communications Corp. is an innovative firm presenting a wealth of publicity resources at reasonable prices. They offer several products and services to help you get national radio, TV, and magazine publicity and to help you with your book and promotion publicity needs. Their clients have been booked by such media outlets as *Oprah, Larry King Live, Good Morning America, Dateline NBC, CNN Headline News, The Los Angeles Times,* and so forth. For full info, call 800/989-1400, ext. 408.

Radio-TV Interview Report is a three-times-a-month trade publication read by over 4,000 radio/TV producers to find interesting guests for interviews. The publication consists entirely of ads (starting at $348) from authors and other experts seeking radio/TV publicity. The *RTIR* staff will write your ad at no charge.

Publicity Blitz Media Directory-on-Disk. These data files list almost 20,000 print and broadcast contacts at magazines, newspapers, feature syndicates, and radio/TV stations. All contacts are coded by subject, so you can quickly find the journalists most likely to write about you. Single copy is $295; a one-year subscription (4 quarterly updates) is $445.

One of the best offers in the industry: Bradley also sells individual media lists—if you don't need all the names in Publicity Blitz and just want to purchase a "slice" of the database (for example, newspaper auto editors, small business magazines, or product editors at women's magazines), Bradley will counsel you on your specific needs, then sell you the short list at a discount from the price of their entire database. Call 800/989-1400 and inquire.

Bradley's Guide to the Top National TV Talk Shows ($75) contains detailed profiles and contact information for the top 100 national news and talk broadcast programs. Published each spring.

Bradley's Guide to Major Book Reviewers ($75) profiles the nation's fifty print outlets which are the most influential when it comes to reviewing books. Published each spring.

Book Marketing ProfitCenter ($100) is a set of data files that lists over 7,000 key book marketing contacts at major wholesalers, bookstores, and catalog firms.

Directory of Printers ($29) lists 791 printers of books, catalogs, magazines, and other bound publications.

Book Publishing Resource Guide ($55) is a printed directory listing over 7,500 book marketing contacts and resources at bookstores, newspapers, magazines, book clubs, book remainder dealers, premium firms, etc.

Direct Mail: Services, Magazines, and Reference Directories

Sandoval Printing

Printing

Gil, Joyce, Chris, & Tony Sandoval
9 Minnetonka Road
Hi-Nella, NJ 08083
Phone: 609/435-7320

Minnetonka Road? Hi-Nella? Yes! I'm serious. Short to medium runs (1,000 to 100,000 pieces; one- to five-color work). While not the cheapest, excellent work from an honest crew. I have known and trusted Gil and his family for over 20 years as my own first choice of printers—and I can be pretty demanding. As his customer and friend, I will personally guarantee his craftsmanship, pride, and the good old-fashioned honest value of any printing he does for you. Quality work shipped promptly, time after time.

Diversified Direct Mail, Inc.

Mailshop

Direct Mail Lettershop Services, Marketing Consultation
Leonard Nock, President
175 Strafford Avenue, Suite 1
Wayne, PA 19087-3396
Phone: 610/668-2000 • Fax 610/668-4355

One of the few shops that will handle smaller numbers: mailings from 1,000 pieces and up, although larger runs are more cost-efficient and handled with the same care. Len has some very unique equipment to handle your direct mail needs.

MailShop USA

Mailshop

Markus Allen, President
4679 West Chester Pike
Newtown Square, PA 19073
Phone: 800/432-9870; 610/359-9870 • Fax 610/359-9840
mailguru@aol.com

One of the best, lowest-cost mailshops in the United States. Markus Allen is extremely knowledgeable about mailing anything, and before you make up any sort of mailing package, talk to him. He'll explain how to lay it out so it gets the best mailing rate, tell you what it needs to meet any of the postal requirements for discounts, and quote you on mailing your material.

Markus is one of the brightest people in the mailing industry, and it's a privilege to do business with his firm. Everyone at MailShop USA is friendly, very knowledgeable, direct, and above all, truly honest. This firm gets my wholehearted recommendation.

National Mail Order Association

Organization

NMOA
2807 Polk Street NE
Minneapolis, MN
Phone: 612/788-1673 • Fax 612/788-1147
www.nmoa.org

An association designed to help and assist entrepreneurs and small business owners who have an interest in mail order. Offers helpful literature and booklets on increasing effectiveness when marketing through the mail. Also offers product marketing and development for its members through its Web site. Good folks, and if you're lucky enough to speak with John Schulte—the chairman— personally (he answers the phone sometimes), you'll find a wealth of information right at your fingertips. Membership is $99 annually.

The Catalog of Catalogs V

Directory

The Complete Mail-Order Directory
by Edward L. Palder
Woodbine House Publications
6510 Bells Mill Road
Bethesda, MD 20817 $24.95 + $4 shipping
Phone: 800/843-7323; 301/897-3570 • Fax 301/897-5838

Contains over 14,000 catalogs in 850 categories—an excellent value. Provides company name, address, telephone number, and a brief description of the merchandise or services. One of the best values in the industry; recommended reading.

National Directory of Catalogs

Directory

Oxbridge Communications
150 Fifth Avenue
New York, NY 10011 $395
Phone: 800/955-0231; 212/741-0231 • Fax 212/633-2938
http://www.mediafinder.com

Over 9,000 U.S. and Canadian catalogs. Listing includes catalog and company names, address, phone, products carried, personnel, and list rental data for direct marketers. Expensive, but thorough, accurate, and nicely put together. No question about it, this is the best book in the industry. Also available on CD-ROM, $495.

The Directory of Mail Order Catalogs

Directory

Grey House Publishing
Pocket Knife Square
Lakeville, CT 06039   11th Edition, $165
Phone: 800/562-2139; 860/435-0868 • Fax 860/435-0867
http://www.greyhouse.com • books@greyhouse.com

7,500 consumer catalog companies. 1997 edition contains over 5,000 presidents, 2,000 marketing managers, 800 buyers, and 500 list managers, with 41 product area chapters. Grey House also publishes the **Directory of Business to Business Catalogs** ($135). The **Directory of Business Information Resources** ($165) lists associations, newsletters, magazines, and trade shows, with 14,000 entries divided into 85 industry chapters. In addition, the **Directory of Overseas Catalogs** ($165) contains 1,350 entries, with catalogs listed by country and by product type. And the **International Trade and Business Directories** ($125) lists over 4,000 worldwide, industry-specific business directories, organized by industry and by country.

Directory of Mailing List Companies

Directory

Todd Publishing
P.O. Box 635
Nyack, NY 10960   13th Edition, $50
Phone: 800/747-1056; 914/358-6213 • Fax 914/358-1059
toddpub@aol.com

Features about 1,000 mailing list companies, including brokers, compilers, managers, and owners of over 30,000 mailing lists. Shows company name, contact name, address, and phone and fax numbers. Provides additional information such as list specialties, if company is broker or manager, etc. Information about companies is presented by alphabetical sequence, list specialty categories, brokers, managers, owners, and general lists.

Guide to American Directories

Directory

Todd Publishing
P.O. Box 635
Nyack, NY 10960   14th Edition, $95
Phone: 800/747-1056; 914/358-6213 • Fax 914/358-1059
toddpub@aol.com

Excellent resource for finding markets. Contains information on publishers and distributors of about 11,000 directories. Directories are published by book publishers, magazines, trade associations,

Guide to American Directories, continued
chambers of commerce, and city, state, and federal government agencies. Categorized under more than 150 industrial, technical, mercantile, scientific, and professional headings. Separate alphabetical index. Just a few examples of the headings are: aging and retirement, alternative culture and lifestyle, amusement industry, bibliographies, book dealers, civil and human rights, colleges and universities, consumer affairs, footwear and shoe industry, franchising, hospital and health care facilities, mail order, marine industry, philanthropy, safety and security, women's affairs...etc.

Encyclopedia of Associations

Directory

Gale Research, Inc.
P.O. Box 33477
Detroit, MI 48232 $460
Phone: 800/877-GALE (4253) • Fax 313/961-6083
Describes nearly 23,000 associations, including trade and professional, social welfare, public affairs, labor union, fraternal, and patriotic organizations, as well as religious, sports, and hobby groups. Includes both large (AAA = 29 million members) and small groups, including the Bald Headed Men of America (12,500 members). After about a dozen phone calls to get a copy to review, I gave up. So I have no idea how good this book is, how easy or difficult it is to use, or how anyone is able to deal with a company like this on any continual basis after the run-around I got. Also available from Gale Research is **Directories in Print** ($345), which contains over 15,000 entries arranged in 26 subject chapters, cross-indexed. Gale Research publishes a catalog of their own books (and CDs) of databases with the reference information available through their publications. Call them (ugh—good luck!) to receive this 154-page catalog, free.

Directory of Leading Private Companies

Directory

National Register Publishing Company
Division of Reed Elsevier PLC
121 Chanlon Road
New Providence, NJ 07974
Phone: 800/521-8110
Reed publishes a good number of reference books. Call for a free catalog.

Catalog Age • also Direct

Magazine

Cowles Business Media, Inc.
11 River Bend Drive South • P.O. Box 4949
Stamford, CT 06907-0949
Phone: 203/358-9900 • Fax 203/358-5811
One year, 12 issues $74
Excellent tabloid-size magazines that have their hand on the pulse of the catalog industry. Editorial supports industry giants such as catalogs from L.L. Bean and Spiegel; not too much for us little guys.

Target Marketing

Magazine

North American Publishing Company
401 N. Broad Street
Philadelphia, PA 19108
Phone: 215/238-5300 • Fax 215/238-5270
One year, 12 issues $65
Excellent resource for direct mail information. Most issues are how-to and information rich! (Be careful of advertorial issues.)

DM News

Tabloid Newsmagazine

100 Avenue of the Americas
New York, NY 10013
Phone: 212/741-2095 • Fax 212/925-8752
Weekly newsprint tabloid, $75/year
Direct marketing and industry news–oriented.

Direct Marketing

Magazine

Hoke Communications
224 Seventh Street
Garden City, NY 11503
Phone: 800/229-6700; 516/746-6700 • Fax 516/294-8141
One year, 12 issues $60
I grew up on this magazine - it set the industry standard for years. (These guys are tough on sample copies.)

(Keep in mind subscription prices shown here are for tourists; most trade magazines are sent free to qualified recipients. To see if you qualify, get a sample copy and fill out the reader response card— and check the new subscriber box.)

Inventors' Magazines

Inventors' Digest
310 Franklin Street, Suite 24
Boston, MA 02110
Phone: 800/838-8808; 617/367-4540 • Fax 617/723-6988
www.inventorsdigest.com
One year, 6 issues $22

One of the best magazines for inventors. Contains pertinent inventor stories and advertising of interest to inventors (inventors' clubs, product evaluation programs, classified ads) mixed with how-to articles about inventing, patents, licensing, and marketing. They even run some of my writing from time to time. Required reading if you have an invention or have lots of ideas and wonder if others have these creative streaks. Worth it.

Dream Merchant
2309 Torrance Boulevard, Suite 104
Torrance, CA 90501
Phone: 310/328-1925 • Fax 310/328-1844
One year, 6 issues $15.95

The other dominant magazine force in the inventing industry. Heavier in how-to articles, and not quite as slick as *Inventors' Digest* (this publication is printed on newspaper stock), but oh, how useful it can be. Anyone reading this publication regularly is privy to all of my own latest articles—they run them in every issue, along with sage advice from Joseph E. Cossman and Barbara Braebeck, to name just one or two notables. The information-rich content makes this subscription a steal for any inventor or marketer.

Lists, Vendors, and Directories

Most of the larger list companies offer a free booklet or catalog of all the lists they sell—which may be thousands. In addition, some of these booklets contain excellent information on specifying lists. All of them are free, and I recommend you call a few companies and get their catalogs, if for no other reason than to see what's out there and check out the thousands of lists that are available.

Firstmark, Inc.

List Vendor

34 Juniper Lane
Newton Center, MA 02159
Phone: 800/729-2600; 617/965-7989 • Fax 617/965-8510
http://www.firstmark.com • fmk@firstmark.com
Business database lists, but primarily health care lists such as Alzheimer facilities, HMOs, physicians by specialty, hospitals, nursing homes, etc. Free demo disk, free catalog of lists. These folks are knowledgeable and a pleasure to work with.

Hugo Dunhill Mailing Lists

List Vendor

30 E. 33rd Street, 12th Floor
New York, NY 10016
Phone: 800/223-6454; 212/213-9300 • Fax 212/213-9245
In addition to their free catalog of mailing lists, Hugo Dunhill publishes several excellent free reference brochures on effective direct mail letters, programs, and profit analysis. If you are fortunate enough to speak with Mr. Dunhill, take his advice—he's forgotten more about direct mail and lists than most people could learn in several lifetimes.

American Business Lists

List Vendor

5711 S. 86th Circle • P.O. Box 27347
Omaha, NE 68127
Phone: 800/555-5335 (business lists);
    800/661-5478 (consumer lists); 402/331-7169
    Fax 402/331-1505
http://www.LookupUSA.com • lists@abii.com
Free book of lists available upon request.

PCS Mailing List Company

List Vendor

39 Cross Street
Peabody, MA 01960
Phone: 800/532-LIST; 508/532-7100 • Fax 508/532-9181
Their free catalog contains almost 100 pages and is a lesson in what's available in lists. Contains thousands and thousands of lists. Check it out!

Dun and Bradstreet

List Vendor

3 Sylvan Way
Parsippany, NJ 07054
Phone: 800/624-5669; 201/455-0900
Free book of lists available upon request.

Best Mailing Lists

List Vendor

888 South Craycroft Road
Tucson, AZ 85711
Phone: 800/692-2378; 520/745-0200 • Fax 520/745-3800
Free catalog of lists available upon request. Nice folks!

CompilersPlus

List Vendor

466 Main Street
New Rochelle, NY 10801
Phone: 800/431-2914; 914/633-5240 • Fax 914/633-5261
Free catalog of lists available upon request. Nice catalog—it will give you a fast ramp up in what's available from a list house. Contains some unusual databases in the mix.

SRDS Direct Marketing List Source™

Directory

(Formerly *SRDS Direct Mail List Rates and Data*)
SRDS
1700 Higgins Road
Des Plaines, IL 60018
Phone: 800/851-SRDS (7737) • Fax 847/375-5001
http://www.SRDS.com
One year, 6 issues $384 (individual lists cost $238 each)

SRDS publishes a huge reference book on lists, just as it does in the magazine industry for periodicals. The *SRDS Direct Marketing List Source*™ delivers detailed descriptions of more than 16,000 business, consumer, and agri-market lists in 212 market classifications. Like the SRDS directory of magazines, this book is well over 1,000 pages and is a complete reference manual in itself. One of the most comprehensive resources available for the list industry. We use this at our own office. Recommended.

National Directory of Mailing Lists

Directory

Oxbridge Communications
150 Fifth Avenue
New York, NY 10011 $495
Phone: 800/955-0231; 212/741-0231 • Fax 212/633-2938
http://www.mediafinder.com

In direct competition with SRDS's directory, this publication shows 15,000 lists available for rent or purchase, with detailed descriptions of each. An excellent resource—we use this at our office, too. Also available on CD-ROM, $595.

Magazine Directories and References

Most of the major magazine directories give a wealth of information about the magazines they list, such as circulation, publisher's editorial profile (which generally indicates if the publication accepts PR), personnel, rates (black and white, color), rate policy, and closing dates. Each directory also gives unique additional information the publisher feels is important, and each presents all the information in its own special way. Be sure to look at all of the directories and select your favorite. Many directories may be found in smaller libraries. Larger libraries carry the rest.

SRDS

Directories

SRDS
1700 Higgins Road
Des Plaines, IL 60018
Phone: 800/851-SRDS (7737) • Fax 847/375-5001
http://www.SRDS.com

Business Publication Advertising Source™ One year, 12 issues, $549. Contains over 7,500 U.S. and 1,200 international business publications broken into more than 185 market classifications. One of the major directories, and one of the best resources available. Recommended highly—we use SRDS here in our own office.

Consumer Magazine Advertising Source™ One year, 12 issues, $529. Detailed descriptions of over 2,700 domestic consumer magazines and card decks arranged into 75 market classifications. Over 300 international publications, and over 300 farm publications.

Newspaper Advertising Source™ One year, 12 issues, $529. Comprehensive information listing over 3,200 newspapers organized by city and state. Another easy-to-use reference from SRDS.

TV & Cable Source™ One year, 4 issues, $380. Over 4,700 listings of commercial stations, broadcast networks, cable systems, cable networks, syndicators and sales rep firms. Includes programming, personnel, format, and positioning statement.

Radio Advertising Source™ One year, 12 issues, $405. If you're planning a radio campaign, this terrific resource contains detailed listings of over 10,000 stations. Includes such information as format, audience profile, personnel, special and syndicator programming—over 1,300 pages.

Interactive Advertising Source™ One year, 4 issues, $249. Brand new from SRDS! Explore the advertising possibilities on the Internet, online services, and websites. Learn about interactive kiosks and displays, interactive telephone and television. Information is clear and easy to use.

Direct Marketing List Source™ One year, 6 issues, 6 updates, $384. Over 16,000 lists in 212 market classifications. Over 600 co-op and package insert programs. See our write-up earlier in this reference section.

Out-of-Home Advertising Source™ Annual, $149. An introduction to going beyond traditional media such as magazines and newspapers (that are delivered to your home). Over 2,000 out-of-home marketing vehicles such as aerials/inflatables, bus bench, outdoor, taxi, transit, airport, hotel, movie theater, sports events, shopping malls, in-flight, in-store, event and mobile advertising, to name but a few of the 19 media categories.

Bacon's Media Directories

Directories

332 S. Michigan Avenue
Chicago, IL 60604
Phone: 800/621-0561; 312/922-2400 • Fax 312/922-3127
Since I've written about Bacon's directories extensively through-
out this book, I'll just list the many directories they publish. All of
Bacon's Media Directories are extremely good products, and I recom-
mend them without hesitation. We use most of their directories in
our own office for our clients' marketing campaigns.

Bacon's Newspaper/Magazine Directory (2 volumes) - $280
Bacon's Radio/TV/Cable Directory (broadcast media; 2
volumes) - $280
Bacon's Media Calendar Directory (editorial calendars and
profiles) - $280
Bacon's Business Media Directory (business media and
contacts) - $280
Bacon's International Media Directory (Western European
media) - $280
Bacon's New York Media Directory - $175. In-depth coverage
in one of the largest media markets.
Bacon's California Media Directory - $175
MediaSource Software (formerly *Directories on CD-ROM*; all
print and broadcast media) - $1095

New York Publicity Outlets
"metro CALIFORNIA media"

Directories

Public Relations Plus, Inc.
P.O. Box 1197
New Milford, CT 06776
Phone: 800/999-8448; 860/354-9361 • Fax 800/588-3827
Subscription for either book (2 editions per year): $185
These two top-notch marketing reference tools are the most comprehensive books for the specific areas they serve. Both publications
contain over 500 81/2" x 11" pages and are strategic for marketing
and PR campaigns in the electronic and news media. They offer the
most telephone numbers for specific individuals of any resource, anywhere. If you're good on the phone, or market in New York or California, these directories are a must.

All-In-One Directory

Directory

Gebbie Press
P.O. Box 1000
New Paltz, NY 12561 $85
Phone: 914/255-7560 • Fax 914/256-1239
Published in a single 6" x 9" spiral-bound 550-page directory. Over 19,000 entries encompassing daily and weekly newspapers, radio stations, television stations, and magazines (including business and farm publications). A handy reference directory that's easy to use and less costly than some of the bigger directories. We use this in our office, too. Recommended.

Oxbridge Communications

Directories

150 Fifth Avenue
New York, NY 10011
Phone: 800/955-0231; 212/741-0231 • Fax 212/633-2938
http://www.mediafinder.com
Standard Periodical Directory - $695. One of the largest reference directories published. Hardcover; more than 2,000 81/2" x 11" pages. Over 80,000 different PR resources shown. Nice book! This is the combination of Oxbridge's magazine and newspaper listing directories. It is the ultimate source. Also available on CD-ROM, $745.
Oxbridge Directory of Newsletters - $595. Most marketers miss the boat by not sending news releases to newsletter publishers. One of the most valuable marketing tools around, this publication—with over 20,000 entries—is the most comprehensive directory of newsletters ever. Recommended.
National Directory of Magazines - $595. Same great directory style and depth, but just magazines—over 25,000 of them. Also available on CD-ROM, $695.
National Directory of Catalogs - $495. The most exhaustive directory of catalogs in the U.S. Over 1,100 pages with up to a dozen listings per page. Contains product lines, personnel, frequency, circulation, target audience, list availability. A wonderfully easy-to-use reference tool, we use this extensively in our office. Recommended.
National Directory of Mailing Lists - $495. See previous write-up under the mailing list heading. An industry standard.
MediaFinder - $995. CD-ROM of ALL of the above books. Wow.
These works from Oxbridge are the best tools in the industry if you need as deep a marketing campaign as you can possibly get. They are the most comprehensive, and the ultimate resource in marketing. Oxbridge Communications is world class in all their directories, and they get my highest recommendations.

Burrelle's Media Directories

Directories

Burrelle's Information Services
75 East Northfield Road
Livingston, NJ 07039
Phone: 800-USMEDIA (876-3342); 201/992-6600
   Fax 201/992-7675
directory@burrelles.com
Burrelle's Media Directories complete five-book set: $550.
Newspapers and Related Media (two-book set): $225.
Magazines and Newsletters (one book): $225.
Newspapers and Magazines (three-book set): $300.
Broadcast and Related Media (two-book set): $225.
Prices for any of this data on computer disk are approximately the same as for the books—a very nice feature. However, when you order the complete 5-book set, Burrelle's also sends all the data on computer disks, free.

Burrelle's also offers a press clipping service, TV and radio transcripts, advertising and newsclip analysis, and database and label services for sending this information.

To limit a PR campaign geographically, or to pinpoint select communities for marketing, Burrelle's also offers media directories by state for Pennsylvania ($85), New Jersey ($60), New York ($95), New England ($95), California ($85), Minnesota ($60), and Texas ($60), plus $4 shipping each. These directories contain in-state newspapers, magazines, radio stations, TV stations, wire services, cable systems, and media ownership information. You can't go wrong with any of Burrelle's directories as marketing tools. I recommend them.

Hudson's Subscription Newsletter Directory

Directory

The Newsletter Clearinghouse
44 West Market Street • P.O. Box 311
Rhinebeck, NY 12572   13th Edition, $159
Phone: 800/572-3451; 914/876-2081 • Fax 914/876-2561
Almost 5,000 subscription newsletters listed in an easy-to-use marketing reference tool. Information is referenced, cross-referenced, and indexed to make using this book a pleasure. Handy 7" x 9" book is 500 pages of pertinent newsletter information. I use this book in my own marketing campaigns, and I recommend it. Information is clear and presented concisely.

Dictionary of Marketing Terms

Dictionary

by Betsy-Ann Toffler and Jane Imber
ISBN 0-8120-1783-8
Barron's Educational Series, Inc.
250 Wireless Boulevard
Hauppauge, NY 11788 $11.95

An excellent, excellent reference book, too great for me not to list here. If you have any interest in marketing, this book will become a lifelong friend. Over 3,500 definitions to help you through any marketing questions. Excellent material at a reasonable price. Softcover. All questions about marketing terminology are answered, and the book is a lesson in marketing itself. Too good not to own—a recommended purchase.

Paper Companies
How To Create Instant Stationery & Brochures
From Your Own Laser Printer

Several paper companies have recently launched new lines of preprinted papers. These papers are printed in two, three, or more colors in a handsome background design that will make your laser-imprinted type look good. Most of the area in these preprinted sheets is left open for your laser or computer imprint. You simply design your type to fit into the colorful graphics already printed on the sheet. Most designs are borders of some variation, to give your document a classy look of a fully printed brochure for your company.

You can buy anything from preprinted letterhead to complete stationery packages with the same design theme carried throughout letterhead, envelopes, and business cards. You can also get matching or nonmatching three-fold brochure paper with handsome borders printed on both front and back, or flat sheet 81/2" x 11" preprinted paper to make flyers. The business cards come to you perforated, 6- or 10-up on a page.

You simply run any of these preprinted forms through your laser printer and voilà, instant brochure, instant stationery, or instant corporate identity package. Cost for this material is usually about $20 per 100 sheets, so very short runs are affordable (but long runs aren't). You wouldn't be able to get a run of 100 sheets printed in 2 or 3 colors at a printer's for a reasonable amount.

Clever use of these preprinted forms can make you look like a big company or a stodgy old corporation that's been around for years. Choose any misconception you'd like, at very little expense. If you use these preprinted papers, take your time to make sure the type and graphics you lay into these designs make your company look good. When done well, these low-cost preprinted formats can be used in place of a data sheet for even greater results. Here's where to get them.

Paper Showcase

P. O. Box 8465

Mankato, MN 56002-8465

Phone: 800/287-8163 • Fax 800/842-3371

Publishes a beautiful 64-page catalog of preprinted letterheads, brochures and mailers, envelopes, business cards, labels, and presentation folders. You can also buy a template (software) that makes it easier to lay out and design these forms in your computer. Request a free catalog.

Paper Direct

100 Plaza Drive

Secaucus, NJ 07094-3606

Phone: 800/A-PAPERS (272-7377)

Fax 800/44-FAXPD (443-2973)

http://www.paperdirect.com

Publishes a smaller-format catalog, 107 pages and still growing, filled with preprinted stationery, certificates, cards, labels, and brochures; also publishes a software template to work with your computer to aid in layout. In addition, Paper Direct sells high-quality paper that is not printed, so you can print your own images. Great for short runs of plain stationery with matching envelopes. Request a free catalog.

NEBS

500 Main Street

Groton, MA 01471

Phone: 800/225-6380 • Fax 800/234-4324

NEBS is one of the largest forms printers in the U.S., and not without good reason. They produce quality work, on time, and stand behind their work 100%. They now produce several lines of preprinted stationery and compete successfully with the other innovative paper merchants. Their selection of preprinted papers is not yet as wide as some of their other resources, but it is constantly growing and changing. Call to request a free catalog.

Queblo

150 Kingswood Road

Mankato, MN 56001

Phone: 800/523-9080; 507/388-8647

Publishes a handsome 48-page catalog of preprinted papers including complete stationery packages of letterhead, business cards and envelopes, awards and certificates, presentation packages, folders, and tri-fold brochures. Call to request a free copy of the catalog.

Quill

100 Schelter Road

Lincolnshire, IL 60069

Phone: 800/789-5813 • Fax 800/789-8955

Just what you've been waiting for—a discount catalog of better-quality laser and inkjet papers. Create stationery, brochures, business cards, and so forth through your own computer printer. Create your own corporate identity swiftly, easily, and now, cheaply. For example, a kit of 420 pieces, which consists of 50 sheets of letterhead, 50 sheets of border paper, 50 envelopes, 100 business cards, 50 brochures, 60 post cards, and 60 labels—all matching—is just $24.95. It's a great way to look like a big firm with all these matching elements in your communication package. Call to request a free catalog.

I believe all the firms listed to be excellent resources: honest, with good pricing, quality products, and fast shipping. I recommend them. Each company has its own specially designed products that make its offerings unique. Get catalogs, decide for yourself. Have fun.

Additional Products and Services from

The Danielle Adams Publishing Company

Package Review
30-minute audio (on cassette) or handwritten corrections of your package. Includes suggestions and direction.

Package Analysis
Deeper package analysis (or review of longer packages) along with additional marketing analysis and instruction.

Market Analysis and Consulting
Two-hour market analysis package. Includes live discussion of your current marketing and suggestions and recommendations on where and how to move forward quickly, at low cost.

Consulting
Marketing, advertising, direct marketing, catalog review, new product development, resources, direction. Fresh, objective views. Jeffrey is quite used to saving clients way more than they spend on his services. On site, or on the phone.

Writing
Retail, catalog copy, direct mail, and technical writing, too. Market action plans. Business letters and campaigns a specialty. Press releases that work. Traditional and direct response copywriting that will make your numbers sizzle. Manuals, instructions, books, annual reports, and ghostwriting - you'd be surprised at whom Jeffrey writes for. Radio and television commercials and scripts.

Traditional Marketing and Advertising
Brochures, including both design and copywriting, business graphics, logos and logo enhancements, from the master of graphics himself. TV and radio commercials - consulting, writing, and scripting. Direct mail and direct marketing letters, brochures, packages. Please call for additional information and pricing.

Speaking
When Jeffrey Dobkin speaks, people laugh.
They also listen & learn. Like his books, Jeff crams a lot of useful information into a presentation. Please have your group or association call for information.

Private Club - Enjoy Jeffrey's writing before anyone else. Receive his monthly columns on small business marketing as soon as he writes them. Be among the first people on the planet to preview his marketing material - and find all his mistakes. Then have an opportunity to buy book galleys, manuscripts, and audio tapes before final edits and publishing. You'll like this insider's service.

HOW TO MARKET A PRODUCT FOR UNDER $500

Just $29.95 + $4 shipping for a signed edition.

UNCOMMON MARKETING TECHNIQUES

Just $17.95.   Please add $3 shipping. Signed.

Audio Cassette Series: Just $49 + $5 shipping.

3 Double-Sided Cassettes. Two studio-made cassettes are highlights of *How To Market a Product for Under $500*. One cassette is an AT&T tele-conference, 70 people on the line and only Jeffrey with an open mike. A brief question and answer period follows. Side two is a 1/2-hour radio interview (WMGK, Phila.) showing a more personal side of Jeffrey.

Two Video Cassettes: $69.95 + $4 shipping.

Watch Jeff as he presents a 40-minute information-rich speech to the members of the Highlander Club at their very first chapter meeting in Baltimore, MD.

Then see Jeffrey loosen up as he presents an hour and a half of solid Multi-Level Marketing information to a group of about 200 MLMers in California.

Finally, see Jeff sweat as viewers call in with the most unusual array of questions when he appears on a segment of CNBC's *The Money Wheel*.

_____Please keep me on your **Mailing List!** _____Send **NEWSLETTER** info!

Send Check, Money Order, or Call to Charge to Visa/MC, Discover, or AMEX.

Name_____

Address_____

City, St_____Zip_____

Telephone_____Fax_____

Products_____Quantity_____

If gift, endorsement should read:

Charging to Credit Card Number_____

Signature_____Expires_____

Amount_____Thank you! For additional orders, photocopy this form or just use a sheet of paper.

THE DANIELLE ADAMS PUBLISHING CO.

~ Satisfaction Always Guaranteed ~

BOX 100 ☆ MERION STATION, PA 19066

610/642-1000 ☆ FAX 610/642-6832

INQUIRIES: 610/642-1000
ORDERS: 800/234-IDEA